# Louisiana's Rogue Sheriffs:
## A Culture of Corruption

### By Tom Aswell

Copyright, 2019

by

Tom Aswell

ISBN: 978-1-7331968-0-2

All rights reserved

# Dedication

    To Betty, my anchor, my compass, and the gentle breeze in my sails for the past fifty years—to Amy, Leah and Jennifer, and to the dedicated sheriffs and deputies who do not appear in this book because they possessed the principles and integrity to resist the seductive temptations of power and money.

# Acknowledgements

Whenever writers take on projects such as this one, family duties are often sacrificed to research, interviews, and writing. This book is no different and I couldn't have done it without the patience and understanding of my wife of half-a-century, Betty. I also owe a special thanks to another family member, Jeanette Herren, who not only created the cover for this book, but has been one of my cheerleaders throughout my writing career, always believing, always encouraging.

Lamar White, publisher of the informative and often provocative web blog *Bayou Brief*, was the primary source for information contained in Chapter 11 about Louisiana Attorney General Jeff Landry. Additionally, he graciously consented to the reproduction of his story about Lafayette City Marshal Brian Pope found in chapter 41. Thank you, Lamar. You're a ray of sunshine illuminating the dark character of Louisiana's shady political operatives.

The more eyes that see a manuscript, the more likely that mistakes in spelling, grammar, and syntax will be caught—not to mention simple the inevitable typos. For that reason, I had two individuals perform the all-important editing task. Thanks to Gloria Weaver and to Steven Winham for their eagle eyes and for their comments, suggestions and support.

I have long been a proponent of independent book stores. I have only one advertisement on my web blog and that's for Cavalier House Books—and I don't charge for it. John Cavalier is my web page guru and has generously provided me with a list of independent book sellers in Louisiana. I cannot find the words to adequately encourage people to read and to support their independent book stores. We cannot allow them to go the way of our newspapers.

Likewise, independent book publishers are disappearing from the landscape. This is nothing less than tragic. For that reason, I want to offer a special thanks to Claitor's Publishing of Baton Rouge. Claitor's primarily publishes law books but also publishes books for authors who want to see and hold a copy of their published works.

Heartfelt thanks to five individuals who took the time to read the manuscript and to offer their observations for inclusion in the book. *New Orleans Advocate* columnist James Gill is a skilled observer of the human condition whose columns are truly priceless. Robert Mann, a veteran of the political wars in Washington and Baton Rouge, holds the Manship Chair in Journalism at the Manship School of Mass Communications at LSU. Additionally, he has authored a number of critically-acclaimed books, including *A Grand Delusion: America's Descent into Vietnam, The Walls of Jericho: Lyndon Johnson, Hubert Humphrey, Richard Russell, and the Struggle for Civil Rights, Legacy to Power: Senator Russell Long of Louisiana, and Daisy Petals and Mushroom Clouds: LBJ, Barry Goldwater, and the Ad That Changed American Politics,* and available on October 1: *Becoming Ronald Reagan: The Rise of a Conservative Icon.* Anthony G. "Tony" Falterman read the manuscript from an insider's perspective. He is not only the retired district attorney for the 23$^{rd}$ Judicial District, which includes the parishes of Ascension, Assumption and St. James, but he also is the retired sheriff of Assumption Parish and the former president of the Louisiana Sheriffs' Association. Thanks to each of you for your generous comments about this book. Another with an insider's view was Rafael C. Goyeneche, III, President of the New Orleans Metropolitan Crime Commission. Rafael has a long-standing reputation as a no-nonsense watchdog of official corruption and to have him offer encouraging words about the book is a major coup to be cherished—and I do, with deep humility. Steven Winham has been a steady voice of encouragement—and caution—for years now and his wise counsel is always welcomed and appreciated. A stickler for accuracy, his endorsement is especially valued.

My undying gratitude goes out to the five of you who took the time to read and offer your critiques.

## Acknowledgements

Finally, and certainly not last, a special thanks to all the dedicated, honest, and hard-working law enforcement officials who did not make this book. That's a good thing. Going out each day to keep us out of harm's way when you literally don't know if you'll be coming home at the end of your shift, while often taken for granted, is nevertheless greatly appreciated. You are what stands between us and anarchy.

# Introduction

The idea for this book is the direct result of my writing about a single sheriff in Louisiana: Louis Ackal of Iberia Parish, located deep in the heart of the state's Cajun Country. Without going into detail about Ackal's iron-fisted rule over the parish—there's an entire chapter devoted to him in the book—suffice it to say he is a microcosm of the political power of sheriffs not just in Louisiana, but throughout the United States.

The unchecked authority of the local sheriff is, without question, the fertile feeding ground of corruption as can be found with the likes of Joe Arpaio (Maricopa County, Arizona), Lee Baca (Los Angeles County), Pat Kelly (Athens County, Ohio), Lawrence Hodge (Whitley County, Kentucky), Chuck Arnold (Gibson County, Tennessee), Tyrone Clark, Sr. (Sumter County, Alabama), Todd Entrekin (Etowah County, Alabama), Mike Byrd (Jackson County, Mississippi), and countless others spread across the nation's landscape. That is not to say, of course, that I have not had my share of run-ins with local sheriffs when my duties as a newspaper reporter conflicted with the manner in which they preferred to run their fiefdoms, that is to say, with unbridled and unquestioned authority. My job, much to their consternation, was to challenge that authority from time to time.

I've had sheriffs in the parishes of St. Landry, Claiborne, Tangipahoa and Bienville issue invitations to me to not return to their turf.

The one incident that stands out in my memory more than all the others, however, occurred in my hometown of Ruston, Louisiana, in the early 1970s. I operated the north Louisiana bureau for the sister newspapers, *The Shreveport Times* and *Monroe Morning World*. Ruston was situated on I-20 between the two cities and my job was to keep readers abreast of events in that part of the state for both publications.

Most of my stories were of a routine nature and were best described as non-memorable.

Until, that is, a drug deal went bad in Dallas, Texas, that left one person dead. The shooting involved individuals from Austin, Houston and Boston. The killer was said to be residing at the time in Ruston with his girlfriend and their baby. As the manhunt, now centered in Ruston, intensified, I suddenly found myself as the point man, "stringing" for papers in Houston, Austin, Dallas and Boston as each paper demanded the latest details of the search for the killer.

It was a Saturday and incredibly, the Lincoln Parish Sheriff's Office, even as the manhunt ensued, would close at midnight and not reopen until noon on Sunday.

Meanwhile, I had a description of the car the killer was driving and I gave that information to the papers in Texas and Boston, as well as publishing it in the Shreveport and Monroe papers.

On Sunday morning, after the papers hit the streets, a high school student named Jim Hilton who ironically, would go on to a successful career as a Ruston police officer, spotted the car on his way to church and notified city police who quickly apprehended the fugitive.

You would normally think law enforcement officials would be grateful that a sharp-eyed citizen had seen the car, but not Sheriff George Simonton.

On Monday morning, during my usual courthouse rounds, a livid Simonton accosted me verbally, accusing me of irresponsible, yellow journalism. "You ran that goddamn description of the car and it's a wonder he didn't get clear out of the goddamn country!" the sheriff screamed at me, veins popping out of his beet-red forehead.

"Sheriff," I replied as calmly as I could under the circumstances, since he blindsided me with his attack, "it's because I published a description of the car that someone recognized it and called city police who caught him. I believe you're a little jealous of city police because your office was closed for business."

His response was not suitable for printing.

It would not be the last encounter I had with Sheriff Simonton although I have the say the next one, about five years later, was, while still confrontational, amusing—at least to me. You can read about that one in the epilogue.

*Oh, so thank your lucky stars, you've got protection*
*Walk the line and never mind the cost.*
*And don't wonder who them lawmen was protectin'*
*When they nailed the Savior to the cross.*

*'Cause the law is for protection of the people*
*Rules are rules and any fool can see.*
*We don't need no riddle speakin' prophets*
*Scarin' decent folks like you and me, no siree.*
--Kris Kristofferson

# Prologue

"We have to be responseful to the public, all the public, even the nuts. In short, this is kind of a kissass business, to put it bluntly."
--*The Natchitoches Parish Sheriff's Deputy Manual*[1]

The office of sheriff is older than the office of the president. Indeed, it pre-dates the republic itself by more than a century, older even than the Magna Carta, signed in 1215. In fact, the office, which originated in England, dates back over a thousand years.[2] In this country, the first sheriff took office in Delaware in 1669—a full 107 years before the Declaration of Independence. (Ironically, it is in that state where efforts have been ongoing for several years to re-define the role of sheriff by revoking the office's arrest powers.)

The office gets its name from the term *Shire Reeve*, meaning the keeper of the county.[3] The sheriff, other than the occasional small-town police chief, is the only elected law enforcement official in America. More than 99 percent of sheriffs in the U.S. are elected. In 42 states, sheriffs are elected to four-year terms. In Massachusetts, the term is for six years. It's for a three-year term in New Jersey and for two years in Arkansas and New Hampshire. In Rhode Island, the governor appoints the sheriff and in two Colorado counties and Dade County, Florida, sheriffs are appointed by the county executive.[4]

There were 3,080 sheriffs in the U.S. as of January 2015, but three entire states—Alaska, which has no counties, Hawaii and Connecticut—do not have a sheriff. Sheriffs' offices range in size from one or two officers in small rural areas to the largest of them all, the Los Angeles County Sheriff's Office, with 16,400 deputies and 400 reserve deputies.[5]

The last line of defense for the citizenry, the sheriff, is the public's protector, the keeper of the peace, the guardian of liberty and the protector of rights. He is responsible for keeping the peace and enforcing the law. While many states, such as California, certain law enforcement qualifications must be met before being able to run for sheriff. In most states, however, there are no such qualifications and anyone can run for the office. Moreover, the office is unique in that sheriffs are accountable directly to the U.S. Constitution and the constitutions of their respective states.[6]

It is those last two factors—the general lack of qualifications (other than just being a good politician) and accountability solely to the federal and state constitutions, to the specific exclusion of the president, congress and the governor—that makes the sheriff the single most powerful person in a county, more powerful even than the district attorney or the judiciary in many cases.

And therein lies the problem. That much power concentrated in the hands of a single individual, who often possesses no concept of basic human rights, is a recipe for abuse and greed. And sometimes the result is even outright lawlessness on the part of the very ones sworn to uphold the law. Intimidation replaces protection; liberty and rights are replaced by fear and persecution. And the sheriff, already all-powerful, becomes even more so.

The Louisiana Sheriffs' Association (LSA) is certainly no exception. "Prior to about 1978 or so, the office of secretary-treasurer was the power of the association," said Anthony G. "Tony" Falterman, retired sheriff of Assumption Parish, one of the original parishes of the Territory of Orleans located along the banks of Lafourche Bayou and the state's largest sugar cane producer.

When Falterman first became sheriff, the LSA "was located in a tiny hole in the wall on Third Street in downtown Baton Rouge," he said. Today it's an ultra-modern, sprawling complex near the LSU campus on Nicholson Drive. The LSA operates its own insurance pool, the Louisiana Sheriff's Law Enforcement Program, which covers more than three-fourths of the sheriffs' offices in the state in liability litigation.

"The LSA secretary-treasurer was provided an automobile and a credit card and represented the association at the legislature and at other functions and meetings," Falterman said. When he defeated Tangipahoa Parish Sheriff Frank Edwards as president of the sheriffs' association, use of a vehicle and credit cards were suspended. He also lobbied the state legislature successfully for what at the time was called hazardous duty pay, today known as supplemental pay. He got approval for the supplemental pay by agreeing that all recipients would be Police Officer Standards and Training (POST) certified. Falterman, as a member of the Louisiana

# Prologue

Commission on Law Enforcement, also helped certify all the academies in Louisiana that applied to train recruits.[8]

With the rise of the sheriff's influence, we have witnessed corruption, says DeKalb County, Illinois Sheriff Roger, with some not living "up to the standards of the badge." That, naturally led to the indictment of some for various abuses, from drunkenness to corruption. Sheriff Henry Plummer of Bannock, Montana, for the most extreme example, was hung by his own constituents in 1864 because of persistent stories that he commanded a "gang of robbers" even as he dispensed justice.

Falterman, who after retiring as sheriff, served as the district attorney for Louisiana's 23rd Judicial District which includes the parishes of Ascension, Assumption and St. James, agreed with Sheriff Scott. "It has always been my opinion that the longer an office holder remains in office, the greater the potential for committing absolutely egregious ethical or criminal violations. The aura of being untouchable and undefeated surrounding an elected official can lead to a tragic downfall and often prison. A vast majority of the men and women in uniform are dedicated to their profession, and the potential for becoming an on the job fatality occurs every time a uniform is worn! We should all be thankful for the jobs being done by a mostly underpaid group of men and women that needs the public's support now—more than ever."[9]

That is the reason for this book. Abuse of power by those entrusted to the citizenry has come under a media microscope on a national scale. With the ambush of law enforcement officers in Baton Rouge, Lake Charles and elsewhere, it is understandable that there is an edginess and more than a little apprehension with the answering of each call for help or with each traffic stop. The headlines in all the newspapers and the TV news stories are ample evidence of this. This book does not address the problem of deliberate attacks on police as weighed against the shootings of innocent victims by police. Most often, these are events that involve snap judgments that result in tragic results which set off community protests and riots.

Nor is this about the vast majority of law enforcement personnel, including sheriffs and their deputies, who go about their duties and meet their responsibilities honestly and with respect for victims and perpetrators alike. Instead, it is the intent of this book to look at behind-the-scenes wrongdoing, abuses of office and of citizens that have become a matter of policy of certain officials. Rather than isolated incidents, we will focus on trends that should—but only rarely do—cause the citizenry to rise up and say, "Enough!"

The problem of bad cops is nationwide but this book will be limited to the dark legacies of Louisiana sheriffs along with a few other Louisiana law enforcement agencies.

# Table of Contents

| | | |
|---|---|---|
| Dedication | | ...... iii |
| Acknowledgements | | ...... v |
| Introduction | | ...... ix |
| Prologue | | ...... xiii |
| | | |
| Chapter 1 | The Kefauver Hearings | ...... 1 |
| Chapter 2 | Louisiana Sheriffs' Association | ...... 13 |
| Chapter 3 | Christopher Columbus Nash, Daniel Wesley Shaw: Grant Parish | ...... 17 |
| Chapter 4 | D.J. "Cat" Doucet, Adler LeDoux: St. Landry Parish | ...... 21 |
| Chapter 5 | Noah Cross, Frank DeLaughter: Concordia Parish | ...... 25 |
| Chapter 6 | Willie Waggonner, Vol Dooley: Bossier Parish | ...... 35 |
| Chapter 7 | Steve Prator: Caddo Parish | ...... 39 |
| Chapter 8 | Bailey Grant, Royce Toney: Ouachita Parish | ...... 41 |
| Chapter 9 | Bobby Tardo, Duffy Breaux: Lafourche Parish | ...... 51 |
| Chapter 10 | J. Edward Layrisson, Daniel Edwards: Tangipahoa Parish | ...... 55 |
| Chapter 11 | Jeff Landry, Charles Fuselier: St. Martin Parish | ...... 65 |
| Chapter 12 | F.O. "Potch" Didier, Bill Belt: Avoyelles Parish | ...... 73 |
| Chapter 13 | Jessel Ourso: Iberville Parish | ...... 79 |
| Chapter 14 | Eugene Holland, Chaney Phillips, Ronald "Gun" Ficklin, Jessie Hugues: St. Helena Parish | ...... 83 |
| Chapter 15 | Cale Rinicker: East Carroll Parish | ...... 87 |
| Chapter 16 | Norm Fletcher: Natchitoches Parish | ...... 91 |
| Chapter 17 | Irvin "Jif" Hingle: Plaquemines Parish | ...... 93 |
| Chapter 18 | Mike Tregre: St. John the Baptist Parish | ...... 99 |
| Chapter 19 | Albert D. "Bodie" Little: Winn Parish | ...... 107 |
| Chapter 20 | Sid J. Gautreaux: East Baton Rouge Parish | ...... 111 |
| Chapter 21 | Harry Lee, Newell Normand: Jefferson Parish | ...... 117 |
| Chapter 22 | Charles Foti, Marlin Gusman: Orleans Parish | ...... 125 |
| Chapter 23 | Dallas Cormier: Jefferson Davis Parish | ...... 139 |

| | | |
|---|---|---|
| Chapter 24 | Jeff Britt, Ricky Jones: Tensas Parish | 143 |
| Chapter 25 | Scott Franklin: LaSalle Parish | 151 |
| Chapter 26 | Jack Strain: St. Tammany Parish | 157 |
| Chapter 27 | Clay Higgins: St. Landry Parish | 173 |
| Chapter 28 | Rodney Arbuckle: DeSoto Parish | 179 |
| Chapter 29 | Joseph Reed Bueche: Pointe Coupee Parish | 185 |
| Chapter 30 | Willy Martin: St. James Parish | 187 |
| Chapter 31 | Greg Champagne: St. Charles Parish | 189 |
| Chapter 32 | Louis Ackal: Iberia Parish | 201 |
| Chapter 33 | Mike Couvillon: Vermilion Parish | 217 |
| Chapter 34 | Jack Stephens: St. Bernard Parish | 221 |
| Chapter 35 | Austin Daniel: West Feliciana Parish | 227 |
| Chapter 36 | Wayne Morein, Eddie Soileau: Evangeline Parish Sheriff's Office, and Ville Platte Police Department | 231 |
| Chapter 37 | Jerry Larpenter: Terrebonne Parish | 239 |
| Chapter 38 | Litigation: The Costs of Bad Sheriffing | 249 |

## The Others

| | | |
|---|---|---|
| Chapter 39 | George D'Artois: City of Shreveport | 255 |
| Chapter 40 | John Guandolo, Keith Phillips and Ekko Barnhill | 261 |
| Chapter 41 | Lafayette City Marshal Brian Pope | 267 |
| Chapter 42 | Jason Kinch, Corey Jackson: Lafayette Parish | 277 |
| Chapter 43 | Marlin Defillo: New Orleans Police Department | 283 |
| Chapter 44 | Lloyd Grafton: An Expert's Perspective | 287 |
| Epilogue | | 293 |
| Notes | | 297 |
| Index | | 343 |

# 1
## The Kefauver Hearings

Nothing grabs headlines like a good congressional committee hearing with an all-star cast of shady characters called to testify and to answer embarrassing questions under oath.

Such was the case in 1951 when the Senate Crime Commission, chaired by Tennessee Sen. Estes Kefauver, held hearings in New Orleans as part of its traveling 1950-51 investigation of organized crime in America. The result was a glaring national spotlight that laid bare the accommodating and even corrupt manner in which four Louisiana sheriffs allowed gambling and prostitution to flourish.

The colorful Frank Clancy, who served as Sheriff of Jefferson Parish from 1928 to 1956, was the focus of the hearings, but the sheriffs of Iberia, Orleans, and St. Bernard proved every bit as lenient, even cooperative, when it came to abetting vice in their parishes. Clancy's tenure spanned the careers of several controversial Louisiana governors, including Dick Leche, O.K. Allen, Jimmie Davis and Huey and Earl Long.

Clancy testified, albeit reluctantly, in Sen. Kefauver's 1950-1951 Senate Crime Commission hearings on organized crime. The Jefferson Parish sheriff, a stereotypical political boss, acknowledged that he had allowed the placement of 5,000 slot machines in the parish by associates of New Orleans crime boss Carlos Marcello. Moreover, Marcello opened three gambling casinos on the east side of the Mississippi River. Slot machines targeted low-income gamblers who could only afford the nickel slots while the casinos attracted more of the silk-stocking clientele.

In addition to sharing in the profits of the gambling enterprises, he also kept the right to hire all personnel below management level, a real plum for someone in a position to dole out political patronage. Clancy testified that gambling had flourished in Orleans and Jefferson parishes and the surrounding parishes for a century and that a candidate could not get himself elected on an anti-gambling ticket.[1]

Gambling not only flourished, but was originally introduced by individuals who were unlike those with organized crime connections who stepped in later, prompting Gov. Huey Long to pressure Clancy to issue a stern but temporary at best warning to gambling establishments. When he appeared before Kefauver's committee 22 years later, he openly admitted that he still allowed illegal gambling because it provided jobs for approximately 1,000 elderly and otherwise unemployable citizens of Jefferson parish. Moreover, he said when he was running for office, he promised voters that regarding gambling, he would be "as dry as the Sahara Desert."[2]

Clancy provided testimony to the Kefauver committee that proved embarrassing to Marcello and when he sharply curtailed illegal gambling in the parish, he quickly found himself at odds with organized crime. In April 1955, a 64-year-old New Orleans bank teller named Frank Bourg was hospitalized following a heart attack; an unidentified assailant entered his hospital room and smashed his skull as he slept.

While all evidence indicated it to be a gangland killing, police never could find evidence of criminal associates in Bourg's nearly 30 years as a bank teller. Finally, it was theorized that Bourg had been mistaken for Clancy, who occupied the adjacent room. Because of his testimony before Kefauver, a guard had been placed outside his hospital room. The morning of the attack on Bourg, the guard was removed on orders of someone representing themselves as the sheriff's wife, the police report said.

Following the Bourg slaying, Clancy promptly ceased his cooperation with federal authorities.[3]

A much more detailed account of how local sheriffs in Jefferson, Orleans, St. Bernard, and Iberia parishes turned a blind eye to the manner in which gambling, drugs, and prostitution were allowed to flourish was provided in *Interim Report No. Three* of the Kefauver Committee, compiled and published by Thomas Hunt on the *American Mafia* Website. In some cases, they didn't just ignore the illegal activity, but protected and profited from it. Those sheriffs, and other law enforcement officials scattered across the state, pretty much lived by the famous quote by former New Orleans Mayor Martin Behrman who said, "You can make prostitution illegal, but you can't make it unpopular." Though Behrman's pithy aphorism was uttered in response to the federal government's shutdown of the Crescent City's fabled Storyville red-light district in 1917, it applied just as aptly to

# Chapter 1: The Kefauver Hearings

narcotics, gambling, and [during prohibition] alcohol—both from the standpoint of consumer and supplier.

The Kefauver hearings focused mainly on gambling, prostitution, and narcotics and it was in those three areas of organized crime that the names of several Louisiana sheriffs and other law enforcement personnel repeatedly popped up in testimony.

Another source, an Internet Web page identified simply as *Historical Text Archive*, cited a couple of others in its feature, *Scenes along the Gulf Coast,* an account of alcohol trafficking along the U.S. Gulf Coast during prohibition. During that brief period, which gave rise to the reputations of Al Capone and Eliot Ness, a largely undefined organization of financiers and rumrunners formed the syndicates that smuggled alcohol from Cuba and other Caribbean nations into Louisiana through the same swamps, bays and bayous used by the Pirate Jean Lafitte a century before.

Whereas Lafitte could count on the cooperation of sympathetic Cajuns to help conceal his whereabouts from authorities, the bootleggers of the prohibition era were abetted by much more valuable ally: local law enforcement, particularly rural sheriffs perfectly willing to accept a percentage of the profits in exchange for looking the other way and sometimes even serving as lookouts.

Undercover federal agent Patrick Needham of St. Helena Parish infiltrated a New Orleans underworld organization by posing as a disgruntled prohibition agent. His furtive work resulted in 34 indictments, including the leader of the Louisiana Republican Party and controller of the New Orleans Customs district, St. Bernard Parish Sheriff L.A. Meraux, and New Orleans police captain Joseph Johnson.

Needham's work and the resulting indictments prompted U.S. Treasury officials to describe New Orleans as a hotbed of bootleggers and the headquarters of gangs that apparently operated without restraint, and that Washington was convinced "that official collusion aided the New Orleans bootleggers..."[4]

Equally prevalent in St. Landry Parish, a half-hour north of Lafayette, was the official protection provided for moonshiners who turned out some of the best home brew in the South. Long before the legendary Sheriff Cat Doucet and his fabled whorehouses was Sheriff Charles Thibodeaux and deputy U.S. Marshal for the West District of Louisiana Dudley Briley. The two lawmen often cooperated in sending advance warnings to the local entrepreneurs when revenuers were about to conduct a raid.

Briley, on the inside by virtue of his position as a federal marshal, would get word to Thibodeaux who would dispatch his deputies into the remote areas of St. Landry to alert the bootleggers. They would immediately begin sounding off with deer hunting horns, warning all moonshiners within earshot to find business somewhere besides deep in the cypress woods where the stills were located. As a result of the collusion of Briley and Thibodeaux, federal agents seized and destroyed stills but logged few arrests.[5]

But the testimony given before the Kefauver Committee, dramatic and eye-opening as it was, illustrated the in-your-face audacity of sheriffs and municipal police officers of the three contiguous parishes of Jefferson, Orleans, and St. Bernard and the contempt they showed for the oaths they were sworn to as officers of the law.

New Orleans, Part B of the committee's Third Interim Report began, represented a microcosm of organized crime on a national scale in that the city presented "a complete case history of how national gambling and racketeering elements align themselves with local operators in a metropolitan area" and how they "depended in large measure on the negligence, the active support, or the participation of some local law-enforcement officials." Moreover, those same law enforcement officials were more often than not able to "nullify the efforts of diligent officials and public-spirited citizens in their own or nearby jurisdictions."[6]

John Bosch was president of the trade association of coin-machine operators, which consisted primarily of pinball machines that paid off in money to winners. He testified before the committee that the association had an attorney on a $300-per-month retainer. He was simultaneously employed as the New Orleans city attorney whose job it was to prosecute pinball machine violations. At the same time, a member of the pinball association's executive committee was one Angelo Gemelli, a full-time New Orleans police officer whose duty was to check pinball operations and to arrest operators who paid off. His unique dual role placed him in an opportunistic position to "persuade" nonmembers to join the association and to pay the steep dues assessed operators. Gemelli received 10 percent of all amounts he collected for the association in his membership "campaigns."[7]

## Chapter 1: The Kefauver Hearings

George Reyer, a former New Orleans police superintendent who also once served as president of the International Association of Police Chiefs, retired in 1946 and took a job with the *Daily Sports Wire*, an illegal betting wire service, at $100-a-week to check for wire taps. Admitting to the Kefauver Committee that he was not a wire expert, he said in his four years with the service, he never found a tap. Reyer also held an interest in several New Orleans-area gambling casinos that linked him to the Club Forest, a swank local casino that featured a restaurant, bar and grill, three large dice tables, a smaller dice table, two roulette wheels, two blackjack games, a football pool and a racehorse book. Club Forest paid nearly $400 a week to *Daily Sports Wire* for its wire service. The Kefauver Committee was unable to establish with any certainty that Reyer's interests in the casinos overlapped his tenure with the New Orleans Police Department.[8]

The sheriff's office in Orleans Parish under John J. Grosch was not averse to taking protection payments from the mob which, it turned out, was the least of his concerns. His divorced wife offered devastating testimony to the committee. In the last six years of their married life, which ended in 1940, she said her husband, then the chief of detectives for the New Orleans Police Department, accumulated $150,000 in a safety deposit box that she had obtained. Following his instructions, she said she purchased the safety box under an assumed name and a false address.

She said he received money each week from a man named Julius Pace, a slot machine and jukebox dealer. She testified that she personally received $39 each week in an envelope given her by another slot machine operator, Larry Copeland. Moreover, she said every Saturday night, a man whom she believed ran a house of prostitution brought her and her husband food for the week. In addition to her oral testimony, Mrs. Grosch, who later became a supervisor of nurses' aides in a New Orleans hospital, provided records that corroborated her testimony. She also produced written agreements made at the time of her divorce from Grosch. One of those gave her $5,000 and the other, a secret agreement, was a settlement of $35,000, both of which gave strong evidence that the sheriff's wealth was far greater than could be explained by his $186 per month salary.[9]

Grosch, of course, was not the only law enforcement official whose net worth belied his modest salary. St. Bernard Parish Sheriff Celestine "Dutch" Rowley, in his testimony before the committee, admitted to a "supplementary" income of from $6,000 to $8,000 over the three-year period leading up to his committee appearance. He owned two vehicles, a 1949 Ford and a 1949 Cadillac that he purchased with cash withdrawn from his own bedroom strongbox. At the time of his testimony, the box contained between $15,000 and $20,000. When asked the source of his funds, he pleaded the Fifth Amendment.

Rowley, who served as sheriff since 1939, said as far back as the 1870s, the local constable and justice of the peace were paid from gambling funds. He also pointed out the irony of the state and federal governments' practice of assessing and collecting taxes on illegal slot machines and then using the tax information to conduct raids to seize the machines.[10]

The committee heard testimony from four sheriffs and two town marshals, each of whom admitted being aware of the existence of gambling, handbooks, slot machines and prostitution in his jurisdiction while at the same time denying ever having personally observed such activities. New Orleans Mayor DeLesseps S. Morrison told the committee that Jefferson and St. Bernard parishes had one of the nation's highest concentrations of wide-open gambling houses. He cited Club Forest, which had 48 from five, ten, 25, 50-cent and one-dollar slot machines.

In addition to the daytime operation that included the features listed earlier, the club's nighttime operation included a keno game, six roulette wheels, small dice games, four tables of blackjack, from two to five tables for big dice games and free drinks and cigarettes for gamblers. Customers who ran out of money could cash checks or obtain loans on jewelry. Its assets at the end of 1949 were given as more than $700,000 on gross receipts of $2 million.[11]

The Beverly Club in Jefferson Parish, which was destroyed by fire in July 1983, was every bit as elaborate and ornate as Club Forest. Opened in 1945, it was previously called the Suburban Gardens Roadhouse. It was run by "Dandy" Phil Kastel and business partners Carlos Marcello, New York mobster Frank Costello and Miami Mafia boss Meyer Lansky. Opulent to excess, it featured silk-covered walls, complimentary lipstick and perfume for female clientele, and a bandstand that could be transformed to a full-sized stage at the press of a button.

Security was considerably tighter at The Beverly than at the Jefferson Parish Sheriff's Office. Besides the generators that served as a safeguard against untoward shenanigans during power failures, floor-to-ceiling bars protected a basement storage room, employees were frisked at

## Chapter 1: The Kefauver Hearings

the beginning and ends of shifts, and a gun mount, concealed behind shrubbery on the front lawn, served as added protection. A loft in a detached building held gaming tables—moved there during occasional raids—just before the arrival of cops, of course.

When the Kefauver hearings came to New Orleans, Kastel was subpoenaed to testify but he refused to answer the committee's questions. He invoked his Fifth Amendment privilege on 56 occasions and was subsequently charged with 56 counts of contempt of Congress.

The Beverly shut down following a statewide crackdown on gambling but Kastel reopened it in 1959 and ran it until his death in 1963. Though the Beverly's gambling era ended with Kastel's death, the Beverly remains something of a celebrated story. Such acts as Carmen Miranda, Rudy Vallee and Danny Thomas performed on its stage over the years of its operation and celebrity visitors interested in illicit gambling included Lana Turner, Ann Miller, Jane Powell, Martha Raye, Dorothy Lamour, Joan Fontaine, Cyd Charisse, June Allyson, Roddy McDowall, Cesar Romero, Jo Ann Worley, Arte Johnson, Fannie Flagg, Bob Crane, and Gary Burghoff.[12]

Gretna, the parish seat of Jefferson Parish and situated on the wide-open west bank of the Mississippi River, had a population of only 14,000 but boasted at least six large gambling clubs complete with horse parlors, Gretna Town Marshal Beauregard Miller told the committee. But he wasn't the only one; Iberia Parish Sheriff Gilbert Ozenne knew of four in his parish and St. Bernard Parish Sheriff Celestine "Dutch" Rowley could rattle off the names of half-a-dozen others in his jurisdiction.[13]

Jefferson Parish Sheriff Frank Clancy was no exception, saying he could not dispute the Kefauver Committee counsel's estimate of 5,000 machines in that parish. The sheriff even admitted that the Dixie Finance Corporation, in which he held an interest, could possibly have loaned money to slot machine distributors. Even citizens' efforts to prompt official action against illegal gambling, led by Rev. Dana Dawson, a Metairie minister, proved fruitless. Dawson testified before the committee that when his group brought a padlock lawsuit against Club Forest, he was approached by Pete Perez, the club's dice foreman who, little shame in doing so, promised funds for Dawson's church's Sunday school building in exchange for Dawson's dropping the suit.

Rather than cracking down on the gambling houses, Clancy instead actually took part in some of the negotiations between the club representative and Dawson, telling the pastor how bothersome it was for him as sheriff to have to try and obtain employment in the clubs for his friends. Clancy bragged that he had placed about 2,000 persons in jobs in the clubs even as he continued to stress the economic value of the clubs to the parish because of the jobs provided. Meanwhile, the owners of four casinos continued to make contributions to not only Dawson's church, but to other churches as well, through both Perez and Clancy.[14]

Clancy, who was a practicing attorney before being elected sheriff, admitted in his Washington testimony before the committee that he had accompanied Perez on his visit to Rev. Dawson and had attempted to persuade Dawson to drop his lawsuit against the casinos. But, his attorney senses kicking in, he became somewhat obstinate when asked if gambling was considered against the law in his parish and whether he had ever made any real effort to enforce any anti-gambling laws that might be on the books. He refused to answer those questions on the grounds of self-incrimination.

But, later, when he returned to Washington in an effort to avoid contempt of Congress charges, he admitted he had done nothing to rein in illegal gambling. He said he failed to take action for the benefit of some 1,000 employees in the half-dozen big casinos, most of them elderly or poor, who depended on their salaries to survive. For their sake, he pleaded, gambling had been allowed to flourish. Gretna Town Marshal Beauregard Miller echoed that sentiment, saying, "Without gambling, the town would be dead. It has a population of 14,000 and its main business is gambling." He added, not insignificantly, that anyone who shut down gambling would certainly be defeated in subsequent elections.[15]

In addition to his selfless concern for the poor and elderly, Clancy also employed another underprivileged person named Cassagne who served as a deputy who made the arrangements for finding jobs in the casinos for Clancy constituents and who served as a collector of protection money from the casinos. Cassagne, whose first name has been lost to the passing years, was a regular in the casinos as he made his rounds collecting for Clancy.

Clancy, for his part, took the Fifth in his testimony before the committee when asked if he had ever received any money from Cassagne. Later, in Washington, he did admit that Cassagne made collections from the gambling houses and that he, Clancy, "might possibly" have taken a cut for

## Chapter 1: The Kefauver Hearings

himself. He insisted, however, that Cassagne's collections were for charity and those who wanted charitable "contributions" often accompanied Cassagne on his collection rounds. Kastel, who operated The Beverly Club admitted that one of Clancy's deputies, Cy Ernst, often drove him home from the Beverly, often when he was carrying large amounts of money with him.[16]

In exasperation, the Kefauver Committee at the end of its New Orleans hearings concluded that Clancy, with his "history and attitudes, his personal and business associations with flagrant lawbreakers, posed flatly and succinctly for the committee the problem of the admittedly negligent local official who eases the path for organized crime and its use of interstate facilities, but who can be dealt with personally only by local action."

The committee said Clancy "typified in effect" the foundation "upon which the entire structure of organized gambling and racketeering rests." The committee report said that without conniving and participating officials like Clancy, "neither the wire services and bookmaking interests emanating from Chicago nor the gambling and racketeering elements allied with (Frank) Costello of New York nor the local criminals like Carlos Marcello and Joseph Poretto could have used the interstate facilities of communication and transportation to further their illegal enterprises alone or in concert with other racketeers from all over the country."

The committee ended the New Orleans section of its report by noting that it was "apparent" that the following patterns of organized crime and gambling were present in New Orleans:

- The association of native gamblers and gangsters with outside racketeers, especially those from the Costello-Lansky-(Joe) Adonis syndicate;
- A deep-seated aversion on the part of law enforcement officials to enforce laws they were sworn to uphold;
- The personal enrichment of sheriffs, marshals, and other law enforcement officials through their failure to enforce gambling laws and other vice-related statutes;
- The interference with attempts by civic and religious organizations to encourage law enforcement;

- The attempt to justify "wide open" conditions by citing so-called benefits through employment opportunities and "by the fact that the 'people' (who are never asked) want it that way;"
- The failure (or refusal) to see that the apology for such wide-open conditions was tainted by the self-interest of the officials who had a vested stake in the continuance of the status quo;
- The brazenness of law enforcement officials, who in gangster style refused to answer questions about their law enforcement activities on grounds of self-incrimination;
- The failure of state government in Baton Rouge to take effective steps to ensure that law enforcement officials enforce gambling and other vice-related laws.[17]

New Iberia town marshal Howard LaBauve testified that in Iberia Parish, situated in the heart of Louisiana's Cajun country, slot machines operated openly and prostitution was allowed in restricted districts of the city all his life and no one ever objected. He said the State health department examined the women to ensure they were free of sexually transmitted diseases. His testimony lent evidence to the belief that law enforcement officials were not only lenient toward vice, but openly obstructive to reform.

Warren Moity, an unsuccessful candidate for mayor of New Iberia, found to his shock that friends were in the slot machine business but that they could operate only if they paid off LaBauve and Iberia Parish Sheriff Gilbert Ozenne. Moity complained loudly enough to prompt a grand jury investigation but the grand jury foreman played the slots and a no-true bill was returned. Next, Moity tried a newspaper campaign but the local paper refused to take his paid advertisements. Finally, unable to beat the devil, he decided to join him by going into the slot machine business himself.

He confided in his business partner, who happened to be the brother of city marshal LaBauve, and within a few days he was contacted by a former Florida slot machine operator named William Webster, who cut himself in for half the profits with Moity and his business partner each taking 25 percent. But when Moity began attempting to obtain locations for his machines, he found there were no good locations left. All the good locations were already held by Sheriff Ozenne's son-in-law and by LaBauve's brother-in-law.

## Chapter 1: The Kefauver Hearings

LaBauve told Moity his machines would be destroyed unless LaBauve and Ozenne were paid protection money. When the expenses of federal and state licenses, trade association dues, and protection payments to LaBauve and Ozenne ate up all the profits, Webster pulled out and returned to Florida, taking his machines with him.

The obstacles to success notwithstanding, Moity went through with the purchase of new machines but refused to pay the protection money. His bucking the powers that be naturally brought threats to both Moity and the owners of the locations where he had machines. On at least one occasion, he was shot at. He was further threatened when it became known that he was planning to travel to Washington to testify before the Kefauver Committee. He attempted to sell his slot machines and even got a prospect to put up a $750 deposit. But when the potential buyer couldn't come to an agreement with LaBauve and Ozenne, he withdrew his offer, Moity testified.

Illegal prohibition-era alcohol, gambling and prostitution, of course, were not the only forms of vice introduced to Louisiana and guaranteed success by the acquiescence of law enforcement. Narcotics, whether entering through the swamps and bayous along the Louisiana coastline or through the Port of New Orleans, one of the busiest ports in the nation, were a problem just as much as in any other part of the country, mainly due to the efforts of organized crime.

Thomas McGuire, agent in charge of the Bureau of Narcotics in New Orleans, told the committee that the drug traffic in New Orleans ranked in importance with that of other metropolitan areas. He said his unit was investigating the participation of Mafia members in the narcotics traffic but that their highly secretive organization made them difficult to penetrate. He said that any place that operates so openly with an abundance of prostitution and gambling was the perfect breeding ground for the narcotics trade by racketeers who were often involved in other illegal activities—with the tacit approval of law enforcement.

Jefferson Parish Sheriff Frank Clancy, for example, could not recall a single instance in which Louisiana Mafia boss Carlos Marcello was arrested for drug trafficking in Jefferson Parish even though he had previously served time for narcotics sales and despite the committee's having information in its possession showing that Carlos Marcello and his brother Anthony owned a goat used in running narcotics into the port of

New Orleans. Both Marcello brothers, in their appearance before the committee, refused to answer any questions pertaining to their narcotics involvement, giving only their names and local addresses, on the grounds of self-incrimination.[18]

The impact of Carlos Marcello, born Calogero Minacore, on New Orleans racketeering is impossible to underrate. The committee found his fingerprints in every line of inquiry it pursued—from his early partnership in The Beverly and the Old Southport, another casino, to running narcotics and prostitution. Phone records connected him with various crime bosses in New York and Chicago, including Mickey Cohen. His influence would continue—and expand into other parts of Louisiana such as St. Landry, Concordia, and Bossier parishes—until the federal Brilab investigation and his eventual conviction, along with former Louisiana Commissioner of Administration Charles Roemer, in August 1981.[19]

Marcello died 12 years later, on March 3, 1993, at his home in Jefferson Parish.[20]

# 2
## Louisiana Sheriffs' Association

The Louisiana Sheriffs' Association was founded in 1938 "to specifically address issues related to the office of sheriff and the changing times," according to a six-paragraph overview of the organization on its Web page. A "group of Louisiana sheriffs" formed the LSA "to become a fervent voice for Louisiana's chief law enforcement officers, representing large and small, urban and rural offices across the state," it added.[1]

The initial charter was issued that same year by the Louisiana Secretary of State's office for the Sheriffs' and Police Training School Association of the State of Louisiana. Seven years later, on July 27, 1945, the first charter for the LSA as a non-profit corporation was granted. Subsequent to that, similar charters were issued for the Louisiana Sheriffs' Mounted Posse Association, Inc. (1963), and the Louisiana Association of Deputy Sheriffs, Inc., LADS (1990). Only the LSA charter has maintained its active status, according to Secretary of State corporate records.[2]

The LSA is made up of the state's 64 sheriffs and almost 14,000 deputy sheriffs. "Its purpose is to maintain the powers of the sheriff as peace officer, to ensure the delivery of first-rate services by sponsoring legislation to promote the administration of criminal justice and to serve as a clearinghouse of information."[3]

Relative to the stated goal of first-rate services via the sponsorship of legislation, it's interesting to note that in 2018's regular legislative session, there were nine bills and six resolutions introduced that pertained to sheriffs. Of the six resolutions, four were to commend sheriffs and deputies in recognition of service. Of the nine bills, five dealt with insurance premiums for sheriffs and deputies.

Of the four remaining bills that actually dealt with procedures and duties, one provided "for an exception to the crime of political payroll padding by a sheriff." The legislative record was essentially the same for the previous year, with eight bills, five of which dealt with insurance premiums for sheriffs and deputies, and seven resolutions with six of those expressing either condolences or commendations. The same pattern is repeated in legislative sessions on a year after year basis as the LSA pushes legislation beneficial to its members with only occasional legislation dealing with actual law enforcement on the part of sheriffs' offices.

So much for assurances of the delivery of first-rate services.

Louisiana sheriffs, the LSA web page is quick to point out, are among their counterparts in other states in that they serve as the chief law enforcement officer, the chief executive officer of the court, and the official tax collector for the parishes in which they are elected. It's not so fast to reveal that its main reason for existence has less to do with law enforcement than with enacting favorable legislation pertaining to medical and retirement benefits for its membership.

The LSA is governed by an executive committee, an executive board, and a president. The executive committee is comprised of the first and second vice presidents, a secretary treasurer and a sergeant-at-arms. The executive board is made up of members and alternates elected from nine districts throughout the state. Working committees are appointed to consider issues of special interest to the LSA. Issues include areas involving legislation, risk management, civil law, emergency task enforcement, jails and prisons, juvenile incarceration, narcotics education and enforcement, law enforcement compensation, tax law, unemployment compensation, contractual services, and conferences.[4]

The LSA's annual conference is generally held in July at a posh resort in Sandestin, Florida, and besides sheriffs and deputies, is usually attended by the head of the Louisiana State Police, the secretary of the Louisiana Department of Safety and Corrections, elected officials and, in election years, by those seeking elective office. Training sessions are offered but over the five-day event, that consisted of a grand total of five hours while committee meetings on unemployment compensation, insurance, and finance took less than four hours.[5]

The 2018 conference, held from July 29 to August 2, seemed mainly designed for vendors, however, with 25 hours set aside for registration, setups and exhibitions. Mostly, the conference is staged as an opportunity

## Chapter 2: Louisiana Sheriffs' Association

for sheriffs and deputies to rub shoulders with vendors and politicians as evidenced by schedules for a golf tournament (entry fee: $125), family fun night, LSA officer installation brunch, Breakfast with vendors, ladies brunch, LSA president's/vendors reception and a second breakfast with vendors on the conference's final day.[6]

The LSA web page lists only two programs conducted by the organization and one of those is the Louisiana Sheriffs' and Deputies' Political Action Committee. The LSA, through its sheriffs' and deputies' PAC, contributed $266,000 to political campaigns during the 2015 election cycle.[7]

If the LSA is active in writing campaign checks, it is downright benevolent in the fees it pays its general counsel, the New Orleans law firm of Usry & Weeks.

Forty-five sheriff's departments are members of the Louisiana Sheriffs' Law Enforcement Program (LSLEP) which serves as a risk management arm of the LSA to self-insure members against public liability for the acts of sheriffs and their deputies. Premiums collected from the 45-member departments come to around $5 million annually. The most recent financial statement available, for the fiscal year ended on June 30, 2016, indicate the LSLEP had total assets of assets of $17.1 million against liabilities of $8.2 million.

The $6.6 million in operating expenses included nearly $4.9 million in claim losses and claims adjustment expenses and $1.5 million in excess insurance premiums, creating an operating income net loss of more than $1.2 million. Total liabilities of $8.2 million included $7.1 million in unpaid claims.[8]

Usry & Weeks represents 36 of those 45 members of LSLEP. The firm has a long-standing agreement with LSLEP dating back to 1986 with its predecessor, the Louisiana Sheriffs' Risk Management Program. Unlike the traditional lawyer-client relationship, Usry & Weeks does not submit detailed invoices with services broken down by the quarter-hour. Nor are the firm's fees allocated on a per-claim basis.

Instead, LSLEP is billed at a flat rate of $150,000 per month, or $1,620,000 per year. "The flat fee has resulted in a substantial savings on premiums charged by the excess insurer to the program as well allowing the LSLEP to set a predictable cost to budget for legal work for over 80 percent of its members," said firm attorney Craig Frosch in a July 34, 2018, letter to the author.

"...The Firm also is engaged as General Counsel for the LSA and has been since 1986," he wrote. "The LSA currently has an agreement with the Firm for a monthly flat fee of $2,400 under which the Firm provides services as General Counsel and legal advisor to the Association. No invoice is generated for this work, and there is no written agreement."[9]

The LSLEP-member parishes represented by Usry & Weeks include Acadia, Allen, Ascension, Assumption, Beauregard, Caldwell, Cameron, Catahoula, Concordia, East Carroll, Franklin, Iberia, Iberville, Jackson, Jefferson Davis, LaSalle, Lincoln, Madison, Morehouse, Ouachita, Richland, St. Helena, St. James, St. John the Baptist, St. Landry, St. Martin, St. Mary, Tensas, Union, Vermilion, Vernon, Washington, West Baton Rouge, West Carroll, West Feliciana, and Winn.[10]

# 3

## Christopher Columbus Nash, Daniel Wesley Shaw: Grant Parish

Easily the ugliest chapter in Louisiana's history was the Colfax massacre in Grant Parish on Easter Sunday, April 13, 1873 and the sheriff of the newly-formed parish was a central figure in the carnage that took place.

Christopher Columbus Nash, a Democrat veteran Confederate soldier of the Civil War who was held for a year and a half as a prisoner of war at Johnson's Island in Ohio, was sworn in as sheriff on January 2, 1873, only three months prior to the riots. Alphonse Cazabat, also a Democrat, took the oath as parish judge on the same date but Governor William Pitt Kellogg issued commissions to Republicans—Robert Register as judge and Daniel Wesley Shaw as sheriff on January 17 and 18.[1]

William Smith Calhoun, a local planter who had inherited a 14,000-acre plantation in what would become Grant Parish, was a former slaveowner who lived with a mixed-race woman. Despite his status as a former slaveowner, he supported black political equality after the Civil War. He led a group of freedmen to vote in November 1868. The ballot box was located at a store whose owner threatened blacks if they voted Republican. Calhoun arranged for the ballot box to be switched to a store owned by a Republican and Republicans received 318 votes to only 49 for Democrats. Whites, refusing to accept the results, threw the ballot box into the Red River and arrested Calhoun, who they accused of election fraud.

Calhoun subsequently drafted a bill which created a new parish, Grant, from parts of adjacent Winn and Rapides parishes. The bill to create the new, black-majority parish was easily passed by the Republican legislature. Tensions continued through the election of 1872 that produced a sharply divided government in Louisiana. Because of the lack of a consensus and with neither party recognizing the other, two sets of officials claimed virtually every office in the state.

The Republicans seized control of the courthouse and took their oaths of office on the night of March 25 and remained there overnight. Their black supporters, afraid that Democrats would try to retake control of the courthouse, began to dig trenches around the building. The Democrats, led by Nash and Cazabat, calling for armed whites to regain control of the courthouse, recruited whites from adjacent Winn Parish and the Republicans countered by recruiting a posse of armed blacks to defend the building.

Nash fed the tensions by spreading the rumor that blacks planned to kill all the white men and claim the white women for themselves. This only served to attract more whites to join Nash in the "struggle for white supremacy."[2]

Nash, responding to Cazabat's orders to put down the so-called riot, recruited an army of more than 300 white paramilitary veterans from Rapides, Winn and Catahoula parishes and began advancing on the courthouse at noon on Easter Sunday. When those occupying the courthouse refused his orders to vacate, Nash gave women and children camped outside the courthouse 30 minutes to leave.

The shooting began soon after and the battle lasted for several hours with only a few casualties. But when Nash's men moved a four-pound cannon to a position behind the courthouse, some of the defenders panicked and fled the building. About 60 ran into a nearby wooded area and Nash's men pursued on horseback, killing most of them on the spot.

When the remaining occupants of the courthouse surrendered, an accidental shooting of one of Nash's men set off the mass killing of all the black men, including unarmed men hiding in the courthouse. Some of the bodies were dumped into the Red River. About 50 blacks survived the carnage and were taken prisoner but later that night they were systematically murdered by Nash's men. One black victim, Levi Nelson, was shot but survived when he managed to crawl away unnoticed. He later served as one of the federal government's witnesses against those who were indicted for the butchery.[3]

While the precise number of dead varied, U.S. marshals visited the site on April 15 and reported 62 fatalities. A military report to Congress two

## Chapter 3: Christopher Nash, Daniel Wesley Shaw: Grant Parish

years later put the number of 81 black men identified by name. The report also said that 15 to 20 bodies had been dumped into the river and that another 18 were secretly buried, putting the total at 105.

As most of the members of the paramilitary group fled to Texas and elsewhere, Nash, in May 1874, formed the first chapter of the White League from his former army, and chapters quickly popped up in other areas of the state. Two months later, the White League threw out Republican officeholders in nearby Red River Parish, assassinating six whites and several blacks who were witnesses. Intimidation employed by followers of Nash allowed the Democrats to regain control of the state legislature in 1876 and to finally dismantle Reconstruction in Louisiana.[4]

# 4
## D.J. "Cat" Doucet, Adler LeDoux: St. Landry Parish

When two sheriffs' deputies, one from West Baton Rouge Parish and the other from Rapides, were arrested in 2014 and 2016, respectively, for engaging in sexual relations with prostitutes, they may have been channeling the late D.J. "Cat" Doucet, longtime sheriff of St. Landry Parish who openly ran prostitution houses in the parish.

In July 2016, the Rapides Parish Sheriff's Office in Central Louisiana fired a lieutenant for an "ongoing sexual relationship with a female engaged in prostitution," according to Louisiana State Police. Stacy Bender, 48, was arrested on six counts of malfeasance in office, two counts of solicitation for prostitution, inciting prostitution, obstruction of justice and two counts of unlawful use of criminal records.[1]

A news release issued by the sheriff's department said Bender "had an ongoing sexual relationship with a female engaged in prostitution. Investigators believe that Bender was on duty during the time he was engaged in these criminal offenses."[2]

Two years earlier, in October 2014, Baton Rouge police arrested West Baton Rouge Parish Deputy Florian Deutsch, accusing him of propositioning prostitutes for free sex, flashing his badge and threatening them with jail if they refused to comply. Deutsch, a 33-year-old corrections officer at the West Baton Rouge Parish Prison, was promptly fired by the West Baton Rouge Parish Sheriff's Office.[3]

The Deutsch arrest and firing were the third in a series of incidents involving West Baton Rouge Parish deputies. Days earlier, Sergeant Brent Ballard was fired after failing to return to work following a three-day suspension for falsely accusing parish inmates of wrongdoing and threatening them with violence. An assistant warden at the parish prison was demoted before that for making inappropriate comments to women.

The allegations against Deutsch stemmed from a pair of incidents. The woman called Baton Rouge police to report that a man later identified as Deutsch propositioned her through an online advertisement but when he appeared at a hotel to meet her, he brandished his badge and demanded free sex or he would take her to jail, so she complied. But when he contacted her a second time later, the woman went to police who set up a sting operation. When he showed up at a hotel room for their agreed-upon rendezvous, he was met by officers who arrested him. The woman was not arrested.[4]

Doucet was one of the most colorful—and corrupt—in the history of colorful and corrupt Louisiana sheriffs. First elected in 1936 with the backing of the Huey Long political machine, he immediately allowed illegal gambling and prostitution to flourish throughout the parish. He quickly obtained the nickname "Cat," as a result of his personal role in the protection of prostitution along U.S. 190 from Krotz Springs to Eunice.[5]

A 1939 FBI memo went even further in charging that Doucet "was operating all slot machines in St. Landry Parish." The following year, as his first term was nearing an end, both the St. Landry district attorney and the Eunice newspaper, the *Eunice New Era*, publicly appealed to the sheriff to clean up the vice in the parish. The newspaper charged that Doucet and other parish officials had failed to perform their constitutionally-mandated duty to shut down the slot machines in the parish.[6]

He lost his bid for re-election in 1940 and that same year, he was indicted by a parish grand jury on charges he had embezzled $3,000. Even though seven of his former deputies testified against him, the charges were eventually dismissed because of "prosecution irregularities." Out of office for 12 years, he was again elected sheriff in 1952 and the following year, another grand jury investigated Doucet for unspecified activity but failed to indict him. He remained sheriff until 1968, winning four consecutive terms and

## Chapter 4: D.J. "Cat" Doucet, Adler LeDoux: St. Landry Parish

surviving a December 11, 1958, *New Orleans Times-Picayune* article which cited "flagrant gambling law violations" in St. Landry Parish.[7]

In 1956, in an interview with Southeastern Louisiana University history professor and author Michael Kurtz, Doucet boasted that the election of Governor Earl K. Long, Huey's younger brother, in 1956 would enable the sheriff to "open up the cathouses again," adding that Long had promised to "let me get my fair share of the take."[8]

Stanley Nelson, editor of *The Concordia Sentinel* in Ferriday, across the Mississippi River from Natchez, has been writing for years about gambling, prostitution, and racial killings during the mid-twentieth century in that parish. A Pulitzer Prize finalist for his coverage of the parish's dark underworld, he once wrote, "To understand the underworld influence in Concordia Parish in the 1960s, one must first understand St. Landry Parish a decade before."[9]

So smoothly did gambling and prostitution operate in St. Landry that when Curt Hewitt arrived in Concordia Parish in 1965 with a blueprint to convert the local Morville Lounge into a gambling and prostitution hall for underworld figures who included among their number the notorious Carlos Marcello, he used as a model the operation he had run in St. Landry in plain sight and apparently with the blessings—and protection—of Sheriff Doucet.[10]

Doucet, like Earl Long, was an astute politician. Both knew the days of Jim Crow segregation in the Deep South were numbered and, again like Long, Doucet could do the math when it came to taking advantage of the African-American vote. Following Long's lead, he became one of the first local white politicians in Louisiana outside New Orleans to endorse the growing civil rights movement by allowing blacks to register to vote.[11]

But it was his legacy of prostitution and gambling that lived on in St. Landry Parish long after Doucet left office. In 1974, a *Baton Rouge State-Times* reporter, John Morris would pull into a club called The Spot alongside U.S. 71 just north of Krotz Springs. Inside, he ordered a beer only to be told by the shapely proprietor, "This ain't no bar, Honey, this is a whorehouse."

That same year the author, working for the same publication had occasion to go undercover in order to cover cockfights in the parish.

Security for the event was provided by deputies of Doucet's successor, Adler LeDoux. Following the furor over the story about the cockfights, the Louisiana attorney general was asked by a legislator to determine the application of the state's animal cruelty laws to the activity. The result was a legal opinion from Attorney General William Guste that cockfighting was not against animal cruelty laws because the roosters were fowl, not animal and thus, cockfights were not illegal.

LeDoux was almost as tolerant of prostitution and gambling as Doucet had been but he did have his limits. John Maginnis, in his book *The Last Hayride*, wrote that the *Times of Acadiana* interviewed LeDoux years after his retirement in 1979. Asked why he had tolerated prostitution and pimps in St. Landry during his tenure, LeDoux was quick to correct the reporter. "No pimps," he said emphatically. [12]

# 5

## Noah Cross, Frank DeLaughter: Concordia Parish

Concordia Parish, more specifically Ferriday, Louisiana, is best known as the birthplace of CBS and ABC newsman Howard K. Smith, General Claire Chennault, piano-pounding rocker Jerry Lee Lewis and his two cousins, televangelist Jimmy Swaggart and country singer Mickey Gilley.

But in the darkened corners away from the spotlight provided by the shared fame of those five favorite sons lies a shadowy side of Concordia Parish, a side that harbors whispered secrets of civil rights murders as well as the assassination of a suspected murderer in another case that implicated former Shreveport Public Safety Commissioner George D'Artois. The D'Artois matter will be examined in more detail later in this book but this chapter will focus on wide-open, payoff-protected prostitution and the simmering racial unrest of the Concordia Parish of Noah Cross, easily one of the most notorious sheriffs in Louisiana history.

Cross, who died in 1974, was the sheriff of Concordia Parish, situated in Louisiana's delta farmland directly across the Mississippi River from beautiful Natchez, on two separate occasions. The contrast between Ferriday and Vidalia in Concordia Parish and Natchez could not be greater (of the two major towns of Concordia Parish, Vidalia is the parish seat and the town that actually sits directly across from Natchez).

One of the oldest and most important European settlements of the lower Mississippi Valley, Natchez was founded by the French in 1716, more than a century before Jackson which replaced it as the state capital in 1822. An important cotton and shipping center, Natchez features many of the original antebellum homes that make the city so beautiful and such a tourist attraction.

## Louisiana's Rogue Sheriffs

Across the river, Vidalia and Ferriday present quite a different picture. A wide four-lane concrete highway slices Vidalia in half before leading into Ferriday on the way to such towns as Clayton, Sicily Island, Winnsboro, Mangham, Wisner, Gilbert, Baldwin, Baskin, Archibald and Rayville. Vidalia, the Concordia Parish seat, and Winnsboro come nearest to resembling real towns, with auto dealerships, farm supply franchises, and courthouses. The others, including Ferriday, stand in stark contrast with their run-down shops and deserted store fronts. Most feature the usual assortment of dollar stores, Walmarts, struggling furniture stores, liquor stores, rundown local police stations, used tire stores, the obligatory fast food franchises and the vast array of Protestant churches. Some may have once been centers of local commerce but now are just waiting to die, their weary stores and shops long since boarded up and abandoned or quickly on their way to that ignominious fate. Poverty reigns supreme in the Delta and nowhere is that more pronounced and evident than in the Louisiana farmland of cotton and soybeans that Concordia Parish calls home.

It was in 1944 that Cross was first elected sheriff, the same year that country and western crooner Jimmie Davis was elected to his first of two terms as governor. In 1948, Cross was ousted by Hartwell Love, the man he had defeated four years earlier. Cross was back to stay in 1952, again defeating Love. He would remain in office until he reported to federal prison in 1973.[1]

In a parish with a strong Ku Klux Klan presence, Cross had one of his deputies, Frank DeLaughter, infiltrate the white supremacy group. The move came not as a means of protecting African-Americans but as a maneuver to gather intelligence on Klan activities in order to protect Cross's own illegal prostitution and gambling enterprises.[2]

Stanley Nelson, editor of *The Concordia Sentinel* in Ferriday, has written more than 200 stories about the brutal killing of a black shoe repair shop owner and the failure by a succession of sheriffs and district attorneys to bring the killers to justice.

Nelson, a native of nearby Sicily Island, is a 1977 journalism graduate of Louisiana Tech University in Ruston. He began his newspaper career at the Hammond *Daily Star* before moving back home to work at the *Sentinel*, the quintessential hometown paper. He could not have chosen a better mentor in the person of the late Sam Hanna, a legendary name in

## Chapter 5: Noah Cross, Frank DeLaughter: Concordia Parish

Louisiana newspaper lore (his son Sam Jr. now runs the family newspapers in Ferriday, West Monroe, and Winnsboro). But make no mistake, Nelson has put his own indelible mark on the *Sentinel*.[3]

Nelson's dogged work laid bare the murderous activities of a group of about 20 men who were members of a secret organization called the Silver Dollar Club, so named because each member carried a silver dollar minted in the year he was born as a token of his membership. The Silver Dollar Club terrorized African-Americans in the Concordia Parish-Adams County (Natchez, Mississippi) from 1964 through 1967. Members, some of whom Nelson described as psychopaths, harbored no reservations about firebombing homes, churches or cars. Nor were they averse to kidnapping black men guilty of nothing more than walking along roadways.

Jerry Mitchell, writing for the *Clarion-Ledger* in Jackson, Mississippi, wrote in April 2014 that shortly after midnight on Dec. 10, 1964, Frank Morris, a black shoe repair shopkeeper, was asleep on a cot in the back of his store when he heard glass breaking. "He bolted to the front of the store and saw two men, one pouring gasoline on the outside of the building and the other holding a shotgun," Mitchell wrote. As a lit match dropped into the gasoline instantly turned the little shop into an inferno, the man behind the shotgun ordered Morris back into the building. By the time he exited the rear of the building, his feet were bleeding, his hair was on fire and the only remnants of clothing remaining were the elastic waistband of his boxer shorts and the shoulder straps of his undershirt. Morris lived long enough to talk to the FBI but told agents he didn't know his attackers.[4]

The Justice Department, however, was too preoccupied with three earlier civil rights murders to actively pursue Morris's killers. Only a few months earlier, the bodies of three civil rights workers had been discovered buried in a levee at Philadelphia, Mississippi (Neshoba County), and Attorney General Robert Kennedy directed the FBI's efforts to solving those murders.[5]

So why was Frank Morris killed? A couple of theories exist and both are plausible for the time. One says because he was the only shoe repair shop in town and because families then could generally afford only a single pair of shoes, both blacks and whites patronized his shop. He waited on whites, particularly white women, outside, on the porch of his store. Still rumors started by local Ku Klux Klan members said he flirted with the white female customers. Another story has it that Morris refused to repair a deputy sheriff's boots at no charge and in so doing, offended the white lawman.[6]

In February of 2007, Nelson who by then was editor of the *Sentinel*, heard the name of Frank Morris for the first time when the Justice Department released a list of victims' names from unsolved killings during the civil rights era. He wrote what he believed at the time would be his only story about the killing. Two hundred stories later, he is still writing. "I thought that 2007 story would be my only one on the subject," Nelson told the author. "But then the FBI reopened the case and the Southern Poverty Law Center got involved as did the Syracuse University College of Law, LSU journalism students, the Center for Investigative Reporting in San Francisco, and civil rights attorney Janis McDonald."[7]

Nelson said "scores of people," including Jay Shelley of the Manship School of Mass Communications at LSU, have helped him in his pursuit of the killers, most of whom died as suspects before charges could be brought against them. One exception is *Silver Dollar Group* member James Ford Seale who, in 2007, was finally convicted in connection with the deaths of the three civil rights workers in Neshoba County, Mississippi. Seale was the only member of the *Silver Dollar Group* to spend a day in prison.[8]

"All of the sheriffs and district attorneys have had these as cold cases all this time and did nothing," Nelson said. "It's their responsibility to investigate cold cases. One could also blame the FBI for not being more diligent, but thank God for the FBI or nothing would have ever been done. We tend to blame others but we all are to blame for this," he said.[9]

When all is said and done, the investigation of these cases comes back to a single person: Stanley Nelson, whose book about the killings, entitled *Devils Walking: Klan Murders Along the Mississippi in the 1960s*, was published in 2016. Along the way, Nelson was named in 2010 as one of three finalists for the Pulitzer Prize, nominated by LSU in the category of Local Reporting.

But rather than the racial violence—that, for the most part, was not really investigated by local law enforcement, after all—it was the payoffs to protect prostitution and gambling that turned out to be the downfall of Sheriff Noah Cross and deputy Frank DeLaughter, Cross's bag man.

## Chapter 5: Noah Cross, Frank DeLaughter: Concordia Parish

In July 2009, Nelson wrote that Curt Hewitt, who had a lengthy rap sheet, moved to Concordia Parish in 1965 to replicate what he had done in St. Landry Parish, further to the southwest of Concordia: to operate the Morville Lounge as a gambling and prostitution hall for racketeering interests that included Carlos Marcello. And while he was well-versed in running gambling and whorehouses, his curriculum vitae did not include dealing with the Klan.[10]

Hewitt, wrote *Sentinel* writers Nelson, Matt Barnidge and Ian Stanford, said he came to Concordia from Eunice in St. Landry Parish. He also had operated the Peppermint Lounge across the Evangeline Parish line in Basile. He had experience running brothels and said prostitution in the St. Landry area was widespread (see chapter on St. Landry Sheriff Cat Doucet).

Shortly before his arrival to help run the Morville Lounge, a club on Horseshoe Lake owned and run by a man named Reef Freeman, was burned to the ground. The Klan was suspected to have been behind the arson, though it was never proven. Hewitt told FBI agent John Pfeifer in 1971, that the Morville Lounge operations included illegal gambling and prostitution. Freeman dropped out of the business because it was feared the Klan faction in the area, which opposed not only civil rights, but immoral behavior as well, might burn that lounge, too. One Klansman told FBI agents that Freeman's Horseshoe Lake club sold hard whiskey although only beer was legal and "has operated women at his club."[11]

The Monterey Klan unit which threatened to burn down Hewitt's lounge was believed to have been involved in the beatings of at least three men in 1965: a white man and two black men. Despite the heavy hand of New Orleans mafia boss Carlos Marcello in gambling and prostitution operations in Concordia Parish, the Klan at the time remained a formidable foe so it became necessary for the club to protect its interests.[12]

Enter Noah Cross and deputy Frank DeLaughter.

In 1967, *LIFE Magazine* reported that Marcello's organization was operating brothels and casinos in Concordia, and that mafia-controlled establishments there received protection from various resurging Ku Klux Klan organizations. FBI documents indicate that after he took over management of the Morville Lounge, Hewitt's girlfriend served as madam, and two assistant managers worked as professional pimps.[13]

In a bizarre twist, it turned out that, along with Marcello, the Morville Lounge, located about 15 miles south of Vidalia, had a second silent partner—the Klan itself. DeLaughter joined the KKK, ostensibly to keep tabs on the organization from a vantage point on the inside. At the same time, DeLaughter was assigned the duty of picking up the weekly payments of $150 to $250 from the clubs. The protection money was paid in cash, stuffed in white envelopes.[14]

FBI reports obtained by *The Sentinel* indicated that hookers were secreted in trailers near the lounge and at a Natchez trailer park. A fleet of cars to take prostitutes to and from the lounge was kept in a garage in Natchez. The garage was owned by the Daughters of the American Revolution (DAR), an organization oblivious to Hewitt's activities. Hewitt also operated a service station to maintain the cars.

W.C. Falkenheiner, who took office as District Attorney in 1967, made it a commitment during the 1966 election to rid the parish of vice operations. He put a padlock on the facility in early 1967, effectively closing the operation for good.[15]

In the early seventies, following a six-year federal investigation headed up by FBI agent Pfeifer, the *Sentinel* reporters wrote, Hewitt, Cross, DeLaughter and others were prosecuted on federal racketeering, perjury and jury tampering charges. The FBI made the Concordia investigation a priority with three goals: to rid the parish of gambling and prostitution, to neutralize violent Klansmen and to remove Cross and DeLaughter from law enforcement.[16]

On May 6, 1972, following a federal grand jury investigation, Cross was convicted on two counts of perjury for having lied to a grand jury about his acceptance of bribes to protect prostitution and gambling in Concordia Parish. In his trial in Alexandria before U.S. District Judge Nauman Scott, two bar owners testified that they made weekly protection payments to Cross or DeLaughter. One of the operators testified that Cross was paid $200 per month to allow him to operate his bar. Though Cross denied taking payments, he was convicted and sentenced to a four-year prison term. Re-elected despite his conviction, he petitioned the court for a re-trial a month before he took office for his seventh consecutive term.[17]

But his legal problems still were not over. Following his perjury conviction, he was charged with jury tampering and obstruction of justice.

## Chapter 5: Noah Cross, Frank DeLaughter: Concordia Parish

Again found guilty in 1973, he was sentenced to six years to be served concurrently with his perjury conviction. After resigning from office, he reported to the federal correctional institution in Texarkana, Texas. He was released after serving half his term. He died in Ferriday on November 22, 1976, and is buried in Natchez, Mississippi.[18]

Frank DeLaughter was as corrupt as Cross and even more prone to violence.

Once the Morville Lounge's original owners got out because of Klan threats, club owner Judsen Lee "Blackie" Drane and his partner, Adams County (Natchez) KKK leader Ed Fuller, brought in gambling tables and hookers. Cross's chief deputy Frank DeLaughter quickly became a familiar—and frequent—visitor soon after that. They were not social calls, however. DeLaughter, by now a Klan member himself, was there to retrieve protection money on behalf of Sheriff Cross.[19]

In October 1965, all three men—DeLaughter, Drane and Fuller—were arrested, and later convicted in federal court, in the beating of William C. Davis, an employee of Drane's accused by the three of the theft of a slot machine motor. Initially investigated by the parish grand jury, the FBI later made it part of its comprehensive Concordia probe and made it an example of local police brutality. Davis, a white man, left the parish under the FBI's protection until a federal trial on the violation of his civil rights could be held in Monroe.[20]

DeLaughter would admit only to "backhanding" Davis a few times. He invoked his Fifth Amendment rights during his trial, refusing to answer any questions. In 1967, Raymond Keathley, a longtime sheriff's deputy fired by Cross the previous year when he ran against the sheriff, said he saw Davis in a jail cell at the old parish courthouse after the 1964 beating. He said Davis' face "was swollen and covered with blood. One eye was completely closed and the other was nearly closed." Davis died from the injuries he received at the hands of DeLaughter.[21]

Keathley testified that DeLaughter became intoxicated while on duty at the jail and physically attacked Davis. DeLaughter removed the victim from the Ferriday jail and took him to Blackie Drane's warehouse where he was again attacked and beaten by DeLaughter and Fuller. Davis was later returned to the parish jail where DeLaughter and Drane were accused of using a cattle prod on Davis.[22]

Meanwhile, Morville Lounge prospered, thanks to the protection of Cross and DeLaughter. Hewitt ran a sophisticated operation, employing twenty prostitutes, some earning as much as $400 in cash per week. Peepholes were placed in doors at the lounge, and pit bulls and an arsenal of weapons were kept on the property to guard against unwanted guests.[23]

But not all of the prostitutes were willing employees, *The Sentinel* learned.

Retired FBI agent Billy Williams of Portland, Oregon, resident agent in Natchez in the mid-1960s, said a teenage white girl, almost naked, escaped from the lounge, ran over the levee and was rescued by a minister and his wife. The girl said she had been taken to the lounge by force and forced to work as a prostitute.[24]

Another woman testified before a federal grand jury that following her arrest in Shreveport, she was bonded out by a man who, unbeknownst to her, was a pimp. She was taken by force to the lounge where she was kept captive for nearly six weeks during time which she was made to "work a date" in Catahoula Parish before leaving. She said she was slapped around by two men while at the lounge, one of whom she identified as Hewitt.[25]

Even with the torching of the lounge on Horseshoe Lake, prostitution and gambling notwithstanding, easily the most egregious criminal act in Concordia Parish's sordid history, most of which featured the ominous presence of DeLaughter occurred on December 10, 1964.

The sound of breaking glass woke Frank Morris from his sleep in the back bedroom of his shoe repair shop. In the darkness, he walked from his bedroom into his shop. He saw two white men standing outside, one of whom was breaking windows and pouring gasoline around his shop. The second man pointed a single-barrel shotgun at Morris as the shopkeeper approached the front door.[26]

"Get back in there, nigger," the man said as he pointed his shotgun at Morris. At the same time, Morris saw the first man, who had been pouring the gasoline, light a match and throw it into the building. Morris' shop was instantly engulfed in flames. Morris attempted to run out of the building but the man with the gun again said, "Get back in there, nigger."[27]

On fire, he ran out through a back door and toward a nearby service station next door. He was taken to a hospital by two police officers who

## Chapter 5: Noah Cross, Frank DeLaughter: Concordia Parish

happened to be nearby. He was unrecognizable to his attending nurses who knew him. Rev. Robert Lee, Jr. visited Morris in the hospital and years later confided in *Sentinel* Editor Nelson that "Only the bottoms of his feet weren't burned. He was horrible to look at."[28]

Morris survived for four days as friends, FBI agents, pastors and family attempted to get him to identify his attackers. Several would tell Nelson years later, they left believing Morris was holding back the identity of his assailants out of fear or reprisals against him or family members.[29]

Potential witnesses began to disappear quickly. One was a black man who happened to be walking by Morris's shop just before the attack. After his house was twice fired on by shotgun blasts, he received a visit from sheriff's deputies who advised him he was no longer welcome in Ferriday, his son told Nelson.[30]

DeLaughter, in an apparent attempt to discredit the reputation and memory of Morris, started rumors that Morris was a bootlegger and drug dealer, saying that the arson was the result of a drug deal that went bad. No one was ever charged with the crime and, for 44 years, Morris's brutal murder faded from public memory. Those guilty of the crime continued to live freely, fearlessly and with impunity until Nelson began asking questions and writing story after story about the killing.

*The Sentinel* reported that a woman said in 2011 that she had been told by a man close to DeLaughter that the deputy and Arthur Leonard Spencer of Rayville had torched the shoe shop. The man, Klan member O.C. "Coonie" Poissot, told the FBI that he had been with DeLaughter only a few hours before the arson and that DeLaughter told him he was going to teach Morris a lesson for being "uppity" after Morris refused to provide free shoe repair for the deputy.[31]

Morris was 51 years old when he was murdered. His business catered to black and white customers alike, and many people of both races considered him a friend. DeLaughter, who is believed to have been in on the planning of the arson attack on Morris, had joined the Ku Klux Klan in order to protect the criminal enterprises of the sheriff's office as well as his own, according to retired FBI agent John Pfeifer.[32]

Pfeifer, who from 1966 to the mid-1970s investigated corruption and crime in the parish, told the *Concordia Sentinel* before his death in April 2012 that while DeLaughter supported and helped carry out KKK activities, his membership primarily was a means of collecting intelligence on Klan projects, especially those which involved violence against prostitution or gambling operations run with the knowledge and protection of Sheriff Noah Cross.[33]

DeLaughter was also believed to have been involved, at least indirectly, in the torture and drowning death of Joseph Edwards, a black employee of the Shamrock Motel in nearby Vidalia. His body was never found.[34]

Though DeLaughter was believed to have been involved in a multitude of other criminal acts, it wasn't until the 1970s that he and Cross were finally convicted in federal court not for the Morris murder, but for their roles in running prostitution and gambling operations at the Morville Lounge. Their convictions were based largely upon Pfeifer's unrelenting investigation.[35]

DeLaughter, who stood six-feet-four and weighed 260 pounds, was sentenced to one year in prison after his racketeering conviction and for violating the civil rights of Davis. Upon his release from prison, he petitioned the court for a pardon so that he could carry a gun and hunt but his request was denied. He was forever barred from working in law enforcement and was prohibited from carrying a firearm. He died in 1997.[36]

# 6

## Willie Waggonner, Vol Dooley: Bossier Parish

Jack Favor was a champion rodeo performer. In 1942, he won $18,000 (a lot of money for that period) riding the notorious bucking bronco Hell's Angel in the Gene Autry Rodeo in Madison Square Garden in New York City. He also held the bulldogging record on four separate occasions, once throwing a steer in 2.2 seconds in a Houston rodeo, a record later tied by James "Big Jim" Bynum.[1]

By 1961, Favor had retired from the rodeo and was Regional Manager for Hydrotex Industries.

Willie Waggonner, older brother of U.S. Rep. Joe Waggonner, was the sheriff of Bossier Parish and his chief deputy and future successor was Vol Dooley. Louis H. Padgett, Jr. was the district attorney and O.E. Price was 26th Judicial District Court judge.

Mr. and Mrs. W.H. Richey operated a bait and tackle business near Haughton in Bossier Parish across the Red River from Shreveport.

Floyd Edward Cumbey and Donald Lee Yates were a couple of hitchhikers whom Favor gave a ride from Tulsa to Bossier City during one of his business trips in 1964. The lives of these nine individuals would converge to produce tragic consequences for the Richeys and to test Favor's religious faith.

Cumbey and Yates, it turned out, thought that the Richeys had $60,000 hidden in their possession. When the couple refused to admit if they had such holdings on their property, they were shot to death.

The case dragged on for two years without a serious suspect. Meanwhile, Favor, a deeply religious man, had no knowledge of the Richey murders. He barely remembered Cumbey or Yates, he told investigators when he was lured in 1966 to Bossier Parish Courthouse in Benton to submit to a lie detector test, ostensibly to support his innocence in the murders. Instead, Waggonner arrested Favor on the spot, and District Attorney Padgett filed murder charges against the former rodeo star.[2]

Following the Richey murders, Cumbey was tried in Missouri for armed robbery but was freed after a hung jury resulted. Brought back to Bossier Parish, Cumbey pleaded guilty as an accessory to the murders and named Favor as the triggerman. Yates had already confessed to authorities his part in the murders but said that the third suspect was not Favor, but someone else. For whatever reason, Waggonner bought Cumbey's testimony while discounting that of Yates. Waggonner obtained Cumbey's release so that he could testify against Favor at trial.[3]

Judge O.E. Price, later elected to Louisiana's Second Circuit Court of Appeal, inexplicably ruled that the jury could not hear Yates's testimony, which could have cast doubt on Cumbey's claims.[4]

Following Favor's trial, Cumbey was allowed to change his murder pleas to manslaughter. Incredibly, he received suspended sentences on each count. Seven months later, Cumbey was taken By Dooley, on Waggonner's orders, to Texarkana, Texas, and released. Jurors who convicted Favor, however, were lied to. They were told Cumbey would serve hard time in Angola. Yates, however, was given life imprisonment in the case.[5]

Underscoring the manner in which Waggonner et al had botched the case, Cumbey killed his former girlfriend and her roommate in Tulsa just two days after his release. Despite evidence to the contrary as to his whereabouts on April 17, 1964, Favor received a life sentence at the Louisiana State Penitentiary at Angola. When his attorney, former State Senator Joe Cawthon, died, his co-counsel, James B. Wells of Bossier City, who believed in Favor's innocence, began to work pro bono to procure a second trial. This required a lawsuit against the then-warden at Angola, C. Murray Henderson.[6]

During his seven years at Angola, Favor took the lead in turning the struggling prison rodeo into a professional production, which was first opened to the public in 1967 and which now attracts thousands of spectators.

Wells filed a writ of habeas corpus on Favor's behalf, which the state courts denied. A federal judge, however, granted a second trial on the premise that Judge Price and D.A. Padgett, had conspired to convict Favor in his first trial. In the second trial, held seven years later, also held in Benton but with a different judge and prosecutor, Favor was quickly

## Chapter 6: Willie Waggonner, Vol Dooley: Bossier Parish

exonerated of the murders based on Yates' confession which was blocked from admission by Judge Price in the first trial. Favor was not tried a second time for W. H. Richey's murder.[7]

Favor filed a $7 million lawsuit against the State of Louisiana for wrongful imprisonment but settled for a fraction of that amount, a paltry $55,000.[12]

Favor long contended that his conviction was the result of collusion among Price, Waggonner, Dooley, and Padgett, who by the time of Favor's suit, had been elected to a judgeship of the 26th Judicial District Court. The small settlement was a result of state officials having immunity in connection with their job duties, a law that gives prosecutors and investigators carte blanche to carry out false incrimination and warrantless prosecution with no fear of reprisals.

Favor died of pancreatic cancer on December 27, 1988, at the age of 77. Waggonner, who was first elected sheriff in 1948, remained in office until his death from a heart attack on May 9, 1976. He was succeeded by Dooley who remained in office until 1988. He died on August 11, 2014.

# 7

## Steve Prator: Caddo Parish

Steve Prator first became a Shreveport police officer in 1973. In 1990, Hazel Beard, the city's first Republican mayor since Reconstruction, named him Shreveport Chief of Police. In 1999, he ran for sheriff of Caddo Parish when incumbent Don Hathaway did not seek a sixth four-year term. Prator received 70.5 percent of the vote to become the first Republican Caddo Parish sheriff since Reconstruction.

Like other sheriffs throughout Louisiana, Prator, who began his fifth term on July 1, 2016, was quick to grasp the benefits of prisoner work-release program that adds about half-a-million dollars per year to the sheriff's office's general fund.[1]

Businesses are given a $2,400 tax credit per year for each work-release prisoner they employ. Caddo inmates are paid only $7.75 per hour, barely more than the minimum wage and under Louisiana Department of Corrections rules, Prator takes 60-percent or $63.50 per day—whichever is less—from the inmate's gross salary. One work release prisoner, after working full-time for 11 weeks, took home $416, or about $38 per week.[2]

When one prisoner noted that the work-release program in Bunkie in Avoyelles Parish took only 50 percent of his paycheck, Prator was quick to point out that the program is voluntary. "If he wants to sit in his cell, and he's not pleased with his room and board coming out of there, then he can go back to the main compound and wait his time," he said. "In the outside world, you have to pay your own way."[3]

The manager of a Shreveport bicycle shop who employs work-release prisoners at a slightly higher rate of $8.50 per hour said transitional work inmates perform jobs others don't want to do. "It's just jobs that aren't desirable, that aren't fun to do, like cleaning up," he said.

Prator's penchant for inmate labor brought him some international notoriety in 2017 when he complained during a news conference about Louisiana Governor John Bel Edwards' program of early release of nonviolent inmates as a means of reducing Louisiana's rate of incarceration, which was highest in the civilized world at the time.

Prator spent most of the October 5 news conference talking in true Trumpian fashion about the dangers of the pending releasing repeat 1,400 offenders he referred to as "the bad ones," comparing them with state prisoners held in parish jails and sentenced to hard labor, prisoners he labeled as "good."[4]

"Let's face it, somebody's got to be number-one and we've got some bad dudes around here," he said. "We've got some folks that need to be in jail."

"In addition to the bad ones...they're releasing some good ones we use every day to wash cars, to change oil in our cars, to cook in the kitchen, to do all that, where we save money. Well, they're going to let them out."[5]

Prator said that about 60 prisoners would be released from the Caddo Correctional Center under the governor's program.

Angel Harris, an assistant legal counsel at the NAACP Legal Defense and Educational Fund said Prator's remarks were "disgusting" and that he was talking about the "economic exploitation of human beings. He's opposing it because he's going to lose good workers. It reeks of the issue of slavery," she said.[6]

Caddo Parish has a history of racial discrimination in its criminal justice system. More people have been sentenced to death per capita in Caddo than in any other county in the U.S. and nearly 80 percent of those executed have been black. A 2015 study revealed that the parish was a hotbed of racial lynchings between 1877 and 1950.

Harris said as shocking as Prator's comments were, they were typical of the attitude they represented. "I think they're a reflection of the way our criminal justice system is functioning now," she said. "I think what's shocking to people is that this man just said this on television. That attitude is what's permeating throughout our criminal justice system."[7]

# 8

## Bailey Grant, Royce Toney: Ouachita Parish

Fraud, identity theft, illicit affairs, obstruction of justice, hearings on proposed attorney sanctions, forgery, botched prosecutions, a class action lawsuit, and a racial killing that produced four bodies but only a superficial investigation resulting in no jail time.

Throw in a couple of lawsuits and you have the Ouachita Parish Sheriff's Office, replete with scurrilous, unethical, corrupt and illegal activity dating back at least to July 13, 1960, and continuing, at least intermittently, for more than 50 years. And almost all of the stories swirl around two former sheriffs: Bailey Grant and Royce Toney.

Normally, in Louisiana, a sheriff holds office as long as he wants, or until he dies. His sweeping power is such that few potential rivals can offer a serious challenge at the polls. If he has any appreciable political skills, he solidifies his base by doing the things politicians do best: help those in the best position to help him and then call in those chits when needed. It was that lack of term limits for sheriffs and district attorneys that former New Orleans Special Agent in Charge Jeffrey Sallet warned about in his interview with the *New Orleans Times-Picayune* as he prepared for his transfer to Chicago. "Is it a healthy environment when the same family controls a parish through one of those means for decades?" he asked. "Do you really want to upset someone who has been in power for 30 years and may never get out of power?"[1]

Bailey Grant was a master of those skills. He remained in office for 32 years, from 1952 to 1984, declining to seek a ninth four-year term. Over the 32 years following his exit, Ouachita Parish has had five separate sheriffs. Two were single-term office-holders and only one served more than eight years.

On July 13, 1960, with Grant midway through the first year of his third term of office, the quiet of a seemingly routine summer morning was shattered by blasts from a shotgun wielded by one Zennie William Fuller, then 35. By the time the shooting was over just after 7:00 a.m., first with the shotgun and then with a pistol from point-blank range, four black men lay dead on his lawn. A fifth, though wounded, escaped on foot. All five were employees of Fuller.

Fuller claimed the five threatened him, but a heavily redacted FBI report on the cold case dated August 27, 2009, indicated that an agent interviewed a witness to the shooting who refuted that claim. Fuller was far behind in paying the men their wages and they appeared for work at his home and asked to be paid, the witness said.

The report said Fuller, who operated a sewer servicing business, "snapped" when the men demanded their back pay and opened fire with a shotgun, striking all five. "Four of them were lying on the ground but were not yet dead," it said. At that point, teenager William Herbert Fuller, identified as Zennie Fuller's son, "walked outside and shot each of the four men (the fifth, Willie Charlie Gibson, escaped on foot) in the head with a pistol to 'finish them off.'"[2]

Fuller, according to a November 30, 2009, story in the *Monroe News Star* about the FBI cold case, said the men came to his house with knives and that one of them swung at Fuller three times before he managed to retrieve his shotgun and began firing.[3]

Zennie Fuller, the report said, then walked back into his house, took a drink of coffee and dialed Sheriff Grant. "Bailey, this is Robert," he is quoted as saying. "You better get down to my house. I just shot five niggers."

Fuller and Grant "were known to be good friends," the report indicated. Fuller was taken into custody and initially charged with involuntary manslaughter but even those inconsequential charges were later dropped.

When Fuller, an active member of the Ku Klux Klan, began receiving threats following the shootings, he sought the protection of the KKK. (He eventually became the grand dragon of the organization.) Meanwhile, Fuller allegedly threatened the only survivor of the shooting,

## Chapter 8: Bailey Grant, Royce Toney: Quachita Parish

supposedly warning Gibson to corroborate his story and testify that he and the others had intended to kill Fuller.[4]

Giving Fuller the benefit of the doubt as to the veracity of his version of events, the execution-style shootings with the pistol by the teenaged William Herbert Fuller certainly should have warranted Fuller's arrest for second-degree murder instead of involuntary manslaughter. The lesser charge is reflective of the prevailing attitudes of the times in the Deep South but by no means can it be justified. To have even those charges subsequently dropped by the legal establishment which by necessity extended into the district attorney's office is itself an indictment of the very system put in place to protect the general population.

The close bond of friendship between Fuller and Grant, along with Fuller's ties to the Ku Klux Klan, only served to further underscore the injustices inflicted on individuals with the "wrong" skin color by that same system. It also raises the logical question of whether Grant, like other Southern sheriffs in the mid-Twentieth Century, willingly turned a blind eye to the Klan as it employed every means of terrorism at its disposal—including threats, beatings, and even murder—in an attempt to stem the groundswell of non-violent activism that defined the civil rights movement.

It would be bad enough if that was the end of Grant's problems as sheriff but as the decade of the seventies arrived, a new set of problems confronted him, thanks to a class action lawsuit and rulings by a federal court over the treatment of prisoners in his jail situated on the top floor of the Ouachita Parish courthouse.

By February 12, 1979, the parish and Grant had entered into a consent agreement with the federal courts that mandated sweeping changes in how the jail was run.

Those changes were precipitated by a class action lawsuit filed by jail inmates for alleged deprivations of rights under the First, Fourth, Fifth, Sixth, Eighth, and 14th Amendments. Among specific complaints were claims of overcrowding, inadequate supervision, lack of access to courts, censorship of reading material, lack of protection from violent, inadequate staffing and sexual attacks, and unsanitary conditions of jail cells.[5]

Prisoner rapes and numerous acts of violence involving weapons of broomsticks, wire, shivs, razor blades, and rope were documented by investigators.

Federal Judge Tom Stagg wrote a lengthy opinion in January 1982 in which he cited the defendants who included Grant, the Ouachita Parish Police Jury (Louisiana equivalent of a county commission) and state officials for several deficiencies, including failing to make legal representation available to inmates. No attorney had ever been appointed to represent a prisoner in a habeas corpus (a writ requiring a person under arrest to be brought before a judge or into court, especially to secure the person's release unless lawful grounds are shown for their detention) proceeding, and prisoner petitions were often deemed frivolous and were dismissed before attorneys could be appointed to represent the prisoners, Stagg said.[6]

Noting that the Ouachita Parish jail "stands in stark contrast to facilities elsewhere," Stagg ordered that the average population of 120 inmates be reduced to no more than 90 "on a normal daily basis" and that "no cell or cellblocks shall contain more inmates than the number of bunks available." This was after investigations found that some inmates had to sleep on cell floors.[7]

Stagg also ordered that more deputies be hired to serve as corrections officers for the jail and that all personnel "shall be adequately and properly trained."

Upon the establishment of constitutional deprivations, Stagg said, "the federal court is bound to discharge its duty to protect constitutional rights. The Constitution does not stop at the prison gate," he said. "It has been both a...principle of the Eighth Amendment (prohibiting cruel or unusual punishment) that penal measures are constitutionally repugnant if incompatible with the evolving standards of decency..."[8]

The Ouachita Parish Sheriff's Office entered a period of relative quiet during the three terms of Grant's successor Laymon Godwin. That quiet was punctuated by sporadic claims of corruption by Internet bloggers during the administrations of Sheriffs Chuck Cook and Richard Fewell. Those assertions were fueled by the firing of several deputies for reported violations of departmental policy. But through all the claims and counter-claims during those 12 years, no verifiable criminal or unethical conduct could be substantiated and no investigations of official wrongdoing were reported.

## Chapter 8: Bailey Grant, Royce Toney: Quachita Parish

### A Giant Step Backwards with Toney

The same cannot be said for Royce Toney's single term in office.

On February 25, 2012, only days after being hit with a wrongful firing lawsuit by former deputy, Gene Caviness who had given damaging testimony in a civil lawsuit against his boss, Toney was arrested by federal authorities for conspiracy, computer fraud, identity theft and obstruction. Arrested with the 64-year-old Toney in the elaborate attempt at covering up Toney's extracurricular sexual affairs was a deputy, Major Michael K. Davis, who worked in the sheriff's IT department.[9]

Toney, who was elected in 2007 but did not seek re-election, was charged along with Davis with engaging in a conspiracy to track a third-party's communication, and when Davis, upon learning of the FBI investigation into the pair's activities, attempted to conceal their involvement. The indictment alleged that Toney and Davis accessed a protected computer without authorization on nine occasions from April to October of 2010 and that Toney committed identity theft by utilizing an e-mail address and password of another person.

Additionally, the two were charged with a single count of obstruction for reformatting and installing a new operating system on a computer, once Davis learned of the FBI probe. Finally, Toney was accused of obstruction by retaliating against a witness who was cooperating with the FBI investigation.[10]

Assistant U.S. Attorney C. Mignonne Griffing initially was in charge of prosecuting Toney and Davis but would encounter her own ethical and legal problems that would result in legal sanctions and result in the necessity of a new trial for two Monroe city council members convicted in a federal trial in which she was the prosecutor.

On February 8, 2011, a team of FBI agents conducted a raid on the Ouachita Parish Sheriff's Office as a precursor to the indictments to come a year later. The raid was initiated at 4:00 p.m. and agents remained, gathering evidence until after 10:00 p.m.[11]

Toney had already been experiencing difficulties prior to the raid. He had been cited on numerous occasions in audits for violations of state public bid laws by using inmate labor on building projects that, because of their size, were mandated by law to be bid out. Inmate labor was used to renovate his office and for work at the sheriff's office's rifle range; Toney had also announced his intentions to again use inmate labor to renovate an old school building to be used to house the patrol division and the department's work release program.

Besides the wrongful firing lawsuit, Toney was also sued by his former chief financial officer for more than $15,000 in back pay. The sheriff came under heavy criticism for apparent campaign finance violations and was named as the "other man" in an acrimonious divorce proceeding after it was learned he was having an affair with the wife of a local attorney.

While he may have survived the lawsuits, the inmate labor issue and the campaign finance violations, it was the adulterous affair with a married woman that ultimately led to Toney's downfall. The details were simply too sordid for a small town in the heart of the Bible Belt to ignore.

The divorce petition of Larry Glen Culp said his wife, Laurie Schween Culp, whom Toney had placed on his office's payroll at $80,000 per year, had been having an affair with Toney for at least two years. He said Laurie Culp and Toney had sex at a training facility inside the fence of Monroe Regional Airport, in Toney's home, in the parking lot of the Monroe Athletic Club and other parking lots throughout Ouachita Parish—including that lot of St. Francis Medical Center on the night Sheriff's Deputy J.R. Searcy was fatally shot.[12]

Even the most inured political observers found it impossible to get past an act of such callous depravity.

During the Culp divorce proceedings, Toney made it official when he admitted under oath that he had a romantic affair with Laurie Culp. He said he had known her about a year and a half and had communicated with her as far back as 2010. For her part, Laurie Culp said that she was employed in landscape design and construction and also worked at the Monroe Athletic Club.[13]

The relationship began unraveling when Toney struck up an affair with another woman named Kim Leija, who would later deny being involved in a physical affair with Toney. The existence of another woman in Toney's life in turn sparked a jealous response from Culp who threatened to go public with what she knew. Prosecutors believed Toney fired her and then set about attempting to hack her emails to learn what she knew.[14]

## Chapter 8: Bailey Grant, Royce Toney: Quachita Parish

In August 2012, Toney entered guilty pleas to nine of the 23 charges, all misdemeanors, and three months later he was sentenced to six months of home incarceration, ordered to pay a $15,000 fine, and serve four years of supervised probation.[15]

The fine, which could have been as much as $100,000 for each of the nine counts, should have been no problem, given Toney's $140,000 per year retirement income.

Terms of Toney's plea agreement and the ensuing sentence did not sit well with veteran North Louisiana journalist Johnny Gunter, who had begun investigating the sheriff even before he took office in 2008.

"Shortly after he was elected in October 2007, the word on the street was that Toney helped out a local businessman who wanted an incarcerated employee released from Ouachita Correctional Center," Gunter wrote in November 2012. "The employee was wanted out of Mississippi on a burglary charge, but he was released. When Mississippi lawmen came to pick up their prisoner, he was not in jail where he belonged."[16]

Gunter also related the story of former Ouachita Parish Police Jury member Frederick "Bo" Boyte. Boyte, who would die from a self-inflicted gunshot wound, was in parish prison after being convicted of corruption in the Ouachita Parish Police Jury where he served as the parish governing body's public works director. While serving in prison and while on the sheriff's work release program, "Boyte was reportedly making $85 per hour as a supervisor for a pipeline company," Gunter wrote. "Most state work release prisoners make $7.50 per hour or standard wages at the places they're employed.

"In the work release program, the sheriff's department receives its expenses from the prisoners' paychecks and the rest is placed into a bank account for the prisoners to use upon release.

"The FBI was informed that the sheriff's work release program was only receiving the $7.50 per hour for Boyte's work." The remaining $77.50 was unaccounted for, he said.[17]

All of the foregoing would be bad enough, but the Toney scandal spilled over into the office of the U.S. Attorney, forcing a new trial for two defendants because of the romantic involvement of federal prosecutor Mignonne Griffing and now retired FBI Special Agent Bill Chesser who "manipulated the justice system" in order to conceal their relationship, according to testimony.[18]

Robert "Red" Stevens and Arthur Gilmore, Jr., two former Monroe City Councilmen, were indicted for racketeering and extortion in June of 2010. Specifically, each was named in a two-count indictment charging violations of the Racketeer Influenced and Corrupt Organizations Act (RICO), and the Hobbs Act, which prohibits actual or attempted robbery or extortion affecting interstate or foreign commerce. Stevens pleaded guilty to violating the RICO Act in May 2013 and Gilmore was convicted by a jury of accepting cash bribe payments in violation of RICO in September of that same year.[19]

Several legal professionals, including assistant U.S. attorneys, defense attorneys, paralegals and even a federal judge testified to Griffing's character and professionalism but the Toney case undermined her position, resulting in her being pulled from criminal prosecution and assigned to handling appeals. She also was suspended for 14 days without pay after it was learned that she may have let her personal emotions enter into the Toney matter.

Toney's attorney said Griffing had assured him that he would be allowed to surrender but instead, he was arrested, cuffed and forced to do a "perp walk" through his office and out the courthouse doors in full view of courthouse staff, the public and the news media.[20]

Griffing denied she had said Toney would be allowed to surrender, but the issue remained somewhat clouded because of Toney's purportedly raising Griffing's ire over his public remarks about her affair with Chesser which led ultimately to the appeals of Stevens and Gilmore. Griffing's attorney, Leslie Schiff, said the relationship between Griffing and Chesser "did not result in any instances of withheld evidence and had no effect on the delivery of justice, even on those cases where Chesser was the lead special agent and Griffing the lead prosecutor."

In the Toney case and in the Stevens and Gilmore cases, Chesser served as the lead special agent for the FBI and Griffing was lead prosecutor. Griffing, who initially denied a sexual relationship with Chesser, later admitted that she had been "very Clintonian in her answers."[21]

## Chapter 8: Bailey Grant, Royce Toney: Quachita Parish

Gene Caviness, the deputy who filed the wrongful firing lawsuit against Toney in February 2012, was hired by the Office of Alcohol and Tobacco Control (ATC) in August.

Former Sheriff Chuck Cook, under whom Caviness had worked, said Caviness had a "bad habit" of criticizing his superiors under fictitious names on Internet forums and Caviness even admitted under oath that he and Toney had conspired to discredit former Sheriff Richard Fewell and narcotics agent Mike Rowan on the Internet blog, *Cop Watch*, at a time when Toney headed the sheriff's detective division.

Troy Hebert, ATC director at the time, would have his own problems before eventually resigning to run for U.S. Senate. He received less than 1 percent of the vote in the 2016 race won by State Treasurer John N. Kennedy. For whatever reason, Hebert waived the interview process in hiring Caviness even though by then Caviness had admitted he lied under oath about possessing tapes of Toney instructing him on when and what to post on *Cop Watch*. He resigned under pressure rather than being fired as he claimed in his lawsuit against Toney, however.[22]

# 9

## Bobby Tardo, Duffy Breaux: Lafourche Parish

Some people take their politics a little more seriously than others.

Take, for example, Cyrus "Bobby" Tardo. Elected sheriff of Lafourche Parish in 1971, he was defeated for reelection by Duffy Breaux in 1975. That he went on to be elected parish president in 1983 was of little consequence to Tardo. Losing in '75 to the man he had defeated four years earlier apparently was more than he could stomach. After all, he had given Breaux a job after Breaux, who finished third in that '71 election, endorsed Tardo over his runoff opponent—only to have Breaux run against him in the very next election.[1]

On December 15, 1988, Breaux and Deputy Daniel Leche were leaving a senior citizen Christmas party at the Thibodaux Civic Center. A grocery bag was on the ground next to Breaux's vehicle and as he approached it, the sheriff kicked the bag with his foot. As he did so, an explosion rocked the still evening air as shrapnel and nails tore into Breaux's leg, nearly severing his foot.[2]

Marshall McClendon, 42, a former New Orleans, Baton Rouge and Gonzales police officer who had once worked for Tardo during his one term as sheriff as well as having served as an Ascension Parish sheriff's deputy, had detonated a bomb by remote control in an attempt on Breaux's life. Tardo had paid McClendon and John Tullier, Jr. of St. Amant, age 23, $8,000 with the promise of another $12,000 if Breaux died. A third man, former Houma police officer Ralph Bergeron, 42, was also charged with conspiracy to violate and of violation of the Organized Crime Control Act and illegal possession of a destructive device.[3]

Bergeron and Tullier conducted surveillance of Breaux several times before the bombing was actually carried out, the affidavit said.

An informant who admitted his involvement in the attempt on Breaux's life told federal agents that Tardo had supplied the money to have Breaux murdered, according to a federal affidavit that outlined allegations against the men. The informant said Tardo also gave McClendon an additional $2,000 for his participation in the bombing.[4]

The affidavit released at a press conference by U.S. Attorney John Volz said Bureau of Alcohol, Tobacco and Firearms (ATF) agents monitored a conversation between Tardo and the informant. It was during that meeting that Tardo affirmed his knowledge of the bombing, admitted to paying McClendon the extra $2,000, gave the confidential source $100 to help him get out of town, and admitted that he, Tardo, had entered into an agreement with McClendon that called for McClendon to maintain silence if arrested.[5]

Tardo, a retired state trooper who was working as a private investigator and an insurance agent at the time the bombing was carried out, was sentenced to 29 years, five-months in prison but served less than three years of that sentence. He died of heart failure on April 30, 1992, in the Medical Center for Federal Prisoners in Springfield, Missouri where he had been transferred after becoming ill. He never left federal custody following his February 2, 1989 arrest. He was only 61 at the time of his death.

Tullier was sentenced to 19 years, eight months while McClendon was given a 24-year sentence and Bergeron was sentenced to 11 years imprisonment.[6]

Breaux, meanwhile, would go on to serve as sheriff for 16 years, until 1992, when he, too, ran afoul of the law.

Breaux, who began his career in law enforcement as a dispatcher for the sheriff's office, pleaded guilty in 1993 to mail fraud, conspiracy and obstruction of justice for deals in which he was involved while sheriff. At the center of the charges was a scheme to defraud Lafourche Parish of more than $100,000 through Shield Land, a company owned by Breaux and his Chief Deputy, Eddie Duet. The sheriff's office contracted with local banks which paid for the storage of mobile homes. Because Breaux and Duet owned the land where the trailers were stored, they profited directly from the transactions.

## Chapter 9: Bobby Tardo, Duffy Breaux: Lafourche Parish

Breaux served more than four years in federal prison in Montgomery, Alabama, and was released in 1997. He died eight years later, on December 13, 2005, of complications from pneumonia. He was 77.[7]

# 10

## J. Edward Layrisson, Daniel Edwards: Tangipahoa Parish

As far as local political dynasties go, it would be hard to one-up the Edwards family in Tangipahoa Parish. In October 2015 State Rep. John Bel Edwards surprised the experts by leading a field of nine candidates for governor to make the runoff with 40 percent of the statewide vote. He would go on to defeat U.S. Sen. David Vitter in the general election the next month.

That same October night he rolled into the runoff for governor, his brother, Daniel Edwards, polled 65 percent of the parish vote to easily defeat four challengers to win re-election as sheriff. Four years earlier, he pulled 80 percent against two opponents of the vote to win without a runoff. He was first elected in 2003. Before that, their father Frank Edwards had served as sheriff as did his father before him.

Sandwiched in between was Edward Layrisson, who defeated Frank Edwards in 1979 and who remained in office for 24 years before deciding not to run again in 2003.

To say the Tangipahoa Parish Sheriff's Office has earned a certain degree of notoriety would be to belabor the obvious. From IRS liens against the department to the attempted bribery of a sitting sheriff by a state official who also just happened to be the wife of a high-ranking member of organized crime, to the release of a dangerous criminal who subsequently committed murder, to the raid by DEA and FBI agents, the department has seen more than its share of controversy.

All that—and more—occurred over a relatively brief span of only about twenty years.

Of course, the story of "Bloody Tangipahoa" dates back more than a full century and criminal activity has become more sophisticated and generally less gruesome than in the days of roadside ambushes, lynchings, and family feuds. Even so, violence still flares and dangerous and lethal acts do still occur.

Take the 1997 case of Aaron Stanley, for example.

On May 17, the Tangipahoa Parish Sheriff's office responded to an obscenity complaint involving Stanley. As the deputy approached Stanley to question him, Stanley pointed a sawed-off shotgun at the deputy who drew his weapon and ordered Stanley to drop the gun. Stanley fled into a nearby wooded area and escaped. The gun, later found in the woods, had been reported stolen.[1]

Stanley was arrested on June 3 on charges of resisting arrest by flight, obscenity, possession of stolen property and aggravated assault. Bond was later set by a 21st Judicial District judge in the amount of $15,000. He was given a return date of August 6, 1997, to appear in court to answer the charges.

On June 7, deputies inexplicably allowed Stanley to sign himself out of jail on his own recognizance without the approval of or consultation with the judge who had set the initial bond or any other judge in the 21st Judicial District.

On August 5, the day before his scheduled court appearance, Stanley broke into the home of Birdie Ellen Barron in Tickfaw, Louisiana. He strangled and severely beat her and she later died as a result of her injuries. Her children filed a wrongful death lawsuit against Sheriff Layrisson, jail warden Randy Pinion, and Stanley. In their petition, the plaintiffs said Stanley had broken into their mother's home in an attempt to steal money with which to escape the court's jurisdiction and to avoid his scheduled court appearance the next day.

The plaintiffs made the damning allegation that the sheriff's office "actively engaged in a practice of negligently releasing inmates to 'create a vacancy,' without court approval, in order to house federal and/or state inmates at a higher per diem rate, thereby increasing revenue for the Tangipahoa Parish Sheriff's Office."[2]

They also said the defendants "knew or should have known" that Stanley "had a history of arrests for violent crimes" and was a threat to flee and that the "negligent release of Stanley was the direct, natural, reasonably foreseeable and proximate cause" of their mother's death.

# Chapter 10: J. Edward Layrisson, Daniel Edwards: Tangipahoa Parish

The district court upheld the sheriff department's claim of no cause of action, thus negating the plaintiffs' claim. They appealed and the appeal was heard by the Louisiana First Circuit Court of Appeal in Baton Rouge. The three-judge panel comprised of Franklin Foil, Vanessa Guidry Whipple and John Michael Guidry, in a two-to-one decision, upheld the district court.[3]

In writing for the majority, Judge Whipple said bond "does not exist for the protection of the public. Instead, as the courts have recognized, it exists to further the goal of ensuring the presence of the criminal accused at trial. Thus, even if the sheriff violated a duty associated with the housing of this pre-trial detainee by negligently allowing him to be released, he could have just as easily committed the same offenses had he been released and at-large pursuant to the judicially-set bond by posting a commercial surety or property bond. Thus, as a matter of law, the trial court acted properly in holding that no cause of action exists herein upon which liability can be imposed."[4]

In his dissent, Judge Guidry wrote that the sheriff's office "negligently allowed Aaron Stanley, a prisoner in its custody, being held on a $15,000 bond previously set by a judge and charged with several crimes, including aggravated assault, to be released from jail without judicial authorization or review."

Guidry wrote that Stanley's dangerous propensities "were known by the sheriff's office. Specifically, the assault charge for which he was being held was a result of Stanley allegedly pointing a sawed-off shotgun at a sheriff's deputy investigating a complaint against him.

"As keeper of the parish jail, the sheriff had a statutory obligation to hold prisoners and/or detainees lawfully confined to his custody. When a detainee has violent propensities known to the sheriff, the duty to keep him incarcerated, consistent with the court's orders, is imposed to protect the public from the risk of injury resulting from intentional, unprovoked violent acts by an unlawfully released detainee. Ms. Barron was clearly within the ambit of protection of that duty. Stanley's violent attack on her was a foreseeable consequence of the breach of the sheriff's duty as statutory keeper of the parish jail to maintain this violent detainee in custody until he made bail or was ordered released by a judge. Therefore, the plaintiffs have stated a cause of action based on the actionable negligence of the sheriff."[5]

## Layrisson and the Mafia Lieutenant's Wife

Not all of Layrisson's courtroom experiences were as a defendant. He had one opportunity to prove that a sheriff could be above reproach—and he seized that opportunity in the highest of high-profile cases.

On October 13, 1980, Nofio Pecoraro, Jr., 31, was one of several caught up in a DEA raid of a warehouse in Washington Parish in which 750 pounds of marijuana were seized.[6]

Pecoraro's mother, Frances Pecoraro, was the assistant state agriculture commissioner and she also chaired the state's Insurance Rating Commission. Even more significant, however, her husband, Nofio Pecoraro, Sr., the younger Pecoraro's father, was a lieutenant in the Carlos Marcello Mafia family of New Orleans.[7]

Two weeks later Jimmie Burrescia, acting as an intermediary on behalf of Frances Pecoraro, met with Layrisson to discuss campaign contributions and, incidentally, the arrest of Nofio Pecoraro, Jr. On October 29, he returned to Layrisson's office and gave the sheriff and District Attorney Duncan Kemp $9,000 in cash as the FBI, tipped off by Layrisson, recorded the transaction. The money was from Frances Pecoraro as a means of ensuring that the younger Pecoraro would not be convicted. A second meeting with Burrescia was held, also recorded, at which a meeting with Frances Pecoraro was scheduled. That meeting, along with several others between Layrisson and Burrescia, also recorded, revealed that Frances Pecoraro wanted—and expected—help from Layrisson and Kemp in keeping her son out of jail.

A subsequent taped telephone call between Layrisson and Frances Pecoraro, who was in Georgia visiting a sick friend, not only provided details of the bribery scheme, but also moved the matter from the local courts to federal jurisdiction under the federal wire fraud statute and the Travel Act which made it illegal to use an interstate wire to facilitate a criminal scheme.[8]

During an evening recess at Frances Pecoraro's trial, a juror answered her telephone late one night and a voice asked if she was on the

# Chapter 10: J. Edward Layrisson, Daniel Edwards: Tangipahoa Parish

jury. When she replied that she was, the caller asked which case. At that point, the juror said she could not talk and hung up and disconnected the phone. When she advised the judge of the call the next morning, she said in response to his questions that the call would not affect her ability to render a fair and impartial verdict. The defense, however, asked that she be excused and replaced by one of several alternates. The judge said to excuse her might encourage other anonymous calls to attempt to disqualify jurors so that "we may end up with no jury at all."

While an appeals court later ruled that the judge had erred in declining to dismiss the juror, it also noted that the defense had waived any right to complain of the court's refusal to excuse the juror because as a compromise, the judge had given defense counsel the right to re-urge the motion to strike the juror or the entire panel at any later time and that the defense had made no effort to do so. "We conclude that this failure to raise the matter again at trial and, in effect, to gamble on a favorable verdict while reserving the objection for appeal constitutes an impermissible attempt to sandbag the judicial process," the Fifth Circuit Court of Appeals said on December 1, 1982.[9]

## Tax Liens and Blank Hard Drives

For Layrisson, that was his moment in the sun. His office didn't fare so well, financially speaking, after that and his successor, Daniel Edwards, elected in November 2003, took office in July 2004 under the suffocating weight of a $722,000 IRS lien, frozen bank accounts, and computers wiped clean and serving no function other than oversized paper weights.

Was it payback for what Layrisson had inherited from Daniel Edwards' father when he succeeded Frank Edwards in the sheriff's office after the 1979 election, or just a continuation of business as usual in the tangled, incestuous history of Bloody Tangipahoa?

The answer will probably never be known but when Frank Edwards lost his bid to retake his old office from Layrisson in 1983 by a 6,000-vote margin, the sheriff's office was in dire financial straits. There were wholesale layoffs of deputies and drug trafficking was on the upswing. Equipment had been sold off to the point that the department had only two patrol units, a few rifles and some microfilming equipment. The office was in disrepair with plumbing fixtures in the restrooms literally falling down.

Frank Edwards, while in office, had somehow found the funds to purchase 35,000 sportsman license holders embossed with "Compliments of Frank M. Edwards, Sheriff," 20,000 pocket-sized first aid kits and 200 boxes of candy-coated gum. A state auditor's report said that Edwards rented his own farm to the sheriff's office for "undercover investigations" for $500 per month and paid Tom Gillen, who managed his unsuccessful re-election campaign, $20,000 for a history of the parish which was never published. Gillen later became publisher of *The Democratic Voice*.[10]

So, 21 years later, the tables were turned on Frank Edwards' son who justified his father's actions two decades earlier, saying that state law required that all sheriffs leaving office do so with a balanced budget.

The sheriff is the only official required by the Louisiana State Constitution to be personally responsible for his debt, retired Assumption Parish Sheriff Anthony G. "Tony" Falterman pointed out.[11]

"Edwards takes office to find IRS puts lien against sheriff's office," read the headline of the *Hammond Daily Star* on July 2, 2004.

The story, written by reporters Aimee Yee and Sylvia Schon, said, "After learning about the IRS lien the night before his inauguration, the new sheriff confirmed Thursday that Sheriff's Office accounts are frozen at AmSouth Bank, which is former Sheriff Ed Layrisson's fiscal agent."[12]

Layrisson's accountant Bruce Harrell said he was unaware of any problem, adding, "This is all going to be cleared up."

Layrisson denied there was ever any money that went unreported, nor was any money ever owed to the IRS or to Social Security. "It was simply a reporting matter," he said. "These liens were put there without our knowledge and were removed when Bruce communicated with the IRS. This is not a money deal where I'm leaving any debt or anything."[13]

Harrell said the problems originated with an unreadable magnetic tape the sheriff's office used to report W2 information to the IRS and to the Social Security Administration for a two-year period during Layrisson's administration. Harrell said the years were 1996 and 1997 while Layrisson said he thought the years in question were 2002 and 2003. Harrell said the reports had been resubmitted to Social Security which apparently had not notified IRS of the updated information.

# Chapter 10: J. Edward Layrisson, Daniel Edwards: Tangipahoa Parish

Whether or not the problem was simply an administrative error, the problems did not end there. Edwards also said that six of the office computers at the sheriff's substation had been wiped clean, including the hard drives. All of the computers, he said, were reformatted but none of the passwords left behind for the new administration. "Every computer so far, no Windows 95, at least half a dozen," Edwards said. "It's pretty stressful."

Edwards also said that Layrisson's chief civil officer did not open the books for his transition team as planned but Layrisson denied that, saying the transition team was made aware of budget details months prior to taking office. He also said he knew nothing about any missing computer information. "I doubt very seriously that anything is missing from any computer that is a public record," Layrisson said.[14]

## FBI Raid

The problems posed by audits, finances, tax liens and wiped computer hard drives paled by comparison, however, to events of December 15, 2016, when upwards of a hundred federal agents descended upon the Tangipahoa Parish Sheriff's Office and the office of the Hammond Police Department, seizing computers, cellphones, and case files.

The raid, which shut down two government buildings in Hammond, was part of a year-long investigation into the U.S. Drug Enforcement Administration task force accused of stealing cash from drug dealers, selling confiscated narcotics and tampering with witnesses. Two members of the task force, both of whom worked for the Tangipahoa Parish Sheriff's Department, were already facing federal charges, and one pleaded guilty earlier in 2016 to state drug conspiracy charges.

Taken in the raid, among other things, was a computer from the office of Tangipahoa Parish Sheriff Daniel Edwards. "They're basically treating these buildings like crime scenes," one law enforcement official said.

While the FBI refused to comment on the specifics of the raids, the bureau did confirm that agents were accompanied by members of the DEA's Office of Professional Responsibility and the Justice Department's Office of Inspector General, agencies that have been seeking to account for an alarming lack of oversight within the DEA's New Orleans field division, according to *The Baton Rouge Advocate*. Search warrants obtained for the raid were filed under seal.[15]

Also implicated was veteran DEA agent Chad Scott who was stripped of his badge and suspended indefinitely. Scott, who led the drug task force, was accused of stealing money from a murder suspect's home while sheriff's deputies Johnny Domingue and Karl Newman were accused of dealing narcotics.[16] Domingue pleaded guilty to state drug conspiracy charges and was also indicted on federal charges. He was said to be in the government's witness protection program. Newman, a veteran DEA task force officer facing nine charges, including robbery and possession with intent to distribute cocaine and Oxycodone, worked for the Hammond Police Department as a young narcotics agent.[17]

Sheriff Daniel Edwards remained in his office until after lunch before finally emerging and climbing into his SUV and driving past reporters without comment. Jeffrey Sallet, Special Agent in Charge (SAC) of the New Orleans FBI office, declined to answer questions other than to tell reporters that the investigation was ongoing.

> Edwards did issue a statement the following day:
> *As many of you know, yesterday the FBI executed search warrants simultaneously at the Tangipahoa Sheriff's Office here and the Hammond Police Department ... in connection with the federal government's ongoing investigation into the DEA task force that had been operating in our parish.*
>
> *Unfortunately, I cannot provide any details either about the search warrant or the investigation because these matters are under court seal by a court order. I would tell you to direct any and all questions you have about these matters to the FBI.*
>
> *I can tell you that my office has cooperated with the federal authorities since the beginning of this investigation and that aside from the two individuals that have been charged so far – Johnny Domingue and Karl Newman – that no one in the*

# Chapter 10: J. Edward Layrisson, Daniel Edwards: Tangipahoa Parish

*Tangipahoa Parish Sheriff's Office has been notified that they are targets of any investigation.*

*Furthermore, we will continue to cooperate fully with the federal government. Additionally, I know that many people were inconvenienced yesterday, especially those who were trying to come in and pay their property taxes. I want to personally apologize to them. I want the public to know that we are open for business and that my staff and the many fine men and women here at the Tangipahoa Sheriff's Office are continuing to do their good work serving the citizens of this parish.*[17]

The ongoing investigation of Scott was expected to have far-reaching impacts on both federal and state cases involving the DEA task force and the sheriff's department. Even as defendants began seeking new trials in the wake of growing numbers of misconduct claims, Tangipahoa Parish District Attorney Scott Perrilloux said his office had been forced to dismiss several cases involving the task force.

Besides Domingue and Newman, Chad Scott was once himself a Tangipahoa Parish sheriff's deputy prior to joining DEA and once at DEA, helped to set up a pipeline of task force officers who began their careers with the Tangipahoa Parish Sheriff's Office. Besides recruiting Domingue and Newman, he also brought former Tangipahoa deputy, Justin Moran into the DEA fold. Moran, like Scott, was subsequently stripped of his badge and placed on "limited duty," which prohibited him from participating in investigations. He was said by his attorney to be cooperating with the FBI probe.[19]

# 11

## Jeff Landry, Charles Fuselier: St. Martin Parish

It was in 1993 that 23-year-old Jeff Landry and roommate Biff James worked as deputies for the St. Martin Parish Sheriff's Department. When a substantial quantity of confiscated cocaine disappeared from the department's evidence room, James was quickly tabbed as the prime suspect.

When deputies came calling at Landry and James's residence, Landry allowed officers to search the home without the benefit of a search warrant, presumably, according to writer Lamar White, without consulting his roomie. Stashed beneath some floor boards, officers discovered the cocaine, which had a street value of $10,000. James was immediately arrested. Landry resigned within a few months but was never charged.[1]

Today, Jeff Landry is Louisiana's attorney general, the chief legal officer in the state. Before that, he served a single term as U.S. Representative from Louisiana's Third District, squeezing out fellow Republican Hunt Downer in the primary election and easily won in the runoff. During that 2010 campaign, the cocaine story resurfaced when the campaign manager of his Democratic opponent said there were only two logical explanations: "Either Jeff Landry was a dirty cop and knew about the drugs, or he was the worst cop ever and couldn't figure out that $10,000 worth of cocaine was being sold out of his house."[2]

When Louisiana lost a seat in the House in 2012 because of the loss of population and the consolidation of his district with that of fellow Republican Charles Boustany, a physician, Tea Party adherent Landry was defeated by a percentage of 61 to 39 in a bitterly-fought campaign.[3]

During his brief stint in Congress, Landry managed to reject an invitation to meet with President Barack Obama at the White House and in 2010, during Obama's address to a joint session of Congress following the

Deepwater Horizon BP oil spill in the Gulf of Mexico, he held up a handmade sign that read: "Drilling = Jobs." Both acts were blatant displays of his ignorance of political protocol and the long-held tradition of respecting the office of the President, if not the President himself.[4]

After losing to Boustany, Landry's political career was in limbo for three years. Far from finished, however, in 2015, he challenged incumbent Attorney General Buddy Caldwell, better known for his Elvis Presley impersonations than for his pursuit of miscreants. Also entering the race were three other candidates. One of those was an African-American female attorney, Geri Baloney, from St. John the Baptist Parish, located a few miles north of New Orleans.

Caldwell ran first in the October primary with 35 percent of the statewide vote. Landry was close behind with 33 percent, followed by Baloney with 18 percent.

Baloney endorsed Landry against Caldwell despite having lambasted him in the primary campaign for his opposition to the Affordable Care Act and same-sex marriage. He won the November runoff with 56 percent of the vote.[5]

Landry subsequently hired Quendi Baloney, Geri Baloney's daughter at a salary of $53,000 per year in what many political observers saw as a political payoff. But what really raised eyebrows was the fact that she was hired to work in the attorney general's Fraud Division despite being a convicted felon on three charges of...fraud.[6]

Once settled into office, Landry took aim at Democratic Governor John Bel Edwards, whom he hoped to unseat in 2019. When Edwards attempted to hire Natchitoches attorney Taylor Townsend, a political ally, to be lead counsel in a lawsuit against oil and gas companies over the destruction of the state's salt water marshlands, Landry blocked the contract, revealing that Townsend had contributed to Edwards's campaign and had served on his transition team after being elected. The implication was that Edwards was engaging in the political pay-to-play political practice so common in Louisiana.

But Landry had his own motives, all of them political. He had received more than half-a-million dollars in campaign contributions from the oil and gas industry and many of those companies had a vested interest in the outcome of the governor's proposed litigation. Moreover, Landry

## Chapter 11: Jeff Landry, Charles Fuselier: St. Martin Parish

never disclosed that he was the sole owner of a company, UST Environmental Service, an underground storage tank enterprise which worked closely with the oil and gas industry.[7]

Jeff Landry has come a long way since $10,000 worth of cocaine was found stashed beneath the floorboards of his home when he was a deputy sheriff in St. Martin Parish back in 1993. But as political careers in Louisiana are more often than not defined by alliances and backroom deals than by qualifications and ability, one need only consider who his mentor was to understand his unlikely rise from obscure deputy to congressman and attorney general.

Charles Fuselier was sheriff of St. Martin Parish from 1980 to 2003. As such, he would have been the one responsible for plucking Landry from the Parks, Louisiana, (pop. 653) police department and making him a deputy sheriff.[8]

Fuselier's tenure as sheriff was a stormy one, to put it mildly. His 23 years were marked by repeated violations of citizens' rights that included illegal asset seizures, verbal abuse, and the physical beating of an innocent suspect with a baseball bat during interrogation.

Fuselier's refusal to take corrective actions, even after obvious violations were revealed to him, prompted a federal judge to observe, "It has been well-established that repeated and widespread abuses have occurred in the St. Martin Parish Sheriff's Department, that these abuses have been brought to the attention of Sheriff Fuselier, and that he has repeatedly failed to respond to them in even the most minimal fashion...[Sheriff Fuselier] was deliberately indifferent in managing his subordinates."[9]

Judge Howell Cobb's comments stemmed from a case in which a motorist, Howard Craig, was stopped by sheriff's deputies at 3:15 a.m. on March 23, 1990, after Craig's vehicle was observed weaving on Interstate 10.

Craig, after producing a valid Alabama driver's license and an Alabama certificate of title to the 1978 Chevrolet Caprice, told deputies he had recently purchased the car and was travelling from his hometown of Leighton, Alabama, to Beaumont, Texas, to purchase more cars. He gave officers oral permission to search the vehicle. Deputies found an amplified citizen band (CB) radio and a radar detector on the front seat and $18,000 in small bills bundled in a paper bag. After finding the cash, Deputy Paul O'Mary called for backup. A later search at the sheriff's department turned up an additional $13,250.

No narcotics, contraband, or weapons were found in Craig's car. Moreover, telephone calls to the car's previous owner, and to Leighton, Alabama, Police Chief Percy Lee Ricks resulted in what Judge Cobb described as only "minor inconsistencies" in Craig's story. Nevertheless, Craig was held incommunicado for approximately eight hours and was questioned at length about the money and the circumstances surrounding his trip. He was shuttled back and forth between four rooms where he was questioned by two deputies and Assistant District Attorney John Haney.

Despite Craig's request that he be allowed to call an attorney, he denied that he ever had such an opportunity and the questioning continued even after his request. Sheriff Fuselier was present at the station at some point during the questioning and was informed of the ongoing investigation.

Craig subsequently signed a disclaimer of ownership of the money and the Caprice but later said he did so involuntarily and only after captains Scott Haydel, Butch Dupuis, and Officer O'Mary told him he would not be released until he signed the disclaimer, a claim denied by the deputies. O'Mary eventually issued Craig two traffic citations—for improper lane usage and no proof of insurance, but not until after he had signed the disclaimer. A fourth deputy then dropped Craig off at the Lafayette bus station and no charges were ever brought against him by the district attorney's office.

Three days after the traffic stop, on March 26, the district court in St. Martin Parish held a forfeiture hearing. Based solely on the skeletal affidavit signed by Capt. Dupuis and the disclaimer form signed by Craig, the court found that probable cause existed for the forfeiture. Craig, who never received notice of the proceeding, did not make an appearance at the hearing.

Ruling on Craig's subsequent federal lawsuit against Sheriff Fuselier, District Attorney Bernard Boudreaux and Assistant DA Haney, Judge Cobb wrote that Craig's Fourth Amendment rights were violated when he was transported to and detained at the police station. "Craig's eight-hour detention at the station is indistinguishable from an arrest and

## Chapter 11: Jeff Landry, Charles Fuselier: St. Martin Parish

must be based on probable cause to comply with the Fourth Amendment," he said.[10]

The defendants argued that their "well-founded suspicions" justified the detention, prompting Cobb to write, "Reasonable suspicion is insufficient as a matter of law to justify the detention in the present case," adding that it "was clearly established that transportation of a suspect to, and prolonged detention at the station was indistinguishable from an arrest and required probable cause." Judge Cobb also cited a 1982 case that said presenting a defendant the choice between signing "such a worthless document" as a waiver of ownership and staying in custody is a deprivation of the right to liberty. "Conditioning release on the waiver of property violates a suspect's right to liberty," the judge wrote. "Under the Fourth Amendment, (the) state ... may not seize property without probable cause to associate it with criminal activity. In the present case, the deputies found a large amount of currency and some radio equipment. However, they did not locate drugs, drug paraphernalia, weapons, or contraband, even with the aid of the department's drug dog. Consequently, this court concludes as a matter of law that there was no probable cause to seize Craig's property. Furthermore, due process requires that Craig be given adequate notice of the forfeiture proceeding.

Judge Cobb held Sheriff Fuselier individually liable for the actions of his deputies because he was present during the detention and questioning of Craig and "acquiesced in the deputies' conduct. Furthermore, the sheriff apparently ratified their actions; when asked whether he agreed with his deputies' action, he stated that 'I would have to think that they acted properly from the evidence of what I've seen, yes.'"

Haney, on the other hand, tried to claim that absolute immunity shielded him from personal liability, a claim that Cobb rejected out of hand. "The evidence before this court establishes that Haney is not entitled to absolute immunity for his role in the detention and questioning of Craig and the seizure of his property. Haney's conduct on the morning in question is indistinguishable from that of the sheriff's officers and is the functional equivalent of police investigation."

Judge Cobb also held Haney liable for his role in the preparation of the disclaimer. "Haney assisted in the preparation by 'suggesting to

[Dupuis] some of the necessary legal things that I felt like needed to be included,'" he wrote in his decision.

Finally, Cobb, citing a 1991 claim against the St. Martin Parish Sheriff's Department and Fuselier, delivered a sharp rebuke directly at Fuselier when he wrote, "...it has been well-established that repeated and widespread abuses have occurred in the St. Martin Parish Sheriff's Department, that these abuses have been brought to the attention of Sheriff Fuselier, and that he has repeatedly failed to respond to them in even the most minimal fashion ... [Sheriff Fuselier] was deliberately indifferent in managing his subordinates."[11]

That 1991 claim cited by Judge Cobb was a case heard by Federal Magistrate Judge Mildred "Mimi" Methvin and she in turn cited a 1986 case which she also heard which had prompted a damning observation from her:

"Defendants admitted that at least 15 civil rights cases have been filed against Sheriff Fuselier, deputies under his supervision, or both. Sheriff Fuselier testified at trial that the allegations of these suits charge him and at least eight deputy sheriffs with brutality or other violations of civil rights."[12]

The 1986 case cited by Judge Methvin was especially egregious in that an innocent black man hauled in for questioning in the murder of a white man was savagely beaten with a baseball bat by deputies who tried unsuccessfully to force a confession out of him.

In November 1986, Detective Eddie Romero requested that Dalton Etienne, a black resident of St. Martinville, come to the sheriff's office for questioning in connection with the recent murder of a white man. Etienne had already been questioned once and released. Before returning for a second round of questioning, Etienne took the advice of his brother, a Houston police officer, and wore a concealed tape recorder during the interview.

The resulting recording was admitted in evidence and was played at the trial.

Etienne was brought into an interrogation room occupied by Romero and Chief of Detectives Roy Bonvillian. Romero told Etienne that the deputies had "a lot of evidence against him," including experts who would testify in court. He repeatedly said, "I'm going to tell you how you killed that old man," and asked Etienne why he was lying by denying his

## Chapter 11: Jeff Landry, Charles Fuselier: St. Martin Parish

involvement in the crime. When Etienne continued to deny his involvement, Romero began shouting at Etienne, calling him a "motherfucker," and threatening to kill him. Romero then picked up an aluminum baseball bat and struck Etienne with it at least four times on the arms and shoulders. Romero's shouts of "come on motherfucker" and "I'll kill you, motherfucker" are interspersed with Etienne's screams of pain on the recording. Romero continued to threaten Etienne, stating, "I ain't gonna put up with your smart black ass," and remarking that there was no one there to witness the events but Romero and Bonvillian.

Etienne, who never wavered in denying his involvement in the murder, was released following his violent interrogation and was never implicated. He turned the tape over to the FBI, which conducted a civil rights investigation culminating in Romero's conviction of just a misdemeanor following a guilty plea in federal court in May 1987. Romero was ordered to pay a token fine, to serve one-year probation, and to perform 40 hours of community service.[13]

"In view of the FBI investigation, Sheriff Fuselier chose not to conduct his own investigation, nor were any state charges ever referred against Romero for the assault of Dalton Etienne," Judge Methvin wrote. "Sheriff Fuselier did suspend Romero for 30 days, placed him on non-detective duty for five months, and passed him over for promotion to Chief of Detectives. However, in January, 1990, the Sheriff promoted Romero to the higher rank of lieutenant."[14]

Bonvillian, Romero's supervisor, was present in the room while Romero verbally harassed, threatened, and then beat Etienne but observed the beating without voicing any objections or taking any action, Judge Methvin said. Only after Romero struck Etienne for the fourth time did he give a hand signal to Romero to stop.

"Sheriff Fuselier did not discipline Bonvillian or take any other action to correct his approach in the future. No notation of the incident was placed in Bonvillian's personnel file, although the Sheriff admitted at trial that a notation should have been made," the judge wrote.[15]

Judge Methvin also noted that Fuselier took office in July 1980 with no previous experience in law enforcement. His background was in civil engineering and construction. In 1980, new state standards were implemented requiring new sheriffs and deputies to complete training under a program entitled "Peace Officer's Standards in Training" (POST). Since Fuselier took office prior to the effective date of the standards, POST training for him was discretionary. For whatever reason, he opted out of taking it. He also chose not to require any of his deputies hired prior to the effective date of the POST standards to undergo the training.[16]

Despite his lax supervision of deputies, more than a dozen complaints of flagrant violations of civil rights, and the beatings of suspects, Fuselier was described as an "icon" and a "visionary." That was because he grew his department from 28 deputies to nearly 200, oversaw construction of a new jail, a juvenile facility and a new substation, launched a parish-wide 911 system. His office became the first in Louisiana to receive accreditation from the Commission on Accreditation for Law Enforcement Agencies.

He served as president of the Louisiana Sheriffs' Association and in 1996 was named National Sheriff of the Year by the National Sheriffs' Association and in 2003, he was a charter inductee in the Louisiana Political Hall of Fame in Winnfield.[17]

# 12

## F. O. "Potch" Didier, Bill Belt: Avoyelles Parish

Prison telephones, wrote *New Orleans Times-Picayune* columnist James Gill in 2012, "are such a scam that operators can afford to kick back at least $15 million to the state over the next five years."[1]

It's small wonder then, he wrote, that prison inmates in Louisiana were "not so much allowed as encouraged" to make collect calls to family members "because the monopolies that provide the phones get to charge such obscene rates," up to 15 times the going rate for the outside world.[2]

Gill was quick to point out that the telephone rate scam "could not flourish without official blessing." The phone contracts for the prisons, doled out by the Department of Corrections or the local sheriff, "pour millions a year into government coffers." The occasional bills to rein in the practice get killed in legislative committees for the simple reason that the state was reliant on its share of the revenue from the operators. "If the state cannot afford to quit fleecing its most wretched citizens, we are poor indeed," Gill wrote.[3]

Perhaps Gill, when he wrote that, was thinking about the indictment of Avoyelles Parish Sheriff Bill Belt and his wife Tracy and Belt's sister five years earlier.

Given the excessive rates imposed on the captive audience (in a most literal sense), it was, perhaps inevitable that an enterprising sheriff, in this case, Belt, would seize upon the opportunity to capitalize on such easy availability of revenue. Even state statutes that prohibited a sheriff from participating in a transaction in which he has a personal substantial economic interest and which involves the sheriff's office or which prohibited the sheriff's office from doing business with any member of his immediate family discouraged him from filing articles of incorporation for three separate companies positioned to do just that.

The companies were Central Louisiana Communications, Inc., and Southern Louisiana Communications, Inc. chartered in 1993, according to papers filed with the Louisiana Secretary of State, and Infinity Communications, Inc., founded in 1997. He was listed as agent and director for each of the three entities. For good measure, there was Cajun Callers of Bayhills, Inc., chartered in 2002, and run by officers Rae Ellen and Joseph D. Johnson.

Records on file with the Louisiana Secretary of State's office indicated that Cajun Callers has been inactive since 2002 but that all three of Belts' companies remained active and in good standing as late as 2017.[4]

It was payments to Cajun and Infinity that resulted in the nine-count federal indictment of Belt, his wife and his sister, Julie Ann Bernard, on August 1, 2007.

The indictment said on October 1, 1988, the three entered into a conspiracy to "promote and cover up the receipt of proceeds...from the operation of phone services provided at jails operated by the Avoyelles Parish Sheriff's Office." As part of the alleged conspiracy, the Belts, "along with other family members, would receive proceeds from the operation of those phones" and that Belt "had an interest in (and) would receive proceeds from the operation of phones" at the jails.[5]

The indictment further charged that on September 6, October 7, and November 1, 2002, checks were mailed by the three to Cajun Callers. They also were accused of mailing checks to Infinity on January 15, 2003, January 6, 2004, April 26, 2006, and May 30, 2006.

Bernard was also indicted for lying to FBI agents in denying she had any involvement with Cajun Callers and had no memory of signing checks issued to Cajun.[6]

U.S. Attorney Donald Washington said in exchange for his approval of the operation of phone services by favored vendors, Belt and family members "and businesses in which the sheriff had an ownership interest all received proceeds from those services." He

## Chapter 12: F.O. "Potch" Didier, Bill Belt: Avoyelles Parish

said Belt and his wife had illegally profited from the proceeds from inmate phone services over a period of 19 years.[7]

When the dust had finally settled in November 2010, however, Belt, his wife and sister, who had retained the services of Alexandria high-profile criminal defense attorney Mike Small, walked out of the federal courthouse in Shreveport to freedom after a jury found them not guilty of all charges.[8]

While easily the most serious in terms of possible criminal liability, the prison telephone indictment was not Belt's only problem.

Pursuant to a 1971 lawsuit by four inmates of the Louisiana State Penitentiary at Angola (*Hayes Williams, et al, v. Edwin W. Edwards, et al*), who had claimed inmate housing conditions at Angola violated the Eighth and 14th Amendments, a state district court entered injunctive relief in 1975 designed to improve the conditions at Angola and decentralize the Louisiana prison system. The decision was affirmed by the U.S. Fifth Circuit Court of Appeals in February 1977.[9]

The Fifth Circuit, however remanded the case for a determination of appropriate inmate population limits and security staffing requirements both for Angola and for other state prisons which had been built to decentralize Angola. The Department of Public Safety and Corrections subsequently prepared a plan outlining proposed staffing patterns and population limits throughout the state. This "Stipulation and Consent Decree" was signed by various state officials and state prison officials, but was not by the inmates themselves. In 1983, this consent decree was approved by the district court.[10]

"Incident to that plan," the Fifth Circuit said on June 4, 1992, "the Department of Corrections called upon many Louisiana cities and parishes to house convicted state inmates to help alleviate overcrowded conditions in the state facilities. As state prisoners began to arrive in numbers at local jails, federal court suits ensued complaining of overcrowded." By 1989, conditions in Louisiana prisons had deteriorated to the point that a "state of emergency" was declared by the district court which appointed an expert, former Angola Warden Ross Maggio, to assist in resolving these problems.[11]

Maggio was directed to inspect "certain conditions of confinement in Louisiana parish jails, including the Avoyelles Parish jails. Sheriff Belt immediately filed a motion to vacate the 1990 ruling by the district court. His motion was denied and he appealed, resulting in the Fifth Circuit's June 1992 ruling.

The court conceded that neither Belt nor Avoyelles Parish was a party to the Edwards litigation. Nor was there ever, the ruling said, "an adjudication of unconstitutional conditions of confinement at the Avoyelles Parish jails. Nevertheless, Avoyelles Parish is a party to a Stipulation and Consent Decree which sets inmate population limits in the various parish facilities, determines the number of guards required to be on duty and agrees that the state fire marshal and health officer may enforce in state court the rules and regulations of their respective offices."

Belt and Avoyelles Parish, the ruling said, "take issue with the September 1990 order on the grounds that the entry of the Avoyelles Parish Consent Decree did not give the district court jurisdiction over Sheriff Belt and Avoyelles Parish. They argue that the Avoyelles Parish Consent Decree does not enable the district court to assert general supervisory authority over the parish jails or permit even more limited supervisory authority over inmate population limits or guard-to-inmate ratios in the absence of a finding of violations of the consent decree.

"We disagree. Whatever may be the case about jurisdiction over Sheriff Belt and Avoyelles generally, a matter which we need not address, the Avoyelles Parish Consent Decree does permit the entry of the September 1990 order which is designed for the narrow purpose of monitoring compliance with the decree."[12]

Belt became sheriff by virtue of the decision by his predecessor, F.O. "Potch" Didier, not to seek re-election in 1979 after five successive terms as sheriff.

Didier, a colorful character, was first elected in 1959 and holds the distinction of once serving nine days as an inmate in his own jail after becoming involved in a political dispute with then-District Attorney Charles Riddle in 1970.[13]

The reasons behind the dust-up between Didier and Riddle have long since been lost to historians, but he was convicted of malfeasance in office in a trial that brought national notoriety to the small rural parish in

**Chapter 12: F.O. "Potch" Didier, Bill Belt: Avoyelles Parish**

Central Louisiana. Jim Levy, former publisher of the *Bunkie Record*, called it "the biggest trial in the parish" and "an amazing spectacle."[14]

Lead prosecutor was First Assistant District Attorney John Boatner and when the air had finally cleared, Potch was sentenced to 90 days in the parish jail. "I remember that first night he began his sentence," Levy said. "He cooked an andouille gumbo."[15]

Didier was released after only nine days (for good behavior, of course) and immediately assumed his role as the parish's top law enforcement official. He was re-elected two more times, the last in 1975. On New Year's Day, 1980, as outgoing president of the politically powerful Louisiana Sheriffs' Association and as a lame duck sheriff, he had a telephone conversation with U.S. President Jimmy Carter who would go on to lose his own bid for re-election ten months later to Ronald Reagan. The subject of their conversation was never revealed. Didier remained active in the Sheriffs' Association after leaving office.[16]

# 13
## Jessel Ourso: Iberville Parish

Jessel Ourso is one of those people on whom it is nearly impossible to pin a single label. He was at once a saint and a sinner, a rogue and a reformer, a charismatic politician and a powerful despot. Known as the Black Stallion, he served only ten years as sheriff of Iberville Parish—two full terms and part of a third—before his death at the young age of 46—but the legacy he left and the controversy he crammed into those ten years makes it seem as though he was in office much longer.

A man who first worked as a Baton Rouge cop and later as a Louisiana State Trooper and whose reputation would reach into the Swiss Alps, he was removed from office by a governor after his failure to account for money paid to the sheriff's office. He was tried on 33 state and five federal charges and was forced to feed his family while working as a pipefitter for three years but yet, never spent a day in jail.

Conversely, he is credited with establishing Iberville Parish's first prison work-release program and its first "Junior Deputy" program. He organized the sheriff's flotilla to cover swamplands and waterways in the parish and introduced the psychological stress evaluator in the investigation of crimes. He established the first parish wide ambulance service and was the first Iberville Parish sheriff to use a helicopter. He constructed a firing range for deputies and opened it up to the public and established substations for the sheriff's office and staffed them with deputies around the clock. Finally, he built a new $2 million jail for the parish that was finished just before his 1978 death.[1]

It was the end of February 2018 and John J. McKeithen was just completing his first term of office. McKeithen had earlier upset long-standing tradition when he managed to change the State Constitution during his first term so that he could run for re-election. Previously, Louisiana's governors were prohibited from serving two consecutive terms. He would set another precedent when he invoked gubernatorial powers under Article IX, Section 8 of the 1921 Louisiana State Constitution which resulted in the heretofore unthinkable act of suspending a sitting sheriff from office. The current State Constitution, adopted in 1974, removed that authority from the governor, but in 1968 it was a potent club for the governor to use to keep local politicians in line.

Iberville Parish is south of Baton Rouge and situated mostly across the Mississippi River from the capital city, on the west bank. It was there that Ourso was first elected sheriff in 1963, taking office in January the following year. He quickly established himself as someone who overshadowed the state's popular governor. While on a trip to Switzerland to promote economic development for the state, a Swiss executive asked McKeithen what he planned to do about the sheriff in Iberville Parish.[2]

The answer wasn't long in coming. When the Louisiana Legislative Auditor questioned Ourso's failure to account for money the sheriff's office received as payment for security from construction and engineering firms erecting chemical plants along the Mississippi River in Iberville Parish, McKeithen first removed Ourso from office in February 1968 and then refused to issue him his commission after his landslide re-election the previous fall.[3]

In Ourso's case, it was just a matter of old-fashioned Louisiana corruption and extortion that prompted McKeithen to take his action. Iberville was in the midst of a construction explosion with chemical plants sprouting up all along the Mississippi.

Ourso placed his brother in a no-show job as a union steward for the Teamsters at one plant and contractors were ordered to lease equipment from Ourso's nephew, State Trooper Jackie Jackson. The tipping point, though, was Ourso's requirement that contractors use a guard service owned and operated by the sheriff.

One witness described an atmosphere of "just plain racketeering and shakedowns through collusion of individual law enforcement officers and labor."

McKeithen's decision to suspend Ourso was based on the recommendation of then-State Comptroller Roy Theriot which in turn stemmed from a report by Legislative Auditor J.B. Lancaster which laid out

## Chapter 13: Jessel Ourso: Iberville Parish

Ourso's strong-arm tactics, including his preventing contractors from firing workers who were performing no work.[4]

The governor's actions forced Ourso to work for the next three years as a pipefitter as he planned his comeback from the politically dead. With McKeithen ineligible to seek a third term under the state's constitution, Ourso was free to run again in 1971 without the fear of again being blocked from taking office. Again, he won and this time, he took office.

Ourso's son, Mitch Ourso, described the 1971 campaign as the race of his father's life.

That was because he was simultaneously running for election and fending off criminal charges in state court and extortion charges in federal court. In the end, his trials ended either in acquittals or hung juries—and he won his election battle against the incumbent the same year another controversial politician, Edwin W. Edwards, would win the first of his four terms as governor.[5]

He was re-elected again, defeating five challengers in 1975, but would not live to serve out his term. He died on August 28, 1978, in a Houston hospital from liver and kidney failure following a lengthy battle with viral hepatitis.

Described by veteran reporter Dee Cruise as "Iberville's most feared and revered political figure," Ourso was a combat veteran, having served 15 months during the Korean conflict. Another reporter, *The Baton Rouge Advocate*'s Milford Fryer described him as a man who "lived hard and fast, and he left behind a legacy of political astuteness not likely to be repeated in Iberville Parish for years to come."[6]

He was elected posthumously to the Louisiana Political Museum and Hall of Fame in Winnfield in 2009, joining only four other Louisiana sheriffs in that honor: Jefferson Parish's Harry Lee, St. Landry legend Cat Doucet, Grant Parish's Leonard R. "Pop" Hataway, and Charles Fuselier of St. Martin Parish. The following year, he was inducted into the Louisiana Justice Hall of Fame by the Louisiana State Penitentiary Museum Foundation.[7]

# 14

## Eugene Holland, Chaney Phillips, Ronald "Gun" Ficklin, Jessie Hughes: St. Helena Parish

In terms of bad luck with sheriffs, St. Helena Parish must hold franchise rights. Three consecutive sheriffs—and a deputy—were carted off to jail between 1996 and 2008. Charges ranged from theft to mail fraud, conspiracy and money laundering to running a chop shop to molestation of a juvenile and aggravated rape.

In January 1997, Sheriff Eugene Holland was found guilty of misuse of government funds (paying personal bills totaling some $28,000 with public money) and property and using prison inmates for personal labor. He received a 16-month prison sentence.[1]

Holland, who was sheriff for 12 years, died on December 14, 2010, at age 76.[2]

His arrest, conviction and imprisonment seemed to be an ominous precursor for things to come. Less than a year later, in August, his successor, Chaney Phillips, who won a special election to succeed Holland, was indicted on 19 counts of conspiracy, mail fraud and money laundering. The charges were for actions federal authorities said occurred while he served as St. Helena Parish's tax assessor.[3]

Prior to the April election to succeed Holland, a state audit revealed the allegations of conspiracy, mail fraud and money laundering. Also indicted on 15 counts of his own was Phillips' friend, Greensburg businessman Emerson Newman. Phillips was accused in the grand jury indictment of falsely listing Newman and his wife, Jean Newman, as employees of the assessor's office in 1990. They were paid salaries and the assessor's office also paid for their insurance coverage. When Jean Newman fell ill, the Newmans received $160,000 in hospitalization insurance benefits, authorities said. After she died, her husband collected an additional $15,000 in life insurance benefits.

Phillips also was accused of spending nearly $2,000 from the assessor's office to buy suits and clothing for himself.[4]

Weeks before the April election, state police arrested four people - including Emerson Newman - charging them with voter fraud. At the time, officers would not say which of the ten sheriff candidates were connected to the alleged vote-buying. 21st Judicial District Attorney Scott Perrilloux said evidence linked Phillips to the alleged vote buying.[5]

Phillips claimed he was innocent of all charges, but in April 1998, almost exactly a year after his election, he was found guilty on charges of conspiracy, mail fraud, theft and money laundering and was sentenced to eight years in prison.[6]

Now it was Ronald "Gun" Ficklin's turn. He would last eight years before he too, faced felony charges.

Ficklin resigned as mayor of Greensburg when he was appointed sheriff after Phillips was forced from office despite testimony from an FBI agent that he had threatened investigators who were looking into vote-buying allegations in connection with Phillips' election. Ficklin later testified that he had made a mistake and apologized for his actions.[7]

Assuming office in April 1998, Ficklin should have learned from the experience of his predecessors. Instead, he became deeply involved in a more bizarre criminal operation than either Holland or Phillips: billing the Louisiana Department of Public Safety and Corrections (LDOC) for work-release prisoners in his charge that he in turn employed in, of all enterprises, an illegal chop shop run by a friend.[8]

In February 2005 Ficklin was indicted on 22 counts of conspiracy, trafficking in motor vehicles with removed or altered Vehicle Identification Numbers (VINs), removing or altering VINs, aiding and abetting the possession of a firearm by a convicted felon, misprision of a felony (the deliberate concealment by failing to report knowledge of a felony) for not reporting a felon with a firearm, and mail fraud.[9]

The indictment charged that Ficklin employed state prisoners in a local car theft enterprise. His friend, convicted felon Barry Edward Dawsey,

## Chapter 14: Eugene Holland, Chaney Phillips, Ronald "Gun" Ficklin, Jessie Hughes: St. Helena Parish

operated an illegal chop shop from B & D Auto Sales in St. Helena Parish. The operation involved buying and selling salvaged and stolen vehicles. When Dawsey was arrested in a stolen pickup truck, officers found a gun and Ficklin's badge in the vehicle.[10]

Baton Rouge television news reporter Ken Pastorick and a cameraman traveled to Greensburg, the St. Helena Parish seat in an attempt to get footage of Ficklin and possibly an on-camera statement. Ficklin was not at the courthouse and as soon as the pair entered the sheriff's office, they felt an overpowering sense of hatred and resentment from the assembled deputies. The lead deputy told them in no uncertain terms that they were unwelcome. "He told us we had best get out of town quickly," Pastorick said, "and we did. Driving down LA. 16 toward Baton Rouge, I glanced back and saw that a deputy was following us. I told my cameraman not to go a mile over the speed limit and to be certain that he never swerved or strayed over the center line. I was actually in mortal fear for our safety."[11]

Dawsey pleaded guilty in 2006 and received a three-year prison sentence. James Jackson, Mitchell Tidwell and Kevin Simmons also pleaded guilty to their involvement in the car theft ring. Ficklin originally was arrested on a ten-count federal indictment. 12 more counts were added as the investigation progressed.[12]

He was accused of fraud for billing LDOC $140,000 by employing LDOC prisoners in Dawsey's chop shop from October 2000 to September 2001. LDOC paid the St. Helena Parish Sheriff's Office nearly $250,000 during that same time period. More than half of Ficklin's federal charges were for mail fraud.

Cori Leigh Clark, Ficklin's son-in-law, and Alton Hoyt McNabb II, the son of Ficklin's girlfriend, were also implicated and were charged with witness tampering, conspiracy and retaliation after they assaulted Louisiana State Police Sergeant Dennis Stewart on July 30, 2005. Stewart had assisted the FBI and ATF officials in Ficklin's investigation.[13]

In February, 2005, Ficklin, the third consecutive St. Helena Parish sheriff to be indicted, pleaded guilty to 17 of the federal charges. He was sentenced to 63 months in prison on each count, to be served concurrently, on October 30, 2007. He reported to prison to begin his sentence in November 2007.[14]

Ficklin, who served as mayor of Greensburg for 14 years before becoming sheriff, died of cancer in federal prison in North Carolina in October 2011, less than a year before he was scheduled to be released in June 2012. He was 57.[15]

He was succeeded by his chief deputy, Nat Williams, the first African-American sheriff of St. Helena Parish, in June 2007. A year later, on June 26, 2008, Louisiana State Police arrested Deputy Jessie Hughes on charges of molestation of a juvenile and aggravated rape. Williams suspended, then fired Hughes as a result of the allegations.[16]

# 15
## Dale Rinicker: East Carroll Parish

Even as total prison population increased by 18 percent from 1999 to 2010, the number of prisoners housed in private facilities was experiencing a tandem jump of 80 percent, from 71,000 to 128,000.[1]

Early on, East Carroll Parish Sheriff Dale Rinicker took a look at the private prison industry which was on the cusp of an explosion in growth and all he could see was dollar signs. Before it was all over, he would be half-a-million dollars richer but would find himself a resident of a federal prison.

In April 1990, Rinicker approached Lake Providence attorney and businessman "Captain Jack" Wyly. He wanted Wyly to finance the construction of a private prison in the parish to house state prisoners. The 72-year-old Wyly agreed and on April 11, East Carroll Correctional Systems, Inc. (ECCS), a subchapter S corporation, was chartered. One hundred shares of stock were issued to Wyly associates and family members. 35 of the 100 shares were issued to 62-year-old Dorothy Morgel, who had worked as Wyly's legal secretary for 35 years. Wyly was listed in Louisiana Secretary of State corporate records as president and Morgel as secretary-treasurer. Only five of those 35 shares were hers, however. The other 30 were earmarked for Sheriff Rinicker in a maneuver that would lead directly to Rinicker's downfall.[2]

Another of Wyly's corporations, Desona Dairy-Corbin Planting Company (he was an officer in about 200 corporations), loaned ECCS its start-up capital. An abandoned school building was purchased and renovations to convert it into the East Carroll Detention Center (ECDC) began. Simultaneously, a favorable lease agreement was executed whereby the East Carroll Sheriff's Office would pay ECDC rent of 25 percent of the funds paid by the Louisiana Department of Public Safety and Corrections to house state prisoners.[3]

By August, the first state prisoners began trickling into the ECDC and the money was quick to follow. Construction loans were paid until May 1993 and only minimal shareholder distributions were paid out to cover tax obligations. After May, the money flow became a gusher.

The enterprise was so successful that Wyly, in June 1990, chartered Northeast Louisiana Correction Services, Inc., and 1992 he started three more private prison concerns: Northeast Delta Correction Services, the Epps Detention Center and the West Carroll Parish Detention Center. There were no records to show whether or not Rinicker was involved in those ventures.[4]

Because Rinicker was personally profiting from an enterprise that did business with the sheriff's office, both an ethics violation and a conflict of interests, even in Louisiana, a convoluted—and necessary—scheme was hatched to conceal his interests. ECCS made payments, based on her 35 percent interest, to Morgel from May 1993 through August 1995.

In reality, however, only 5 percent went to her. The remainder went to Rinicker, but was not paid to him directly. Rather than launder the money through her own checking account at a bank in Lake Providence where she resided, she opened a second account in another bank in nearby Oak Grove. Her ECCS checks were deposited in the Oak Grove account and she wrote more than $286,000 in checks, most for less than the $10,000 amount that triggered the federally required transaction reporting.[5]

Each of the checks was made payable to Rinicker friend Glen Jordan, who then cashed the checks at a Monroe bank. Rinicker's sister worked at the bank and helped facilitate the transactions. Rinicker then received the proceeds. Jordan was paid a small amount from each check for serving as the conduit. But then the participants got reckless, committing a blunder that sent up red flags to federal authorities. ECCS issued six checks, payable directly to Rinicker and totaling more than $54,000.[6]

Jordan, Wyly and Morgel lied to state auditors and the FBI when asked to explain the payments but Jordan soon capitulated. Once he decided to cooperate, apparently in exchange for immunity since he was never charged, he provided a detailed explanation of his part in laundering the money to Rinicker through ECCS, Morgel and Jordan—with an assist from

## Chapter 15: Dale Rinicker: East Carroll Parish

Rinicker's sister, Myra Jackson. A federal grand jury indicted Wyly, Morgel, ECCS, Rinicker and Jackson on charges of mail fraud, conspiracy to launder money, and money laundering.[7]

The indictment sought forfeiture of a certificate of deposit purchased by ECCS; the remaining balance in the ECCS bank account; all funds in Morgel's Oak Grove account; all ECCS assets and property, all rental payments from the sheriff's office, estimated at nearly $3 million, and approximately $340,000 paid to Rinicker.[8]

In a pre-trial deal, Rinicker entered a guilty plea in a deal in which he agreed to testify for the government at trial. In exchange for his cooperation, charges against his sister were dropped.

Morgel claimed several times that she had not received any financial benefit from the scheme. Morgel and Wyly relied on their defense that they did not specifically intend to violate the law; that, instead, Rinicker extorted them and they, being much older, were afraid of him.

They claimed at trial that Rinicker had a violent temper and was the scheme's mastermind. They said he "extorted" them through fear and intimidation into abetting his scheme. But the prosecution said that rather than fearing Rinicker, they had actually cheated him out of $195,000. "There is no honor among thieves, obviously, because the thieves were stealing from the thief," they said.[9]

Although the government had neither questioned its witnesses, nor cross-examined Morgel, and because counsel for Morgel and Wyly failed to object to these arguments at trial, the appellate court dismissed their claims.

Because the government, through oversight, failed to produce any evidence at trial as to the amount of money seized from Morgel's Oak Grove bank account (claimed by her legal counsel at trial to be less than $6.000 but later amended to $15,000) or the source of this money, the court reversed the forfeiture of her bank account.[10]

Wyly, Morgel, and ECCS were convicted on all counts. The jury found the charged property to be subject to forfeiture. Wyly received a sentence of 48 months imprisonment and ordered to pay a fine of $17,500. Morgel was sentenced to prison for one year and one day and fined $12.500. ECCS was fined $4.8 million. Moreover, Wyly, Morgel, and ECCS were ordered to forfeit their interests in the property described in the forfeiture verdict.[11]

Despite Rinicker's cooperation with prosecutors, the district court refused the government's request for lenience for Rinicker and sentenced him to five years imprisonment and ordered him to pay a $10,000 fine.[12]

Mark Shumate, who succeeded Rinicker as East Carroll Parish Sheriff in 1999, fared a little better in his brush with federal authorities. He got off with three years' probation after entering a guilty plea on April 1, 2014 to the charge of allowing a convicted felon to possess a firearm. Shumate, evidence showed, was aware that a convicted felon was not allowed to possess a firearm when he and a convicted felon had gone hunting together in January 2014.[13]

Shumate's indiscretion didn't seem to upset the citizens of East Carroll Parish, however. He was re-elected in 2003, with 52 percent of the vote in the First Primary over five challengers and again in 2007 with 58 percent of the vote.[14]

# 16
## Norm Fletcher: Natchitoches Parish

Saying "I let my compassion overtake my better judgment," former Natchitoches Parish Sheriff Norm Fletcher walked out of court on August 3, 1989, after receiving a three-year suspended sentence and a $12,600 fine.

"I'm glad the whole thing is over," he said after entering a plea of guilty to conspiracy after the fact and misprision of felony (an offense under English common law no longer active in many countries) in connection with his helping a man escape from the parish jail while awaiting trial on a 1984 burglary charge. Fletcher had originally entered an innocent plea to a six-count federal indictment.

The charges stemmed from Fletcher's failure to report the whereabouts of Fred Bates, Jr., following his escape from jail and the sheriff's failure to make use of the National Crime Information Center's database to check out an alias Bates may have been using.

Bates was captured in August 1988 in St. Thomas, Virgin Islands.

During the investigation of Fletcher that followed his recapture, Bates told federal authorities that Fletcher granted him special privileges at the jail in return for sexual favors, a claim that Fletcher denied. He did admit to granting special privileges to Bates and other prisoners—including allowing them to attend college courses—because he believed it helped in their rehabilitation. No charges were ever brought in connection with Bates's allegations.

In return for Fletcher's guilty plea, the remaining four charges against him were dropped by the Shreveport U.S. Attorney's Office. Those included one count each of conspiracy, aiding and abetting unauthorized flight to avoid prosecution, accessory after the fact and conspiracy after the fact.[1]

The ugliest part of Fletcher's tenure as sheriff, however, came during his re-election campaign in 1983 and rather than casting Fletcher in a bad light, it actually elevated his status in the parish, thanks to the less-than-graceful innuendoes offered up by a challenger who ended up with only 3 percent of the vote.

Fletcher was one of the few sheriffs in Louisiana with no real law enforcement background, having established his reputation as owner of the local radio station. And when opponent Clarence Noel started throwing around hints that Fletcher, a widower, was gay, the ploy backfired. Fletcher, rather than wallow in the political mud with Noel, chose, for the most part, to ignore Noel's claim that it was "time to get homosexuality out of the sheriff's office."

When he finally did accuse Noel of putting everyone in the sheriff's office under a cloud, the challenger put on his best "who, me?" face, declaring, "I said we didn't need to elect a homosexual sheriff. I didn't say anyone in particular was a homosexual. We don't need to elect a homosexual congressman or a homosexual president. My platform is I am against drugs, alcoholism and homosexuality. Anyone who attacks my platform must be for what I am against."[2]

Another rumor had Fletcher being arrested in Shreveport in the mid-sixties. A check of Caddo Parish records turned up only an arrest of....Clarence Noel—for failure to pay child support.[3]

# 17
## Irvin "Jif" Hingle: Plaquemines Parish

In 1992, Irvin "Jif" Hingle defeated two-term incumbent Sheriff Ernest Wooton for sheriff of Plaquemines Parish by a 54-46 percent margin. Wooton would go on to serve in the Louisiana House of Representatives. Hingle would remain in office until his forced resignation in October 2011.

Along the way, he survived a 1995 comeback bid by Wooton, defeating the term-limited legislator by 51-49 percent. But he also got greedy while in office. The greed was fed by the easy money to be made with post-Hurricane Katrina cleanup contracts. Hingle would eventually plead guilty to bribery and conspiracy to commit wire fraud. He would receive only three years, ten months in prison because he cooperated with authorities by wearing a wire in August 2011 to trap Aaron Bennett of Benetech Software of Kenner, the person who bribed him.

On October 5, 2011, U.S. Attorney Jim Letten announced that Hingle had been indicted by a bill of information on charges of accepting bribes and conspiracy to commit mail fraud. A bill of information in lieu of a grand jury indictment is generally considered a strong indication that a suspect was cooperating with investigators.

Hingle accepted two payments of $10,000 each from Bennett in March and April 2008 shortly after he approved an invoice for $333,000 from Benetech for federally funded disaster recovery work. He was also charged with falsely reporting campaign expenditures of more than $100,000, which prosecutors say was used for personal purposes and not for campaign expenses.

At the same time, Bennett was charged with bribery and conspiracy.[1]

The Bill of Information charged that the Plaquemines Parish Sheriff's Office entered into a contract with Benetech to provide services relating to recovery from damages due to Katrina and future natural disasters. In early- to mid-2008, on two separate occasions, Hingle approved Benetech's invoices and issued checks to Benetech in connection with work purportedly done under the 2007 contract.

Besides the U.S. Attorney's office and the FBI, the case was also investigated by the Internal Revenue Service Criminal Investigation Division.

Within weeks of approval of the invoices, the FBI said, Bennett, owner of Benetech, twice made separate $10,000 cash payments to Hingle, paid with the intent of influencing him in connection with the contract. Moreover, the indictment charged, Hingle falsely listed over $100,000 in expenditures as campaign-related when, in fact, they were for personal use.[2]

"We place greater trust in our law enforcement officials, trust that they will maintain and display ethical and lawful conduct, said David Welker, Special Agent in Charge of the Federal Bureau of Investigation's New Orleans Field Office. "Conduct as detailed in the Bill of Information reduces the opportunity for fair business and severely reduces the public's trust in our elected officials."

Letten said the charges "reflect our sacred commitment in federal enforcement to maintain a zero tolerance for any public corruption."[3]

Those charges would be bad enough, but emails obtained by an investigative reporter for a New Orleans television station revealed that the shakedowns and influence-peddling were even more widespread.

Lee Zurik, who consistently breaks major news stories for WVUE-TV, revealed the email chain that was first initiated in June 2009, prompting Rafael Goyeneche, president of the New Orleans Metropolitan Crime Commission to comment, "It's more of a horror movie, from Louisiana's point of view."[4]

Robert Isakson, managing director of the DRC Group, a disaster recovery company out of Mobile, Alabama, first wrote about an upcoming trip to Fort Lauderdale to attend the convention of the National Sheriffs' Association.

The DRC group had already made "tens of millions of Louisiana tax dollars" since Hurricane Katrina through lucrative disaster recovery contracts, Zurik said.[5]

## Chapter 17: Irvin "Jif" Hingle: Plaquemines Parish

"Sheriff Jiff Hingle and we are hosting a formal dinner for about 30 or so sheriffs on Monday night at the nicest steak house in Fort Lauderdale," he wrote. Hingle, for his part, sent out invitations to the event sponsored by DRC. At least 34 invitees returned their RSVPs to the event, paid for by DRC.[6]

Two weeks later, DRC and Isakson hosted a second dinner at the Louisiana Sheriffs' Association Convention in Destin. "If that was intended to influence the sheriff to continue to give him business, or to facilitate future contracts to that vendor, I think you may be approaching the criminal line with that," Zurik quoted Goyeneche as saying.[7]

Meanwhile, Isakson sent separate emails on August 1 to Hingle and his driver, Maj. Brandon Mouriz. The subject of that email was Jails on Demand, a portable holding cell. It said Isakson's attorneys had determined if Hingle desired to lease portable jails from DRC, there would be "no obligation to follow the public bid law."[8]

Two days after the BP Deepwater Horizon well blew up, Isakson received an email from Kristy Fuentes, DRC Group's Louisiana regional manager, who wrote that Mouriz "called today to see if we would sponsor a dinner in Destin during the Louisiana Sheriffs' Association Convention. Jiff is being inducted as president." An hour later, Isakson replied, "Absolutely, let's do this supper and anything else we can do to assist him in this honor."[9]

The relationship between Hingle and Isakson was especially egregious because for a full decade before forming the DRC Group, Isakson headed up the public corruption unit in the FBI's New Orleans office.[10]

In 2009, DRC paid for Hingle and Mouriz to attend the LSU-Alabama football game in Tuscaloosa. Then, following the BP Deepwater Horizon catastrophic oil spill, Isakson and DRC gave Hingle and Mouriz a $100,000 loan to help start an equipment rental company and then DRC hired the company, paying nearly half-a-million dollars with BP money. Additionally, DRC also paid a like amount to another Mouriz-affiliated company, Delta Security, and paid Hingle's marina another $250,000. If that was not sufficient, DRC and Isakson separately hired Darren Angelo, Hingle's business partner at the marina, and paid him personally $304,000 and Angelo's company, Fleet Intermodal, $300,000.[11]

And in return for all that largesse, DRC was paid $34 million by the Plaquemines Parish government between 2007 and mid-2012.

From 2003 through the April 20, 2010, oil spill, DRC had no contracts with Hingle's office. But after that 2009 LSU football trip, the loan, the BP-related work for Hingle, his driver and his business partner, the money began to flow from Hingle's office to Isakson's company.

In January 2011, Hingle awarded DRC a $1.2 million contract to build a temporary 22-bed jail and a few months later gave DRC another contract for $1.9 million to construct a temporary facility for the sheriff's office.[12]

Mouriz made $125,000 in 2010—almost $50,000 of that in overtime. Goyeneche said he wondered how Mouriz could earn that much money in overtime when, in the same year, Mouriz companies earned $912,000 from DRC for BP-related work. When Michael Lafrance was named acting sheriff after Hingle resigned in October 2011, one of his first acts was to fire Mouriz.[13]

One month after his resignation from office, on November 30, Hingle entered a guilty plea to one count of conspiracy before U.S. District Judge Sarah R. Vance.[14]

Judge Vance, saying, "Corruption from the top leads to corruption all around," sentenced Hingle to a jail term of three years and ten months for conspiracy to commit mail fraud and bribery from Bennett whose company constructed the parish jail. She also fined him $10,000.

Hingle had been out of jail on a $50,000 bond since October 5, 2011, when he was charged with the felonies and simultaneously resigned from office.

Bennett had pleaded guilty to bribing Hingle that same October. Following Hingle's guilty plea the following month, U.S. Attorney Letten credited Hingle with stepping forward to help federal agents catch Bennett. The Justice Department, citing Hingle's cooperation with investigators, had recommended a sentence of two years and seven months but Judge Vance said, "I will not reduce the sentence to the extent requested by the government."

The judge said that the sentence took into account Hingle's cooperation because Hingle could have been charged with mail fraud, which could have carried a sentence of up to twenty years in prison

## Chapter 17: Irvin "Jif" Hingle: Plaquemines Parish

instead of charging him with conspiracy to commit mail fraud. The conspiracy charge carried a maximum sentence of five years. The plea bargain did carry a stipulation that the government would not charge Hingle with any other crimes he might have committed.

Hingle also admitted that he diverted more than $149,000 from his political campaign for personal or sheriff's office expenses. Of that, Hingle claimed more than $100,000 in campaign expenses for personal or sheriff's office services was paid to a production company for promotional videos and other media. Those falsified reports were mailed by Hingle, prompting the mail fraud charge.

Hingle said upon exiting the courtroom that after Hurricane Katrina he "began to feel entitled. I think after the storm, as hard as the storm was, things got way too easy for me. I would raise more in one night, campaign-wise, than I would raise in a four-year period prior to that. I became feeling entitled, which was a huge mistake. I just wasn't thinking right."[15]

Despite his sentence, Hingle was still entitled to receive $104,000 per year in retirement benefits for the rest of his life, according to the state Sheriffs' Pension and Relief Fund. Louisiana voters passed a law in 2012 that gives state judges the latitude to deny retirement benefits to public officials who are convicted of felonies. Hingle's guilty plea, however, pre-dated passage of the bill. Moreover, the bill, a state law, applies only to state courts and Hingle pleaded guilty in federal court.[16]

Even with Hingle out of office after he reported to a federal facility in Edgefield, South Carolina on September 16, 2013 to begin his sentence, Plaquemine Parish continued to suffer from his actions.

Hurricane Katrina destroyed the 800-plus bed state-of-the-art Plaquemines Parish Detention Center, an overbuilt facility that threatened to wreck the parish's budget with the demands of maintaining empty cells.

Prior to Katrina, Hingle hoped to cash in on the trend of building larger detention centers to house state and federal prisoners. When Katrina hit, only 127 of PPDC's 457 prisoners belonged to the parish. PPDC still had more than 300 empty beds.

"On his better days – his best year – he was almost $1 million in the hole," said Hingle's successor, Sheriff Connie Greco. "He had everybody else believing he was making money on this, and he wasn't."

Hingle nevertheless moved forward with building a 210,000-square-foot jail with 870 beds at a cost of $118 million. It sits on concrete pylons surrounded by concertina razor wire fencing and able to sustain 150-mile-per-hour winds.

"You've got a bunch of sheriffs who have built these big facilities looking to make ends meet (by filling beds)," Greco said. "Jails don't make ends meet. Jails just break-even—if you're lucky. I don't like that it was built so big. Jails, at one time, were the thing to do. It's not the thing to do anymore," he said. "We're going to run it, and we're going to run it as frugally as we can. The thing is you've got to be very careful about what you accept. You'd have to show me numbers because I'm not going to go into the hole for anybody."[17]

Hingle died on January 9, 2018, of complications from pneumonia while being treated at M.D. Anderson Cancer Center in Houston.

# 18

## Mike Tregre: St. John the Baptist Parish

On December 20, 1993, Leonardo Alexander and Arizona Batiste became embroiled in an argument over property Batiste said Alexander had stolen from his home. The confrontation ended when Batiste shot and killed Alexander when he said Alexander first pulled a chrome-plated handgun on him. Batiste panicked, flagged down a passing friend, Jerry Lewis, threw both guns in his truck with instructions to "get rid of them," according to Lewis, who said he threw the pistol in a canal.

When deputies arrived at the scene of the shooting, one of the officers, Paul Schnyder, was a first cousin to the victim Alexander. Schnyder, because of the conflict of interest, turned the investigation over to his partner, Allan Wayne Schaeffer, but remained on the scene as interviews were conducted with four witnesses, each of whom said Alexander had a handgun. That would seem to collaborate Batiste's claim of self-defense but deputies instead accused the witnesses of lying, saying they had fabricated the story of the second gun.

Lewis said sheriff's deputies went to the canal in search of Alexander's weapon and he seemed to remember there were divers at the canal who were not mentioned in the subsequent report filed by Schaeffer. "They had divers out there," Lewis said.

Carl Butler, an attorney for the sheriff's office, would deny that the sheriff's office had an "official" diving team but Edward Nowell, commander of the Marine Division of the sheriff's office at the time, confirmed that the sheriff's department had access to divers.

Upon their return from the canal, Lewis said deputies pressured him to lie and say there was only one gun, repeatedly asking him, "You gonna continue to lie for Arizona?" Though Lewis said he never changed his story, the investigative report filed by deputies following their last interview with

Lewis said he told them there was only one gun, quoting Lewis as saying he "only received one gun from Batiste, that being the 12-gauge shotgun that killed Alexander. The actual transcript of the interview, however, differs radically from the detectives' report, with no mention of any questions about the gun. Instead, Lewis refused to answer questions and demanded an attorney.

Charges against Lewis were eventually dropped after Batiste's trial because he had produced Batiste's shotgun for deputies. The detective who interviewed him, Mike Tregre, asked, "Have any threats or promises been made to you or has pressure of any kind been applied to induce you to answer questions or give up any of your rights?"

"No," said Lewis, who would later say, "They (the sheriff's deputies) were putting a lot of pressure on me," adding that he was in fear of retaliation against him by Tregre.[1]

In December 1995, two years after the shooting, Schaeffer faxed a file to St. John Assistant District Attorney GeorgeAnn Graugnard which said a silver handgun recovered in the Batiste investigation was being held by the sheriff's office for "safekeeping."

When Batiste's new attorney, Gwyn Brown, discovered the fax, she confirmed with the sheriff's office that it was still in possession of the gun that deputies had denied ever existed. When Batiste appealed for a new trial, cooperation was less forthcoming, saying records of the investigation had been destroyed by Hurricane Katrina in 2005.

The only problem with that was while New Orleans was inundated by floodwaters, St. John the Baptist Parish was not. Instead, it served as a staging area for recovery efforts into New Orleans and the sheriff's department's own annual report boasted there was "no flooding and no looting. Power outages inconvenienced us all but thankfully, damage was mostly limited to roofs." No mention was made of any damage to sheriff's facilities. Nor did the sheriff's office ever file any insurance claims for damaged facilities from the hurricane. Faced with the prospect of explaining how files could have been damaged when nothing else was, the department changed its story to say, "The case files you see were relocated to a mobile trailer following Hurricane Katrina damage to the CID (Criminal Investigations Department) building where they were stored. However, those files cannot be currently located."

## Chapter 18: Mike Tregre: St. John the Baptist Parish

The District Attorney's office likewise claimed that the existence of a second gun was not concealed from Batiste's original attorney, J. Sterling Snowdy, now a district court judge. In denying Batiste's earlier claim that prosecutors suppressed evidence, Judge Madeline Jasmine wrote, "According to testimony, on the morning of the trial, Graugnard phoned defense attorney J. Sterling Snowdy and notified him about the gun."

But if Snowdy knew about the gun, he never brought it up at trial. In fact, during the trial, Snowdy fought with the district attorney because they had been denied access to evidence. "Upon information and belief, defendant contends that the state is in possession of (the victim's) handgun," Snowdy wrote in an August 1995 motion, demanding that the state produce Alexander's handgun.[2]

The sheriff's deputy who Lewis said was putting pressure on him to change his story would be elected sheriff of St. John the Baptist Parish in 2011.

Mike Tregre captured 64 percent of the vote in the first primary, easily defeating two other candidates.[3]

He was sworn into office in July 2012 and six months later, on January 18, 2013, his son, Jared Tregre, was sworn in as a reserve deputy while still a student in high school. He wore a badge and "represented himself as a deputy" during a ceremony for fallen officers in Washington, D.C. Among those honored at the event were St. John deputies Brandon Nielsen and Jeremy Triche, who were killed in 2012. Moreover, by virtue of his still being four months from graduating from high school, Jared Tregre could not legally be commissioned as a reserve deputy since the law requires deputies to have a high school diploma or to possess a GED, said Rafael Goyeneche, president of the New Orleans Metropolitan Crime Commission (MCC), a nonprofit citizen watchdog organization.

"If you desired for your son to attend this event, he could have done so without wearing the very badge that these heroic fallen deputies earned by their hard work, courage and sacrifice," read a letter of criticism of the action from the MCC.

The letter of August 8, 2016, noted that Tregre had given his wife and two children reserve deputy commissions that included badges. "It's a violation of the nepotism law, it is not permitted," said Goyeneche. "He was elected to follow all the laws of Louisiana. As a lawman, it's his burden to set the standard or example."

Goyeneche cited the Louisiana nepotism statute which says, "No member of the immediate family of an agency head shall be employed in his agency." He also alluded to an opinion from the Louisiana Board of Ethics which said the son of a sheriff is prohibited from joining the reserve force of a sheriff's office either on a compensated or non-compensated basis.

"We believe the applicable law and ethics opinion require that you rescind the reserve deputy commissions you issued to your wife, son and daughter," Goyeneche wrote.

Records obtained by the MCC showed that Tregre commissioned 51 people, including his wife and children, in the volunteer reserve deputy division. Another 27 "honorary clergy" commissions were doled out by Tregre. Neither his wife nor children had been certified in Peace Officers Standards and Training (POST) nor had they completed firearms training as required by law for deputies.

Goyeneche said his office has had ongoing concerns over what he described as a common practice of law enforcement officers in Louisiana bestowing commissions that are often accompanied by badges. While the commissions are honorary and not meant to confer law enforcement authority, they nevertheless carry the potential for abuse, he said, calling the commissions "get out of jail free cards."

Goyeneche said his office had received complaints about the commissions, specifically that of Jared Tregre. Edie Triche, mother of the late Jeremy Triche, said her family attended the event in Washington and that she was upset to see young Tregre wearing a police badge. "I don't know what the reason, what the purpose was for him wearing the badge, but to me, it was a dishonor to my son and Brandon for him to do that," she said. "He knows he's not a deputy. His dad gave him the commission. He's not commissioned to do law enforcement work."

Goyeneche's letter described Jered Tregre's action of walking around Washington "with a badge around his neck with people thanking him" for his service as a "disgraceful breech of conduct."

The MCC president also raised concerns about the personal behavior of Jared Tregre in a couple of traffic incidents. In one, he was

## Chapter 18: Mike Tregre: St. John the Baptist Parish

involved in a collision with another vehicle on July 28, 2013, at 5:50 a.m. In that accident, a state trooper cited him as being "at fault for this crash but was not cited." The trooper noted that Tregre was "apparently asleep."

A little more than a month later, on September 10, he was booked with drunk driving by Baton Rouge police at 2:26 a.m. The report said his blood alcohol content was .157 percent, which in Louisiana, was eight times the legal limit for a driver under the age of 21. Even though he was not an official employee of the sheriff's office, his designation as a commissioned reserve deputy should have triggered an internal affairs division review of his DWI arrest but did not, prompting Goyeneche to further admonish Sheriff Tregre by calling the lack of a review "yet another example of the improper procedure and double standard you have applied to your son.[4]

Following is a copy of Goyeneche's letter to Tregre:

Page 2
St. John Parish Sheriff's Office

The MCC has obtained photographic evidence that your teenage son while in your presence wore a badge around his neck and represented himself as a deputy during the May 2013 National Police Week ceremonies in Washington, D.C. which honored the line of duty deaths of Deputies Brandon Nielsen and Jeremy Triche (Exhibit 8). If you desired for your son to attend this event he could have done so without wearing the very badge that these heroic fallen deputies earned by their hard work, courage, and sacrifice. The privilege you granted your son at this solemn event undermines the credibility of the St. John Parish Sheriff's Office and dishonors the memory of two deputies who made the ultimate sacrifice for their fellow deputies and the citizens of St. John Parish.

Further proof of this disgraceful breech of conduct can be found in your wife's Facebook post of June 10, 2013 which reads, "Well it's official! Ever since we went to Washington, DC for National Police Week and Jared Tregre got to walk around with a badge around his neck with people thanking him for the service "he" provides, he has been 'bit by the Badge Bug'!!! Today, he officially changed his major to criminology at LSU and like it or not Sheriff Mike Tregre probably has another law enforcement officer in the making over here!!" (Exhibit 9). Your wife made additional statements regarding the illegitimacy of Jared's badge when she responded to a Facebook comment by the wife of Louisiana State Police Colonel Mike Edmonson. Mrs. Tregre's comment reads, "tell the colonel to just forget those little "impersonation" charges he talked about the first time he met Jared. He's going to make it official soon!!" Three years later, the Louisiana Commission on Law Enforcement still has no record of your son's employment with a law enforcement agency.

Also, the MCC has documented that Reserve Deputy Tregre has a history of problematic driving incidents. This includes a traffic accident in St. John Parish on July 28, 2013 at 5:50 am. The report confirms that Jared was found "at fault for this crash but was not cited" even though the trooper noted the contributing factors as "apparently asleep/blackout" and "careless operation" (Exhibit 10). The MCC learned of a second incident in which Reserve Deputy Tregre was arrested for Driving While Intoxicated (DWI) by the Baton Rouge Police Department around 2:26 a.m. on September 10, 2015. The enclosed police report confirms your son's blood alcohol content was .157% which was 8 times the legal limit for someone under the age of 21 (Exhibit 11). Communications Division recordings confirm that a Baton Rouge Police officer called your office at 2:32 a.m. stating, "I need to get in touch with the sheriff. His son is under arrest for DWI for being in an accident."

The St. John Parish Sheriff's Office Employee DWI policy confirms that any on or off-duty employees arrested for DWI must notify their commander and the commander must inform the Internal Affairs Division (Exhibit 12). Jared's personnel records indicate this policy was not followed as his arrest was never reviewed by internal affairs. The personal notification you received and the failure of your department to conduct an internal affairs investigation into his DWI arrest is yet another example of the improper procedure and double standard you have applied to your son.

The MCC respectfully urges that you immediately revoke the reserve deputy commissions and badges you gave your wife, son, and daughter.

Sincerely,

Rafael C. Goyeneche, III
President

Enclosures
AR/MF

## Chapter 18: Mike Tregre: St. John the Baptist Parish

So, what was Tregre's response to Goyeneche's revelations that he had broken the law?

In an interview with a reporter from *The Baton Rouge Advocate*, he rattled off a laundry list of reasons he had done nothing wrong, none of which would exonerate an ordinary street criminal in the eyes of the law:

- Ignorance.
- He only did what his predecessor did.
- He knew other sheriffs who had done the same thing.
- The commissions were for "identification purposes only."
- "No one has abused anything," and, the most curious explanation of them all,
- "I'm being blamed" for the deaths of the two deputies honored in Washington. "That's what this is all about."

And then he hung up on the reporter.[5]

# 19
## Albert D. "Bodie" Little: Winn Parish

It began in February 2011 with the first official word that Winn Parish Sheriff Albert D. "Bodie" Little was under investigation by the Louisiana Attorney General's office. What was not said at the time was that he was assisting his much younger girlfriend in her distribution of methamphetamines. The announcement came on the heels of the execution of warrants and the collection of evidence at Little's home and office by state police.[1]

A year later, he stood convicted by a federal jury of drug trafficking charges.[2]

Seven months after that, he was sentenced to more than 14 years in federal prison after a jury found him guilty on one count of conspiracy to possess 50 or more grams of methamphetamine and two counts of facilitating drug trafficking through the use of a communication device.[3]

The attorney general's office became involved when local District Attorney Chris Nevils recused himself because of ongoing personal issues with Little. Louisiana is somewhat unique in that the attorney general does not normally intervene in local investigations unless requested by local officials as the result of a provision pushed by local district attorneys over the objections of then-Attorney General William Guste during adoption of a new state constitution in 1974.

Federal charges resulted from an investigation by the Drug Enforcement Agency Task Force. The U.S. Drug Enforcement Agency, Louisiana State Police, the Caddo Parish Sheriff's Office, Shreveport police and Bossier City police participated in the investigation. Ten people were indicted along with Little, who was in his first term as sheriff.

U.S. Attorney Stephanie A. Finley said, "When law enforcement officers disregard the law it hurts all citizens. Former Sheriff Little knowingly chose to break the law and now he is paying the price for his betrayal of the trust the citizens of Winn Parish placed in him. We hope that this case, and the sentences imposed, sends a message that drug trafficking and corruption of those charged with protecting society from such crimes will not be tolerated and will be prosecuted to the fullest extent of the law."[4]

Little, a former Louisiana state trooper and former Winn Parish tax assessor was elected sheriff in 2007 and took office in 2008. Besides his drug trafficking charges, he twice asked the Louisiana Bond Commission to let him borrow hundreds of thousands of dollars to keep the office financially solvent. Revenues rose more than 29 percent from when he took office in June 2008 to 2010, from $1.7 million in the 2007-08 fiscal year to $2.2 million in the year that ended June 30, 2010. Despite that, Little incurred a $700,000 deficit in the fiscal year that ended June 30, 2010.

The State Bond Commission rejected Little's latest request to borrow another $750,000 to fund operations. The Winn Parish Police Jury also refused to give Little any more money, citing the increases already given him. "Winn Parish wants good law enforcement," the police jury president said at a special meeting, adding that taxpayers wanted the sheriff's office run with the current revenue.

Little's response was to threaten to close the Winn Parish jails and to curtail operations.

"What's getting you in trouble is your deficit spending," Said State Rep. Jim Fannin of nearby Jonesboro who was Chairman of the House Appropriations Committee. Looking right at Little, he said, "We try to work with you to keep you out of trouble."

Fannin said commissioners looked at tax revenue the Sheriff's Office has received over the years and at how much Little has borrowed. Members also noted how expenses increased and how Little had not reduced labor and other costs.

"That throws a red flag up at the Bond Commission," Fannin said. "They ask me what's going on. It puts me in an embarrassing situation."[5]

## Chapter 19: Albert D. "Bodie" Little: Winn Parish

Little was also accused in 2010 of allowing a convicted DWI offender to leave the parish jail early, in violation of a state district judge's order.

The investigation, indictment and conviction of his drug trafficking, however, reads more like the product of an overactive imagination of a TV detective series scriptwriter run amok.

Little, 61 and married, was accused of helping his girlfriend cover up her drug deals as a means of preventing her arrest. A state trooper who testified in Little's trial, said, "It's clear he wanted everyone arrested except his girlfriend."

When Little was indicted by a federal grand jury in August 2011, Federal Magistrate Judge Mark Hornsby said A.D. "Bodie" Little must get "out of the business of being sheriff" as a condition to getting out of jail.

Hornsby set Little's bond at $100,000. Additionally, Little was ordered to take a leave of absence from the sheriff's office, wear an ankle monitoring bracelet, and submit to alcohol and drug testing.[6]

Little initially pleaded not guilty. His attorney Taylor Townsend of Natchitoches, said the arrest was political. Through Townsend, Little released the following statement:

*A search warrant issued today at the request of an Investigator from the Attorney General's Office in Baton Rouge has been characterized by Sheriff Little as totally unnecessary and an attempt to embarrass and intimidate the Sheriff according to his attorney T. Taylor Townsend. This search warrant sought to obtain a file from Sheriff Little's office, which is a public record, and permission to take photographs of Sheriff Little's home in Winnfield, Louisiana. Sheriff Little was completely and totally cooperative and the requested file was handed over and photographs were taken of his home.*

*Since taking office in July, 2008, Sheriff Little has worked tirelessly to rid Winn Parish of its drug problem and to see that its citizens are protected from drug dealers who were preying on young people in the Parish. He has worked hard to ensure that schools are safe and free of drug activity. He has obviously stepped on some toes along the way.*

*Sheriff Little's political enemies have proven that they will stoop as low as necessary to embarrass, harass and intimidate him. This search warrant ordeal could have been avoided if they had simply called Sheriff Little and asked for this information. Sheriff Little would have simply handed over the file and allowed the Investigator access to his home because he has nothing to hide.*

*The root of this search warrant is a drug dealer trying to cut a deal to get out of jail. Obviously, this is more of the same—a political witch hunt by those who are either jealous or offended by his tough stance against drugs in Winn Parish according to Townsend.*[7]

# 20

## Sid J. Gautreaux: East Baton Rouge Parish

Ignorance of the Law is no Excuse (unless, apparently, you *are* the Law)

Michigan sheriff Tom Bensley avoided prosecution after it was learned he had issued illegal quotas and incentives to deputies as a means of punishing or rewarding them based on the number of tickets they wrote.

Bensley had offered deputies a paid day off in exchange for writing at least five tickets. After being informed by prosecutors that the quota system was illegal, dozens of tickets and citations issued during the time of the quotas were dismissed and refunds issued to those who had already paid their tickets.

Bensley, taking a tact that law enforcement officers generally reject out of hand for the motoring public, said he didn't know what he did was illegal.[1]

And then there are these laws:
- In North Carolina, it is illegal for a wedding ceremony to be performed at a skating rink.
- You may be placed in jail for up to five years in Tennessee for shooting a hole in a penny.
- In Bettendorf, Iowa, it is against the law to rob a bank and then shoot at the bank teller with a water pistol.
- If two trains meet on the same track in Wyoming, neither shall proceed until the other has passed.

These are just a few samplings from around the country of absurd laws still on the books but not enforced for obvious reasons.

## Louisiana's Rogue Sheriffs

In Louisiana, however, it didn't matter that the Supreme Court ruled anti-sodomy laws unconstitutional in 2003; it was still on the books in Louisiana so the East Baton Rouge Parish Sheriff's Office continued arresting men for it from 2011 through mid-2013. Only after *The Baton Rouge Morning Advocate* exposed the illegal undercover sting operation did Sheriff Sid J. Gautreaux admit that he didn't know the law.[2]

While having sex in public places is still illegal, consensual sex in the privacy of one's home is not. Still, undercover officers continued to pick up a dozen gay men at a local park. They were then lured back to the privacy of their own apartments where they were arrested when it was presumed they'd be having sex even though no money was exchanged, which would have made it illegal. The local district attorney wisely refused to prosecute, saying the men had done nothing illegal.

When a firestorm of criticism rained down upon the sheriff's department, with some of the harshest words coming from straight Metro Councilman John Delgado, Gautreaux issued a public apology, saying his department "made mistakes" and it would no longer use an unconstitutional law to arrest people at public parks.[3]

"Does he know that slavery is no longer around?" an outraged Delgado told *The Advocate*. "Does he know that we have cars and no longer horse and buggies?"[4]

"The Sheriff's Office apologizes that the way these investigations were handled made it appear that we were targeting the gay community," *The New Orleans Times-Picayune* quoted Gautreaux as saying. "That was not our intent. The Sheriff's Office also apologizes to anyone that was unintentionally harmed or offended by the actions of our investigations. Our agency made mistakes; we will learn from them; and we will take measures to ensure it does not happen again."[5]

The U.S. Supreme Court ruled anti-sodomy laws unconstitutional in 2003 in its Lawrence v. Texas decision, though -two states still carried some version of the law on their books with 13 of those specifically targeting same-sex couples. In Virginia, Attorney General Ken Cuccinelli even sued to keep the law intact.[6]

Gautreaux's office didn't help matters with its initial public statement following *The Advocate*'s story:

## Chapter 20: Sid J. Gautreaux: East Baton Rouge Parish

The Sheriff's Office has not, nor will it ever, set out with the intent to target or embarrass any part of our law-abiding community. Our goal is to Protect and Serve the public. When we receive calls from the public about lewd activity near our children, we have to respond. Our park operations, conducted at the specific request of the BREC Park's Ranger, were an attempt to deter or stop lewd activity occurring in the park near children. The deputies in the cases were acting in good faith using a statute that was still on the books of the Louisiana criminal code. The deputies used a statute that they felt fit the situation in order to remedy the concerns of the parents and park officials. The deputies presented sworn affidavits of probable cause, a set of circumstances that would lead a normal person to believe that a crime has been committed or will be committed, to judges for review. In the cases we have reviewed, the judges set bond, in effect concurring that there was probable cause for arrest. To our knowledge, the Sheriff's office was never contacted or told that the law was not enforceable or prosecutable.

In hindsight, however, we feel we should have taken a different approach. We will consult with others in the legislative and judicial branches to see what can be done to remove this law from the criminal code that each deputy receives and to also find alternative ways to deter sexual and lewd activity from our parks.

We want to reiterate our intent in these cases. It was NEVER to target a certain segment of our population. It was only in response to parents, park officials and members of the public concerned that our parks were not safe. When we receive reports of public masturbation, sex and other lewd activity in a park where children are playing, we MUST take these concerns seriously. Our intent was honorable; our approach, however, is something we must evaluate and change. The Sheriff's Office is not concerned with what consenting adults do in private residences. We are concerned with what is going on in public, especially a public place frequented by children. In light of new information, we feel that we need to work with our deputies to provide them with better resources and training to deal with these issues in more appropriate ways. It is very important to us that the public understands our intent and agenda was safety and never prejudiced toward any group.[7]

The outcry was immediate as national news outlets and Internet blogs picked up the story and the sheriff's office's Facebook posts on the subject prompted dozens of critical comments from gay rights and other organizations.

Bruce Parker, a managing director for Capital City Alliance and a coalition manager for Equality Louisiana, asked even if the law was enforceable, "How on earth is this a priority in a city with a murder rate this high?"[8] Baton Rouge's murder rate at times has exceeded that of Chicago, considered one of the deadliest cities in America.

"The people of Baton Rouge are entitled to a law enforcement system that actually enforces the law," said The American Civil Liberties Union of Louisiana in its statement on the controversy. "That means protecting people whose conduct is legal – such as adults engaging in conversation about anything they choose in public places."[9]

Gautreaux, along with his apology, said he had:
- Met with the East Baton Rouge Parish district attorney to improve communication between the two offices to ensure such arrests are not made based on unenforceable laws;
- Contacted the district attorney, Louisiana legislators and the Louisiana Sheriffs' Association to discuss having unconstitutional sections of Louisiana's "crimes against nature" laws repealed;
- Informed sheriff's office employees that they are not to use the unconstitutional law;
- Met with Capital City Alliance, a local group that represents the lesbian, gay, bisexual and transgender community, to "further the dialogue:"

## Chapter 20: Sid J. Gautreaux: East Baton Rouge Parish

- Undertook an evaluation of his office's undercover operations to make changes to "ensure better supervision, training and guidance."[10]

All made necessary because the sheriff was ignorant of the law, a law ruled unconstitutional a decade earlier.

# 21
## Harry Lee, Newell Normand: Jefferson Parish

Because of his right-leaning politics and his heavy-handed treatment of blacks in his sprawling, majority-white Jefferson Parish suburb of New Orleans, it would be accurate to describe Harry Lee as possibly the only redneck Chinese sheriff in America.

Sheriff Lee, when he was alive, could be described as a lot of other things, as well: lawman, jailer, tax collector, process server, issuer of various licenses, attorney, power broker, and a confidant, pal to and sometimes business partner with some of the South Louisiana's shadiest characters, including the late New Orleans crime boss Carlos Marcello.

Article 39 of the Jefferson Parish Sheriff's Office operations manual says employees should avoid associating with criminals and those under investigation or indictment.

Lee, however, said the rule applied to deputies but did not apply to him.[1]

Accordingly, he felt no professional or moral restrictions that would have prevented him from continuing his personal and business relationship with Robert Guidry who had admitted to bribing former Gov. Edwin Edwards and others in order to obtain a license for a New Orleans casino. Nor would it, under Lee's unique moral code, have prevented him from associating with Frank Caracci, a convicted felon whom federal authorities linked to organized crime in New Orleans. In fact, Lee testified on Caracci's behalf during State Police hearings in 1994 on whether to pull Guidry's video poker license over Guidry's business association with Caracci.

Nor did Lee hesitate to spend the night as the guest of Marcello at the don's Grand Isle and Boutte camps—on several different occasions, according to a former State Police intelligence officer.[2] The first word of

Lee's stay at the Grand Isle camp leaked out during his initial campaign for sheriff.

At the time he first ran for sheriff, Lee was a partner in the Jefferson Parish law firm of Lee, Martiny and Caracci. The other two partners were Daniel Martiny and Mark Caracci. Mark Caracci is Frank Caracci's son and Martiny would go on to election to the Louisiana State Senate.

No sooner did Lee take office as sheriff in 1980 than he retained his old law firm to defend his department. It wasn't until three years later, in 1984, when nearing the end of his first term, that he finally severed professional ties with the firm, though he was sold a one-third interest in the firm's office building for $65,000, a fee he was never required to pay. Nor was he required to pay his share of the firm's mortgage.

The Louisiana Board of Ethics, held a dog and pony show investigation of the arrangement that it concluded was in violation of Louisiana's code of ethics which prohibited Lee from having a contractual relationship with the law firm at the same time of the purchase agreement. Another provision of the code prohibits public servants from receiving anything of economic value from any person who has or is seeking to obtain a contractual, business, or financial relationship with the public servant's agency.

The upshot of all the hoopla of the ethics hearings was the imposition of fines of $1,000 each on Lee and the firm for the contractual agreement and additional $1,000 fines against Lee and the firm for the prohibited payments by the firm to Lee in the form of Lee's portion of the mortgage payments.

But, the ethics board added somewhat incredulously, "No governmental purpose would be served by the execution of these fines and accordingly, they are suspended...because of the board's belief that the sheriff was acting in good faith."[3]

And while Lee was no longer officially associated with the firm, it did secure a profitable contract with the Louisiana Sheriffs' Association Risk Management Program. Lee, conveniently, was a member of the board that ran the program.[4]

Lee was never shy about his friendships with characters of questionable repute. He openly admitted during testimony in the hearing into Guidry's video poker license that he recommended to Guidry that he

## Chapter 21: Harry Lee, Newell Normand: Jefferson Parish

partner with Frank Caracci, convicted in 1970 for bribing an Internal Revenue agent, adding that while he did not know of Caracci's criminal background, it wouldn't have mattered to him even if he had known. "I'm not sure I knew Mr. Caracci had a conviction," he testified. "I would have no problem with that. I have a lot of friends convicted of felonies. A lot of people are uptight about that. I'm not."[5]

Other jewels to emanate from the mouth of Harry Lee:
- "We know the crime is in the black community. Why should I waste time in the white community?"—on why he beefed up patrols of black neighborhoods but not white.
- "The sheriff (of Jefferson Parish) is the closest thing there is to being a king in the U.S. I have no unions, I don't have civil service, I hire and fire at will, I don't have to go to (the parish) council and propose a budget. I approve the budget. I'm the head of the law-enforcement district and the law-enforcement district only has one vote, which is me."
- "I would have shot the little bastard myself."—following the shooting of a 16-year-old suspected shoplifter who tried to run over a deputy.
- "My job is to catch crooks. My hobby is to expose hypocrites."
- "I'm old enough and ornery enough that I don't have to appease anybody."[6]

---

The year 2016 was not especially good to Jefferson Parish Sheriff Newell Normand.

Jefferson Parish is a mostly white suburb of majority black New Orleans, situated immediately west of the Crescent City. Normand, as chief deputy to the hugely popular Sheriff Harry Lee, literally inherited the office upon Lee's death from leukemia on October 1, 2007, less than three weeks before he was to stand for election to his eighth consecutive term. Because state law requires qualifying for election to reopen if a candidate dies before an election, Normand was able to qualify to run against three challengers. He easily overwhelmed his opponents with 91 percent of the vote.

## Louisiana's Rogue Sheriffs

Barely two years into his administration as Lee's successor, Normand faced his first public relations hiccup, brought on by, of all people, actor Steven Seagal,. Seagal, a pal of the late Harry Lee, had an A&E Network television reality show called, appropriately enough, *Steven Seagal, Lawman*, which entitled him to carry a special sheriff's deputy badge and to ride with Jefferson Parish deputies as they patrolled the parish, busting prostitutes and drug dealers.

Lee demanded that his deputies raise money for his campaigns, and he took loyalty into consideration when handing out assignments. He once considered running for governor but decided against it, saying he'd rather be king. Ever conscious of the value of good PR, he often buddied up to celebrities, singing with Willie Nelson, dining with Bill Clinton, and making Seagal a reserve deputy after their friendship was cemented by a mutual fondness for firearms.[7]

He recruited Seagal to train his deputies in shooting and martial arts, brought him along to charitable events, and to go on patrol with his deputies, which eventually led to the A&E series.

But then Kayden Nguyen entered the picture, filing a lawsuit against Seagal in which she accused him of holding her against her will and using her as a sex slave during the second season of filming his show. Before the merits of Nguyen's lawsuit could be determined, Normand took decisive action in pulling the plug on the show and invited Nguyen to file a criminal complaint, saying, "I will treat Mr. Seagal no differently than any other employee of the Jefferson Parish Sheriff's Office."[8]

Eleven months later, Seagal popped up again, this time as a special reserve deputy for the infamous Maricopa County (Arizona) Sheriff Joe Arpaio. Normand apparently had no problem with that until Seagal said in an interview that he was "on loan" to Arpaio "out from Louisiana."[9]

Seagal made the claim in an interview immediately following a massive raid by the Maricopa County Sheriff's Office on a home in Laveen, Arizona, which netted exactly one subject suspected of promoting cockfighting.

That prompted an immediate response from Normand through Jefferson Parish Deputy Col. John Fortunato. Seagal, Normand said through his spokesman, "was facing an internal affairs investigation immediately following the outcome of his lawsuit. And he refused to return to Jefferson

## Chapter 21: Harry Lee, Newell Normand: Jefferson Parish

Parish, at which time he tendered his resignation." Nguyen's complaint was later dropped but pursuant to his resignation, Seagal was no longer affiliated with the Jefferson Parish Sheriff's Office, the statement added.[10]

But the Seagal fiasco was only a minor embarrassment since it was Lee, and not Normand, who first brought the actor into the department. Like his mentor Lee, Normand can be controversial at times, even in the absence of illegal activity. Three other events, all in 2016, proved to be much more problematic for the Republican sheriff who, simply because of his distaste for fellow Republican candidate U.S. Senator David Vitter, was instrumental in the 2015 election of Democratic Governor John Bel Edwards in a decidedly red state.

No sooner had Normand laid to rest news reports that the FBI and the IRS were investigating him and a company in which he was part owner than another story cropped up. That story involved his wife's selection as legal counsel for the Louisiana Stadium and Exposition District, more commonly known as the Superdome Commission, whose members are appointed by the governor.[11]

Less than three months after the election of Edwards, the commission chose Shawn Bridgewater-Norman, a partner in the prestigious New Orleans firm Chaffe McCall. Larry Roedel of the Baton Rouge firm Roedel Parsons Koch Boache Balhoff & McCollister had held the contract since 2004. The firm had billings of about $300,000 per year for the firm during its 12-year run.[12]

Though Roedel Parsons was originally appointed by Gov. Kathleen Blanco, the firm was retained throughout Bobby Jindal's eight years in office. It didn't hurt, of course, that Roedel Parsons contributed more than $30,000 to Jindal between 2003 and 2012. Neither Normand, his wife, nor her firm made any contributions to Edwards, according to his campaign finance reports.[13]

Near the end of 2016, Normand appeared to face his biggest crisis over a road rage incident that began on the bridge connecting New Orleans to Jefferson Parish's west bank area and ended in the shooting death of a former NFL player.

Joe McKnight, 28, played on three state championship football teams at John Curtis High School in River Ridge, suburb of New Orleans before starring at Southern California. He played for the Kansas City Chiefs and the New York Jets before an injury derailed his professional career.

He was working for a New Orleans mental health clinic when he became involved in an altercation with Ronald Gasser on the Crescent City Causeway, the Mississippi River bridge connecting New Orleans to the Jefferson Parish west bank. Both drivers exited the causeway in Gretna and when McKnight approached Gasser's vehicle, Gasser fired three shots from inside his car, two of the bullets striking McKnight once in the hand and twice in the upper body.

The real controversy erupted when Normand's office declined to book Gasser for the shooting. The decision to not arrest Gasser proved to be a major PR snafu for Normand as protests erupted almost immediately and Normand's response to the protests during a press conference didn't help assuage feelings among the African American community.[14]

The sheriff attempted to explain his office's lack of action with several puzzling pronouncements. "If you rush to judgment from the beginning and make a strategic error," Normand said, "it makes it very difficult to recover later." He then acknowledged that Louisiana's "stand your ground" self-defense law might come into play. He also said, somewhat incredulously, that there was no evidence that the shooting was racially motivated—McKnight was black and Gasser white—and pointed out that McKnight's stepfather once served as a deputy in the Jefferson Parish Sheriff's Office.[15] His threat to arrest protesters only served to make a bad situation worse.

Reporter Jarvis DeBerry was particularly critical of Normand in a column he penned in the December 10, 2016, issue of the *Times-Picayune*. DeBerry noted that Normand spent the first 21 minutes of a press conference assailing those "who didn't exhibit complete and unquestioning faith in the integrity of Normand's office."[16]

Sounding as though he might have been channeling Donald Trump, Normand attacked his critics while heaping praise on those who had supported him in the first days of the growing controversy. Citing elected officials who publicly supported him and black leaders who, in a December 2 press conference had urged restraint while discouraging public demonstrations against the sheriff's office, he said, "You are true leaders. You are credible leaders."

## Chapter 21: Harry Lee, Newell Normand: Jefferson Parish

But to a reporter who asked that given some high-profile cases of blacks being shot by police officers around the country, couldn't he understand that blacks might be upset at the idea of the decision to release Gasser, Normand shot back, "What you're trying to articulate is misdirected." To a black person who attempted to ask a question, Normand was more than a little dismissive and insensitive when he referred to data that reveal that the majority of blacks killed in Jefferson Parish were killed by other blacks.[17] That the McKnight shooting was completely unrelated to those statistics appeared not to have occurred to Normand, DeBerry observed.

At the sheriff's press conference, DeBerry wrote, "Normand was continuing to wear blinders, pretending not to be able to conceive of black people's fears (or) worries when Gasser wasn't immediately arrested. "…The least the sheriff could do is try to understand people's emotional reactions to Gasser's being initially allowed to go home. If he couldn't do that, he could have just focused on the details of the alleged crime, but his lack of empathy and lecturing tone were a brutal combination.[18]

Normand's controversial tenure came to an end in mid-2017 when he abruptly announced that he was stepping down after 37 years with the Jefferson Parish Sheriff's Office, the last ten as sheriff, to move into his new career as a talk show host for a New Orleans radio station. Making his announcement on July 25, he set his retirement date as August 31. Normand insisted the timing of his announcement was "a coincidence at best," and had nothing to do with the federal indictment of his veteran chief deputy Craig Taffaro.[19]

Taffaro, father-in-law of Louisiana Lieutenant Governor Billy Nungesser, was indicted by a federal grand jury just five days earlier, on July 20 for tax evasion and filing a false tax return in connection with CTNN, an offshore supply company that he co-owned with Normand. His indictment in turn, came a little more than a month after his retirement following nearly 50 years with the Jefferson Parish Sheriff's Office.

CTNN (Craig Taffaro, Newell Normand) apparently did little but collect commissions on sales between two other companies. Equipment and goods were actually purchased by Harvey Gulf, a billion-dollar marine transportation enterprise owned by Republican donor Shane Guidry. They were purchased from a company called Pelican Marine which was owned by Nungesser, Taffaro's son-in-law, who upon his election as lieutenant governor, placed Pelican's assets in a blind trust assigned to....Taffaro. Guidry, for his part, also served as special assistant to Attorney General Jeff Landry, who once served as Guidry's personal attorney. Guidry was hired to oversee the attorney general's criminal investigations unit at a salary of $12,000 per year.[20]

# 22

## Charles Foti, Marlin Gusman: Orleans Parish

Sheriffs' offices, as is the case with all public agencies in Louisiana, routinely undergo state audits. It's an annual process for sheriffs and the audits are generally carried out by outside auditors. These are commonly referred to as contract audits. On those occasions, however, where there is suspected fraud, abuse, or theft, the Louisiana Legislative Auditor's Office comes in for what is called an Investigative Audit.

Legislative Auditor Daryl Purpera's office did just that with the Orleans Parish Sheriff's Office and on March 30, 2016, issued a withering report of deficiencies in Sheriff Marlin N. Gusman's office that included a deputy illegally operating a private security business, deputies fraudulently billing for work ostensibly performed during official working hours, and failure to comply with public bid laws in awarding construction contracts. The entirety of the following chapter is taken directly from that audit report.

### Deputy Sheriff Operated Private Security Business in Possible Violation of State Law

From March 2009 to March 2015, Colonel Lucien Roy Austin owned and operated a personal security business in possible violation of a state statute which prohibits deputy sheriffs from holding an ownership interest in any company that performs any services of a law enforcement nature. Although Col. Austin's OPSO job duties included organizing off-duty details performed by OPSO personnel, it appears that Col. Austin organized off-duty details during his regular work hours for his personal business, a Slidell-based Louisiana for-profit corporation named Austin Sales and Service, Inc." Additionally, records indicated that Col. Austin billed customers for services "that do not appear to have been performed." Several of the checks payable to individuals appear to have been endorsed and negotiated by Austin Sales and Service, including by Col. Austin himself. "By owning a corporation for which he provided services of a law enforcement nature during his regular OPSO work hours, Col. Austin may have violated OPSO policies and state law. Further, by charging customers for services not performed and by negotiating company checks payable to others, Col. Austin may have violated state and federal laws.

Louisiana state law allows for sheriff's deputies to perform private security work for a firm where such work does not conflict with their regularly-assigned hours as deputy sheriffs, the audit pointed out. The Orleans Parish Sheriff's Office (OPSO) Employee Manual had policies and procedures in place under which personnel were allowed to work off-duty security details while wearing their uniforms and utilizing sheriff's office equipment. These policies and procedures require prior authorization from an appropriate supervisor, limit the number of off-duty hours that can be worked during a seven-day week, prohibit employees from taking leave ... to work off-duty security details, and require each deputy to have a fee of $1 per detail hour worked deducted from their paycheck to reimburse (the sheriff's office) for equipment used while performing off-duty security details," the report said. Pay earned by deputies working off-duty details is handled independently from the sheriff's office.

We found that Chief Deputy Gerald Ursin, Jr.; Orleans Parish Prison Chief Gary Bordelon; and Col. Austin's assistant, Deputy Rynika Stewart, assisted Austin Sales and Service, Inc. with arranging and coordinating private security details. In addition, according to OPSO and Austin Sales and Service, Inc. records, Col. Austin, Chief Deputy Ursin, Chief Bordelon, and Deputy Stewart used

## Chapter 22: Charles Foti, Marlin Gusman: Orleans Parish

OPSO computers and other equipment during their regular work hours to arrange, coordinate, and invoice off-duty details while working their regular OPSO schedules. For example, email correspondence shows that Chief Deputy Ursin appears to have assisted Austin Sales and Service, Inc. with handling invoices and coordinating details for the New Orleans Jazz and Heritage Festival (Jazz Fest), Super Bowl XLVII in 2013, and the 2014 NBA All-Star Game.

As part of our audit, we examined OPSO computers and OPSO email accounts used by Col. Austin, Chief Bordelon, and Deputy Stewart. These examinations found that many of the Austin Sales and Service, Inc. invoices for security details were created using OPSO computers, printed on OPSO letterhead, and sent to customers of Austin Sales and Service, Inc. using OPSO email accounts. Although these invoices requested that payment be made to Austin Sales and Service, Inc., the invoices thanked the customers on behalf of Sheriff Marlin Gusman for using the Orleans Parish Sheriff's Office for their security needs. Deputy Stewart, who was responsible for scheduling details and preparing invoices on behalf of Austin Sales and Service, Inc., stated that she believed that handling these off-duty details was part of her regular job duties.

Although deputies are to perform private security work while not on official duty, "state law prohibits a deputy sheriff from holding an ownership interest in any partnership, company, or corporation where the venture is to perform any services of a law enforcement nature," the audit pointed out. Further, in order to provide private security services, state statutes require private security companies and individuals who perform private security services to be licensed by the Louisiana State Board of Private Security Examiners (Security Board). Although active law enforcement officers are exempt from the licensing requirements in their jurisdictions, security companies are required to have at least one agent/officer licensed by the

Security Board. According to Security Board Administrative Supervisor Jane Ryland, neither Austin Sales and Service nor Austin individually was licensed to provide security services during this time period, according to a security board administrative supervisor. "Due to his ownership and operation of an unlicensed security company that primarily provides services of a law enforcement nature, Col. Austin may have violated state law.

### Austin Sales and Service, Inc. Billed Customers for Services Not Provided

During our audit, we obtained Austin Sales and Service, Inc.'s off-duty detail schedules, invoices and other documentation from the OPSO e-mail server, Col. Austin's office and OPSO computers used by Col. Austin, Chief Bordelon, and Deputy Stewart. These schedules appear to have been used to track the hours worked by OPSO deputies and other individuals on security details and to determine the amounts billed to customers of Austin Sales and Service, Inc. We compared the schedules of 29 off-duty security details to the amounts billed to customers by Austin Sales and Service, Inc. and to Austin Sales and Service, Inc. payroll records. These records indicate that, from March 2010 to December 2014, Austin Sales and Service, Inc. billed customers at least $78,173 for services that were not provided or that were provided by individuals who were not P.O.S.T. (Peace Officer Standards and Training) certified or licensed by the Security Board to provide security services.

We attempted to speak with Col. Austin regarding these billings; however, he declined our request for an interview and referred all questions to his attorney. By billing for services that were either not provided or were provided by individuals who had no legal authority to provide security services, Col. Austin may have violated state law.

## Chapter 22: Charles Foti, Marlin Gusman: Orleans Parish

### Questionable Check Endorsements

Our review of Austin Sales and Service, Inc.'s bank records revealed 18 checks related to the 29 overbilled off-duty security details totaling $5,737 that were payable to 12 individuals but appeared to have been endorsed by the payees and either Col. Austin or Chief Bordelon and then cashed or deposited into bank accounts owned by Col. Austin and/or Chief Bordelon. Multiple individuals to whom these checks were made payable confirmed that the endorsement signatures on the back of the checks were not their signatures. These individuals also confirmed that they did not receive, return, or donate any of the checks or proceeds of the checks to Austin Sales and Service, Inc. We attempted to speak with Col. Austin regarding these checks; however, Col. Austin declined our request for an interview and referred all questions to his attorney. Based on the statements of the individuals who claim they did not endorse the Austin Sales and Service, Inc. checks made payable to them, it appears that Col. Austin and Chief Bordelon may have negotiated checks from Austin Sales and Service, Inc. that were payable to others.

By charging Austin Sales and Service, Inc. customers for services that were not performed and by negotiating company checks payable to others, Col. Austin and Chief Bordelon may have violated state and federal laws. On March 25, 2016, Col. Austin was charged in a federal bill of information with one felony count of conspiracy to commit wire fraud.

The audit report included copies of billings for private security services by Austin Sales & Service that were generated on Orleans Parish Sheriff's Office letterhead.

### Deputies Worked Off-duty Details during OPSO Working Hours

Moreover, the sheriff's office paid 16 deputies $4,698 for the same hours during which these deputies appear to have performed off-duty security services in apparent violation of both departmental policies and procedures for off-duty details and state law.

During our audit, we compared Austin Sales and Service, Inc. records to Col. Austin's OPSO time sheets and discovered instances in which Col. Austin appeared to have performed security services during his regular work hours and without taking leave. Auditors also obtained time sheets from the Orleans Parish Clerk of Court - Criminal District (Clerk) for OPSO deputies who provided off-duty security services for the Clerk during elections. By comparing those time sheets to the deputies' OPSO time sheets, auditors found 156 instances in which 16 OPSO deputies (including Col. Austin) appear to have worked off-duty security details during their regularly-scheduled work hours. From October 1, 2010 to November 4, 2014, OPSO paid these deputies a total of $4,698 for 203 hours during which the deputies appear to have been working security details.

The amount of time deputies were shown to be working off-duty details during regularly-scheduled work hours ranged from ten minutes to 12 hours per day. For example, Col. Austin reported working off-duty security details during nearly 95 regular work hours without taking leave. At his regular OPSO hourly rate of $32.83, Col. Austin appears to have been paid $3,103 by OPSO for the same hours during which he was providing off-duty security services.

**Failure to Properly Apply Public Bid Law for Work**

From March 31, 2012 to March 14, 2013, the sheriff's office paid Gulf State, LLC, $231,820 for renovations to shower stalls at the House of Detention (HOD) jail facility. Although this was a public works project as defined by state law, Gusman failed to publicly advertise the project in accordance with the Public Bid Law. In addition, an unlicensed contractor was allowed to perform

## Chapter 22: Charles Foti, Marlin Gusman: Orleans Parish

work without a written contract "and appears to have paid for materials that did not conform to the bid specifications," the report said. By failing to properly apply the public bid law, allowing an unlicensed contractor to perform services without a written contract, and paying for materials that did not conform to the bid specifications, OPSO management may have violated the Louisiana Constitution and state law.

OPSO records indicate that Gulf State, LLC was paid a total of $231,820 to waterproof the inmate showers at the HOD. According to OPSO records, employees, and vendors, this work was performed from March 2012 to April 2012. Documentation supporting the bid process indicates that in October 2010, OPSO advertised a request for proposals to waterproof all shower stalls in the HOD. The scope of work required the vendor to strip and clean all showers down to the concrete and apply waterproofing solution. In addition, all vendors were required to give a complete price of the full job and provide separate pricing for the cost of the waterproofing materials, cost per shower, emergency call outs, and approximate time to respond.

During the course of the audit, it was discovered that the epoxy coating used by Gulf State, LLC did not meet the requirements of the October 2010 request for proposals. According to the request for proposals, the vendor was required to cover the HOD shower stalls with a 3/16$^{th}$-inch coating of waterproofing solution composed of "a Cementitious Polymer Admix overlay which provides outstanding compressive, flexural, tensile and bonding strength. This product waterproofs and is acid resistant, salt resistant, mold resistant, non-flammable and non-toxic, and is a one-step process. The product should be ANSI-61 approved for use in conjunction with potable water." Auditors spoke to Gulf State officer Kendal Marquar, who stated that the waterproofing materials for this project were purchased at a local Sherwin Williams store. "Auditors obtained the receipts for these purchases which indicate that Gulf State, LLC provided an epoxy waterproofing solution that was not acceptable for use in conjunction with potable water, as required by the October 2010 request for proposals," the report said.

Marquar said the HOD renovations were not put out to bid in 2012. He said that John Sens, former OPSO purchasing director, called him and said that federal inspectors were coming to inspect the HOD and that OPSO needed to renovate the showers. "Mr. Marquar stated that Mr. Sens instructed him not to use the materials specified in the 2010 bid specifications, rather they were to use a different sealer and begin renovations on the showers immediately," the report said. Marquar said he never saw a contract between Gulf State, LLC and OPSO. "By failing to properly apply the public bid law, allowing an unlicensed contractor to perform services without a written contract, and paying for materials that did not conform to the bid specifications, OPSO management may have violated the Louisiana Constitution1 and state law," auditors said.

### Ineligible Employees Received State Supplemental Pay

From January 2011 to September 2014, the Sheriff's Office received Deputy Sheriff's Supplemental Pay totaling $1,026,083 from the state of Louisiana for what appears to be ineligible employees who performed purely clerical or non-enforcement duties. "By requesting, receiving, and distributing state funds to employees who performed clerical or nonenforcement duties, (sheriff's office) management may have violated the Louisiana Constitutional and state law."

The audit report ended with a list of 14 recommendations for the sheriff's office:
- Seek legal advice regarding the appropriate actions to be taken regarding supplemental pay obtained by OPSO employees;
- Implement detailed policies and procedures to ensure that only eligible employees, as defined by state law, receive supplemental pay;
- Use the appropriate forms to request supplemental pay funds and update written policies and procedures to ensure that each employee's eligibility for state supplemental pay is re-evaluated when a change in position or job duties occurs;

## Chapter 22: Charles Foti, Marlin Gusman: Orleans Parish

- Implement additional written policies and procedures to ensure that employees do not work off-duty security details during regular working hours;
- Implement written policies and procedures regarding funds withheld from employee paychecks for having worked off-duty security details;
- Require employees to sign an annual certification in which they disclose ownership in any businesses that perform law enforcement services;
- Maintain an electronic database containing information such as the dates, times and locations of all off-duty details worked by OPSO deputies;
- Ensure that all laws (La. R.S. 38:2211, et seq.) pertaining to contracts and public bids are followed;
- Ensure that vendors and professional service providers have valid, written contracts prior to providing services;
- Ensure that contracts and related documentation are maintained in an organized manner and in a central location;
- Endure that all payments are made in accordance with the terms and conditions of the contract;
- Ensure services meet all contractual requirements prior to payment;
- Require proper review of invoices to ensure each payment has a legitimate public purpose as required by the Louisiana Constitution; and
- Require detailed invoices and documentation of the business purpose for all expenditures.[1]

State auditors were not the only ones casting a critical eye at the New Orleans Sheriff's Office and Sheriff Gusman and his predecessor, Charles Foti. Federal judges and the U.S. Justice Department had been trying for more than a decade to get the Orleans Parish Jail to measure up to even minimal humane standards. Efforts to force implementation of basic rights, including health care, sanitary conditions, suicide and violence incident reductions and the cessation of beatings of prisoners by deputies had largely been ignored to the growing frustration of judges and prosecutors.

The nation's attention was first drawn to the conditions of the Orleans Parish jail in the aftermath of Hurricane Katrina in 2005. That's when thousands of inmates were left in sewage-fouled, chest-high flooded cells with no electricity, drinking water, food, or ventilation in the late August-early September stifling heat and humidity of South Louisiana.[2]

Saddled with a long history of cruelty and neglect that predates Katrina and current Sheriff Marlin Gusman, the Orleans Parish Jail, located in America's 35$^{th}$-largest city, is the nation's ninth-largest local jail in terms of population.[3]

Foti, who became Louisiana's attorney general for four years beginning in 2004, had been hit by a $10 million fine by a federal court which found that the sheriff's department under his administration had illegally strip-searched and conducted body-cavity searches on more than 60,000 minor-offense arrestees. It was the largest civil-rights settlement by any law-enforcement agency in Southeast Louisiana, according to attorney Mary Howell, the attorney on the case who has sued both Foti and Gusman. Howell described the Orleans Parish Prison as "40 years of failure."[4]

On a given day, the facility housed as many as 6,500 inmates, more even than the infamous Louisiana State Penitentiary at Angola. And as many as 60 percent of that number included inmates not formally charged with a crime or who were serving time for minor municipal infractions such as drunk and disorderly. They were among those abandoned for days in the wake of Katrina.

As bad as that was, it was almost routine for inmates who were beaten by deputies or other inmates, to attempt suicide. In June 2005, less than two months before Katrina struck, two Orleans Parish deputies were indicted for beating an inmate to death after he was arrested for public drunkenness. In August 2001, a 24-year-old inmate being held on traffic charges died of dehydration when he was held in restraints for 42 hours. Another inmate died of a ruptured peptic ulcer after suffering in agony for 12 hours before collapsing.[5]

Still another inmate was cut down after attempting to hang himself in his jail cell. Two days later, he ate a large quantity of toilet paper which caused him to asphyxiate. The problems at the Orleans Parish Prison (OPP)

## Chapter 22: Charles Foti, Marlin Gusman: Orleans Parish

were so serious that the U.S. Marshal's Service, which had been paying Sheriff Gusman to house federal prisoners, announced that it was pulling its prisoners from the jail because of "concerns about conditions and safety."[6]

On September 11, 2009, Loretta King, acting assistant attorney general for the Civil Rights Division of the U.S. Department of Justice, fired off a 32-page letter to Gusman in which she laid out conditions found at the parish prison during on-site inspections conducted by a team of federal investigators in November, 2008.

The Southern Poverty Law Center noted that during a single month in 2012, OPP dispatched 23 prisoners to the hospital emergency room with severe injuries that ran the gamut: fractures, stab wounds, lacerations, puncture wounds.[7]

On April 1, 2012, the Southern Poverty Law Center (SPLC) filed a federal lawsuit against Gusman, charging that his indifference had created "brutal and inhumane conditions at the Orleans Parish Prison where prisoners endure rampant violence, multiple sexual assaults and neglect."

Filed in United States District Court for the Eastern District of Louisiana, the lawsuit described what it termed abusive treatment suffered by prisoners with mental illness, including a denial of mental health services that leaves the prisoners "extremely vulnerable to physical attacks." The suit said prisoners in need of mental health treatment or protection from suicide "are held practically naked in overcrowded cells that reek of human waste."

The majority of those who cycle through the jail, the suit said, "eventually come home after enduring unspeakable abuses."[8]

The SPLC legal filings included 19 affidavits from plaintiffs and others who claimed to have experienced abusive conditions at the jail.

Three weeks following the filing of the SPLC lawsuit, on April 23, 2012, Jonathan M. Smith, chief, Special Litigation Section, Civil Rights Division of the U.S. Justice Department, followed up King's September 2009 letter with a 21-page letter to Gusman and to his legal counsel, T. Allen Usry, in which he said Gusman had been sent a draft consent decree on November 8, 2011. "Since that time, you have failed to seriously negotiate. In March, five months after our initial settlement offer, we finally received your first substantive response. In the interim, OPP prisoners have needlessly suffered and staff members' safety has been at risk, contrary to the best interests of the people of New Orleans."[9]

Then, apparently addressing Usry, Smith wrote:

"Given the seriousness of the problems in OPP, we urge your client to:

- Take immediate steps to address the concerns raised in this letter regarding the most basic measures to ensure prisoner safety, health, and well-being, and
- Engage in an aggressive schedule of negotiations with the Special Litigation team to reach an agreed-upon remedy embodied in a federal consent decree with a monitor."[10] (APPENDIX C)

On March 11, 2013, attorney Howell wrote her own letter to Judge Lance Africk of U.S. District Court, Eastern District of Louisiana. In her eight-page correspondence in support of the consent decree, she presented an account of "just a few of the deaths and serious incidents which have occurred at the jail in recent years.

"I would urge the sheriff to take this opportunity, in the context of the consent decree, and with the oversight and assistance of the court and the monitor, to closely examine the attitudes and behavior of top level personnel at the jail, especially in the medical and mental health departments, to determine whether the persons currently in these positions are capable of embracing and instituting real and meaningful reform."[11]

Another four years went by before the Justice Department, by now having lost patience, filed for contempt against Gusman on April 25, 2016, for what the DOJ called his "non-compliance" with the consent decree.

Announced by Principal Deputy Assistant Attorney General Vanita Gupta, head of DOJ's Civil Rights Division, and U.S. Attorney Kenneth Polite of the Eastern District of Louisiana, the news release noted that the case was initiated four years before (by SPLC) as a private prisoner class action. DOJ intervened in the SPLC suit pursuant to the Civil Rights of Institutionalized Persons Act, which authorized DOJ to seek a remedy for a pattern of conduct which violates the constitutional rights of individuals confined in a jail, prison, or other correctional facility. DOJ's motion was filed jointly with the plaintiff class, represented by the MacArthur Justice

## Chapter 22: Charles Foti, Marlin Gusman: Orleans Parish

Center, part of Northwestern University School of Law's Bluhm Legal Clinic.[12]

---

One might normally think that with all the pressure being applied by the Justice Department dating back at least to 2005 when prisoners were stranded in the Orleans Parish Prison following Katrina, some progress would be made over the next decade to improve conditions at the prison. The 2013 consent decree would also seem to underscore the probability that there would have been some progress made in that direction.

But one would be wrong in making such assumptions.

More than 12 years post-Katrina, in December 2017, an online publication advocating prisoner rights, *Prison Legal News*, published a story that indicated local political turf battles stymied reform efforts.

Drawing upon New Orleans news services, *Prison Legal News* noted that U.S. District Court Judge Lance Africk was "clearly upset" at the lack of progress. Africk, who assumed oversight over operations at OPP, forced Gusman to appoint a new compliance director but the rate of assaults on staff and prisoners continued unabated.

Metropolitan Crime Commission (MCC) President Rafael Goyeneche said efforts at reform had been blocked because of the political battle between the sheriff's office and the New Orleans City Council. "The sheriff has repeatedly called for more resources, but it hasn't been granted," he said.

"I just don't know how I can make it any clearer," said Africk in 2016. "I'm starting to get more and more frustrated with the slow pace." He added that there was a general consensus that the jail had not reached the point where inmates were safe from possible violence.[13]

# 23

## Dallas Cormier: Jefferson Davis Parish

Dallas Cormier was sheriff of Jefferson Davis Parish for 12 years, from 1980 to 1992.[1]

Two years after leaving office, he applied for a federal pardon which would allow him to possess a firearm so he could go hunting again. The application was necessary because on March 29, 1993, Cormier was sentenced in state court to three years of supervised probation.[2]

Cormier pleaded guilty to one count of obstruction of justice in 31$^{st}$ Judicial Court in Jennings. The last two years of probation were dropped on March 30 by Judge William Knight at the request of the former sheriff's probation officer. He was also sentenced to 500 hours of community service and ordered to pay a fine of $10,000 over a three-year period.

As part of a plea bargain, prosecutors dropped 35 other charges accusing Cormier of crimes ranging from improper use of inmate labor to using public money to purchase trucks, tires and guns for his personal use.[3]

Cormier and his former chief criminal deputy Ted Gary were indicted by a Jefferson Davis Parish grand jury on July 26, 1990, following three days of hearing evidence. The grand jury returned nine separate indictments containing the 36 true bills. Those included 13 counts of theft from the general fund, one count of criminal conspiracy to obstruct justice and 22 counts of malfeasance in office dating back to 1983.

Cormier was facing a maximum penalty of 200 years in prison and $100,000 in fines if convicted on all counts. Gary was looking at 150 years in addition to the 12 months imprisonment after pleading guilty on April 24, 1990, to federal embezzlement charges.[4]

Gary would serve only that 12-month sentence because he entered into his own plea agreement on the state charges whereby, he agreed to testify against Cormier in exchange for leniency.[5]

The indictments came as Cormier, 65, was recuperating from coronary bypass surgery in a Lafayette hospital.

District Attorney Wendell R. Miller said all the charges represented violations of the public trust. "I think the indictments themselves will speak volumes," he said.

Cormier was hit with nine separate counts of malfeasance, including charges that he:
- Misappropriated merchandise from an accident scene on the nearby Interstate 10 involving a K-Mart truck;
- Misappropriated a tire and rim from another accident, also on I-10;
- Intentionally failed to enforce state statutes relative to driving while intoxicated violations;
- Knowingly allowed two deputies to fail to enforce state DWI statutes;
- Tampered with results of a Breathalyzer test conducted on a DWI suspect;
- Filed false reimbursement invoices with the Louisiana Department of Corrections (DOC) for several inmates housed in the Jefferson Davis Parish jail (the indictments said that Cormier knew the inmates had not been housed during all or part of the period for which he billed the state).

Together, Cormier and Gary were named in 13 other counts each of malfeasance in office and theft. They were accused of:
- Allowing employees under their authority to use public funds for personal vacations;
- Using DOC inmate labor to perform work for deputies as well as for a Lake Charles wrecker service;
- Allowing DOC inmates to have furloughs and temporary releases without DOC approval, which constituted a half-dozen felony counts;
- Theft of more than $4,000 used to purchase a pickup truck for Cormier, nearly $2,000 used for repairs to the truck and for the purchase of two tires for the truck;

## Chapter 23: Dallas Cormier: Jefferson Davis Parish

- Theft of more than $1,000 for the purchase of a vertical twenty-ton log splitter for Cormier;
- Theft of more than $1,000 used to purchase miscellaneous items from a school fair and a livestock show;
- Theft of more than $1,100 for the purchase of miscellaneous items for Cormier at a church bazaar and for the purchase of two pair of boots for Cormier;
- Theft of $1,000 used to purchase a horse saddle for Gary;
- Theft of $2,500 cash for Cormier's personal use;
- Theft of up to $500 for the purchase of a pistol for Cormier;
- Theft of more than $500 used for the purchase of a rifle and scope for Cormier;
- Theft of more than $500 used for the purchase of a shotgun for Cormier.

Additionally, Cormier and Gary were charged on one count of criminal conspiracy to obstruct justice by adding their personal funds to the sheriff's office general fund in an effort to distort the results of an ongoing criminal investigation.[6]

Judge Knight, noting that Cormier, despite his plea bargain, still had not admitted to any wrongdoing, said that public officials should be held to a higher standard of behavior than ordinary citizens. He said he was setting the $10,000 fine that high because Cormier would not serve a day in prison for his misdeeds.[7]

# 24
## Jeff Britt, Ricky Jones: Tensas Parish

In 1998, Louisiana Legislative Auditor Dan Kyle began receiving disturbing reports from private citizens in Tensas Parish regarding alleged illegal activities by Tensas Parish Sheriff Jeff Britt. The reports, though mostly anonymous, were of sufficient validity that Kyle ordered an investigative audit of the sheriff's office.

Investigative audits differ from routine audits in that auditors are looking not at normal oversights or minor irregularities but for suspected criminal activity. What they found through thorough examination of financial records, interviews with sheriff's office employees, and reviews of applicable state and federal laws confirmed what the reports had been saying.

Britt, auditors found, had used a sheriff's office credit card to obtain cash advances totaling nearly $4,600 as well as having obtained cash advances of $1,200 from a local grocery store. Additionally, the sheriff's office paid more than $8,200 on Britt's personal credit card account and Britt also received payments for travel expenses and "special investigations" totaling another $15,700. "Sheriff Britt has not provided adequate documentation or explanation to support the business purpose of the advances and payments," said the audit report, dated December 8, 1998.[1]

In addition to the cash advances, the sheriff's office was charged $117 for ATM access fees, $300 for personal medical lab work, $225 for late fees, $564 for insurance, and $1,568 for finance charges. "Sheriff Britt has provided no documentation to support that these payments were related to the official business of the sheriff's office," the audit report said.[2]

Britt explained that a portion of the cash advances that he obtained was used while traveling on sheriff's office business but he was unable to produce any supporting documentation of that claim nor was he able to explain for what public purpose the money was used. He also was unable to explain how nearly $6,000 was used other than to claim it was for official travel. Moreover, some of his explanations did not agree with other information and documentation examined by auditors.

He claimed that some of the money in question was used to pay two informants and though he claimed to have documentation of the money provided to one of the informants, that documentation was never provided, Kyle said.[3]

The sheriff's office maintained a special investigation fund to purchase information and illegal drugs, the report said. The special investigation fund was supplemented by a federal grant, which would have made any misapplication of funds a federal offense. Guidelines of the federal grant require that each officer maintain receipts for money given to informants. Britt said he was not diligent about keeping up with receipts A deputy interviewed by auditors said that neither Britt nor Chief Criminal Deputy Karl Jones had submitted any receipts for special investigation money even during the period between July 1994 and July 1997, when Britt received $7,570 and Jones received $7,079 of special investigation money. "Sheriff Britt did not provide receipts or documentation to support this use of the funds he received," the audit said. "Mr. Jones provided documentation to support $3,075 of the money he received. Mr. Jones stated that when he was terminated, he left the remaining supporting receipts in his desk at the sheriff's office. The records were not located during our investigation."[4]

Britt said he obtained a $500 cash advance and incurred a $22 advance fee at the Hilton Flamingo in New Orleans in July 1996 for travel to the Louisiana Sheriff's Convention in that city. Records showed, however, the audit said, that he also received a $250 travel advance for that same convention and that Britt "obtained a 4500 cash advance in the form of a check made payable to the Hilton Flamingo Casino."[5]

The audit, embarrassing as it surely must have been, was the least of Britt's worries, however. Earlier, in March 1998, he petitioned a federal judge to allow him to have his gun back while he awaited trial on civil rights charges. He was accused of beating a handcuffed prisoner in January 1977 and then lying about to the FBI.[6] His trial ended in a hung jury.[7]

## Chapter 24: Jeff Britt, Ricky Jones: Tensas Parish

A month earlier, in February 1998, three Tensas Parish deputies pleaded guilty to two counts of civil rights violations of inmates involved in an incident at the privately-operated Tensas Detention Center in October 1996.[8]

In May 1999, former Lafayette, Louisiana, police chief Gary Copes was also indicted by a federal grand jury on 12 counts of aiding and abetting inmate abuse while working as a warden at Tensas Detention Center, located in Newellton, Louisiana, which, though privately operated, was owned by the Tensas Parish Sheriff's Office.

Copes was accused of conspiring with Sheriff Britt to "injure, oppress, threaten and intimidate" prisoners in that October 1996 incident at the prison. The indictment quoted Copes as telling Britt, "If you want me to kick ass, I will" and then looked on as deputies beat inmates with batons.[9]

Copes was also charged with witness tampering for allegedly telling a grand jury witness "to deny everything" when questioned about the beatings. He pleaded innocent, was released on $75,000 unsecured bond and promptly went to work as a warden at another private prison in Basile, Louisiana, on the border of Acadia and Evangeline parishes (counties). Both the Basile and Newellton prisons are operated by Louisiana Correction Services.[10]

He was eventually tried on the jury tampering charge and six counts of violating prisoners' civil rights. The jury deadlocked on the civil rights charges and he was acquitted of witness tampering. In 2003, he was employed as Executive Warden for yet another Louisiana Correction Services facility in Pine Prairie in Evangeline Parish.[11]

Britt, meanwhile, pleaded guilty to malfeasance on May 17, 1999, in exchange for a dismissal of the federal charges. He was sentenced to four years' probation and ordered to pay $21,568 in restitution. As a condition of his plea bargain, he resigned before the completion of his term and agreed to make restitution and to never work in law enforcement again.[12]

The Louisiana State Board of Pardons recommended a full pardon for Britt in January 2017, a recommendation granted by Gov. John Bel Edwards in April. Britt, prohibited from working in law enforcement, nevertheless remained closely involved when he began working in the prison commissary business, providing snacks to sheriffs throughout north Louisiana for resale to inmates. In July 2018, Edwards appointed Britt to the Louisiana Used Motor Vehicle Commission. The board, which meets monthly, oversees licensing and disciplining of used-car dealers and members are paid per diem of $75 per meeting.[13]

Though the three deputies were convicted and Britt was forced into resigning, the beating at the Tensas Detention Center served as one of a growing number of examples of the risks in the federal government's policy of housing detainees in local public and private prisons and relying on local officials to police themselves. When detainees are farmed out to local law enforcement agencies who are paid to take the prisoners, the Immigration and Naturalization Service has no direct involvement in the hiring, training or monitoring of the facilities, which leaves the system open for abuse.

Britt's resignation came at an opportune time for Ricky Jones, who finished second in the October 1999 primary but won the runoff in November. His win set the stage for a bizarre confrontation with two municipal officials of the town of Waterproof eight years later.

Approximately an hour east by northeast of the site of the Jena Six incident that rocked the town of Jena and focused an unwanted national spotlight on the community, Waterproof (pop. 800) is nestled near the southern tip of Tensas Parish.

Tensas, located two parishes from Jena and LaSalle Parish, holds the dual distinction of being the smallest parish in terms of population, with only 6,000 residents, and the parish with the state's fastest decline in population in a state of declining population. With a 2010 per capita income of $15,200, it was also the second-poorest parish in the state in the fourth-poorest state in the U.S.

Louisiana had a median income of $45,700 and Waterproof ranks 355th among 389 Louisiana cities and towns with a per capita income of $9,500 per year.[14]

Bobby Higginbotham was elected mayor of Waterproof in 2006 and took over a town whose fiscal books and police department were in a mess. In 2007, Higginbotham hired Miles Jenkins as chief of police. Jenkins was retired from the U.S. military after a 30-year career and held a master's degree in public administration from Alabama's Troy University.

The only other jobs for African-Americans in Waterproof, which is 60 percent black, were working for the white farmers. "You were going to ride the white man's tractor," Jenkins said. "That's it." Prior to becoming

## Chapter 24: Jeff Britt, Ricky Jones: Tensas Parish

the last Louisiana Parish to allow blacks to register to vote, when the first 15 black voters did so in 1964, not a single one of 7,000 blacks living in the parish was registered to vote in Tensas.

Before taking the job, he said the police department was all but non-existent. "You called the Waterproof police for help before," he said, callers would be told "Wait 'til tomorrow. It's too hot to come out today."[15]

When Higginbotham purchased two new patrol cars for the police department and began issuing citations to speeders, it didn't take long to attract the attention of the parish's white political power structure—Sheriff Ricky Jones and District Attorney James Paxton. And if a sheriff is generally considered the most powerful local political power, the district attorney is not far behind.

By stepping up the town's police department activities, Jenkins was posing an overt challenge to the sheriff's political power while simultaneously taking away a source of income for Jones. Before Higginbotham appointed Jenkins, all traffic tickets went to the sheriff's department. Now revenue from tickets within Waterproof were staying in Waterproof instead of being sent to St. Joseph, the parish seat.

Jack McMillan, an African-American deputy sheriff who worked with Jones, tried to warn Jenkins to be more low-key. "You've got to adapt to your environment," he said he told the chief. "You can't come to a small town and do things the same way you might in a big city."

Higginbotham and Jenkins paid no heed and Jenkins would later claim that the white political infrastructure of Tensas Parish, led by Jones and Paxton, felt threatened by their actions. Documents filed in Sixth District Court said the group set about orchestrating actions against the two black officials that included clandestine meetings, false arrests, harassment and even physical violence designed to prevent Jenkins "from performing his law duties as police chief and forced plaintiff to leave the town of Waterproof."[16]

Court documents said because of the dominance of the white power structure, even local office holders, who tended to be African-American, were "powerless to control their own destiny." Jenkins said that Paxton once boasted that he controlled the votes of Waterproof's black aldermen.

He said he was arrested and declared a flight risk by Paxton even though he lived and owned property in Tensas Parish. He was even cited for disturbing the peace for an incident where individuals threatened him for issuing traffic citations. When he arrested individuals who shoved his patrol car into a ditch, Paxton refused to press charges. When he arrested the former town clerk for illegal entry, he was charged with kidnapping. "That's the most ludicrous notion I've ever come across," said attorney Ron Wilson. Jenkins said he was attacked and choked by a deputy sheriff who he said shouted, "Shut up. We are in charge. We are the sheriff and the sheriff controls Tensas Parish. The sooner you all learn this the better off you will be."[17]

Using a state audit of the town, Paxton and Jones struck. A parish grand jury returned indictments of Jenkins and Higginbotham. Higginbotham was charged on 44 criminal counts on the basis of that audit, which covered the fiscal year ended June 30, 2006.[18]

Higginbotham wasn't elected until September of 2006. All but two of the counts were dropped but the nightmare for Higginbotham and Jenkins was far from over. An Internet blogger published a one-page post calling Jenkins "crazed" in announcing their arrests for running what the blogger referred to as a federally funded "speed trap town."[19]

The reference to Waterproof's being a "speed trap town" was apparently gleaned from a report issued by the Legislative Auditor's office on June 6, 2007, when Jenkins and Higginbotham had been in office for less than a year.

That report showed that Waterproof derived 37 percent of its annual revenue from traffic fines, which placed the town 33rd in the state in the percentage of city revenue received from traffic fines. Of the 304 cities and towns surveyed by the auditor's office, 50, or slightly more than 16 percent, received 25 percent or more of their funding from traffic fines.

Breaking that number down further, 32 towns received a higher percentage of city funding from traffic fines. The top five, in order or percentage, were Baskin (87.41 percent), Robeline (85.73 percent), Lillie (85.59 percent), Georgetown (85.33 percent) and Dodson (78.57 percent).[20]

Waterproof's 37 percent would hardly be sufficient to classify Jenkins as "crazed." Still, the prosecution went forward on the two remaining charges of credit card abuse and what prosecutors called theft via an illegal pay raise for the mayor—a raise approved by the town's board of

## Chapter 24: Jeff Britt, Ricky Jones: Tensas Parish

aldermen but nonetheless pursued by Paxton and Jones. Jenkins was tried on charges related to his enforcement of traffic tickets.

In a town of 60 percent African-American population, Higginbotham found himself being tried by a jury consisting of exactly one black person. His legal counsel was disqualified by Paxton and the public defender had a conflict of interest. That left the mayor representing himself pro se. An accused is guaranteed the right of discovery of all evidence in the possession of prosecutors so that he may formulate his defense. Two days before the trial began, Paxton turned over ten boxes of files. Higginbotham's request for an extension in order to obtain legal representation and to examine the mountain of files, normally a formality that is routinely granted by a presiding judge, was denied.

In a trial, both sides have what is known as preemptory strikes. That is where a prospective juror may be challenged for a lack of impartiality. During jury selection, Higginbotham, forced to act as his own attorney, attempted to strike one juror who had relationships with several witnesses. Despite his still having challenges remaining, he was told he could not strike that juror. Transcripts of trials are critical in the appeal process but the sound recorder being used by the court reporter "malfunctioned," eliminating the transcript for at least two witnesses' testimony.

Higginbotham was convicted but the worst was yet to come. He admitted misuse of the town credit card but despite his conviction for a grand total of $60,000 in fraud and theft—an amount that would normally result in probation at worst for a first-offender—Higginbotham, who, like Jenkins, was from Waterproof, was ordered held without bail during his appeal. The judge did not set excessively high bail; he set no bail at the same time that people like Jack Abramoff, William Jefferson and Tom Delay were out on bail.[21]

New Orleans attorney Rachel Conner, who represented Higginbotham in his appeal, said, "Essentially, every single thing that you can do to violate someone's constitutional rights from beginning to end happened in his case. The vindictiveness, and whatever else is going on under the surface, I think that's where it shows itself. And then you've got a guy with errors in his trial from A to Z. They didn't even set $3 million as his bond. They set *no* bond."

"People need to see exactly what is going on in these little southern towns around here," Jenkins said.[22]

Jones, when asked to comment on Jenkins's lawsuit that claimed harassment and intimidation by the sheriff's office, denied that race was a factor. Instead, he insisted that Jenkins had abused his office and that many local citizens who filed complaints against him were black. "I'm not going to support any type of corruption," Jones said. "Certainly not from him."[23]

Higginbotham, who insists that he and Jenkins tried to bring a degree of professionalism to Waterproof, ended up spending 19 months in jail.[24] And Jones, though by no means alone in the orchestrated political assassination of Higginbotham and Jenkins, certainly appeared complicit, along with Paxton and presiding trial judge John Crigler, in efforts to take them down.

The saga of Higginbotham and Jenkins had a bittersweet ending, at least from Higginbotham's standpoint, in 2012. When the Second Circuit Court of Appeal reversed his conviction and vacated his sentence. The substance of the charges against him were not addressed by the appellate court which instead, focused on irregularities, primarily the missing transcripts from the trial.[25]

# 25
## Scott Franklin: LaSalle Parish

Did an otherwise innocuous remark about sitting under a certain shade tree at a high school result in a 2009 retaliatory drug raid led by the LaSalle Parish sheriff on Jena's African-American community?

The answer to such a loaded question depends, of course, on whom you ask. LaSalle Parish Sheriff Scott Franklin said a lot of drugs and drug dealers were taken off the street in the pre-dawn raid that resulted in 13 arrests and the seizures of vehicles, a home and a barber shop. Marijuana confiscated by authorities from a kitchen table, however, turned out to be broccoli stems left over from a dinner the previous night, according to one resident who was nevertheless arrested and whose ten-year-old car was impounded as "evidence."

The raid by 150 officers from ten different agencies occurred on July 9, 2009. It immediately sparked speculation that the show of force in the name of law and order was continued white establishment payback for an ugly incident at Jena High School back in 2006 that brought international notoriety to Jena in the form of the cause célèbre that quickly became known as the "Jena Six."

On August 30, 2006, at a back-to-school assembly during which male students were being briefed on basic school rules and dress codes, an African-American student, perhaps joking, perhaps not, asked if blacks would be allowed to sit under a tree that served as an unofficial gathering spot for white students. In an apparent answer to the query, three white students hung nooses from the tree as a joke, albeit a joke in extremely poor taste. Despite assurances from local police and the FBI that the nooses were not racially motivated, school officials nevertheless assigned the perpetrators to an alternative school for one month after which they served a two-week suspension, all of which did little to assuage simmering tension that quickly surfaced in the form of racial confrontations that culminated in a fight during which a white boy suffered a head wound that required stitches. Then, on December 4, a gang of eight to ten black students attacked an 11th-grade white student, beating him into unconsciousness. The white student, Justin Barker, had nothing to do with the noose incident that had occurred more than three months earlier. Barker spent nearly three hours in the local hospital emergency room and six blacks, who would become known as the Jena Six, were charged with attempted second-degree murder. The gang's leader, 16-year-old Mychal Bell, who had already been on probation in connection with a battery incident and a property crime a year earlier, was tried as an adult. Charges against the others were reduced to aggravated battery and conspiracy.

An all-white jury of five women and one man found Bell guilty. When the jury notices went out, none of the blacks who were summoned appeared at the courthouse. As a result, the jury pool was necessarily all-white.

The ensuing publicity over the trial and conviction outraged blacks throughout the nation and their anger did not subside even when District Court Judge J.P. Mauffray, Jr. vacated Bell's adult conviction and ordered that he be retried as a juvenile. Tens of thousands of demonstrators, mostly black and including such civil rights luminaries as Jesse Jackson and Al Sharpton descended upon the small central Louisiana town of 3,000. Bell subsequently pled guilty to second-degree battery and to intentionally inflicting serious bodily injury on another person. He agreed to serve 18 months in juvenile custody. The five remaining defendants received fines and unsupervised probation.[1]

Fast forward three years to July 9, 2009.

It was four in the morning and Franklin was pumping up his troops at the Jena Rodeo Building at the local fair grounds. Those under his leadership this morning included SWAT teams from the Louisiana State Police, a U.S. Marshal Fugitive Task Force, agents from the FBI and the Bureau of Alcohol, Tobacco and Firearms (ATF), the Pineville Police Department and, of course, deputies from his own office. "This is serious business we're fixing to do," he lectured, possibly forgetting that he was addressing experienced lawmen with considerably more experience in these matters than he himself possessed. "If you think this is a training exercise

## Chapter 25: Scott Franklin, LaSalle Parish

or if you think these are good ole boys from redneck country and we're going to good ole boy them into handcuffs, you're wrong. It's going to be like Baghdad out in this community at 5:00 a.m."²

It was a performance worthy of a bad Jean-Claude Van Damme movie, except a Jean-Claude Van Damme movie might've been less macho.

Franklin called the raid "Operation Third Option," named after his campaign slogan in which he said drug dealers had three options: quit dealing drugs, leave LaSalle Parish or go to jail. Good campaign rhetoric, to be sure, but this was the real world and when the dust had settled and more than a dozen suspects herded like cattle onto the fairgrounds for public viewing, the fact remained that there was little to show for the massive display of power in the way of drugs or other physical evidence other than a few joints.

That didn't stop the search teams brought in to dismantle homes and businesses. Franklin said body cameras worn during the raid provided visual evidence of the effectiveness of the operation. "We're completely satisfied with the results," he said following the roundup, adding that he had begun planning the operation in November 2007, less than two months following the protests over the Jena Six. To skeptics, the admitted timing appearing unmistakable in its message.

The sister of Robert Bailey, one of the Jena Six, was Catrina Wallace. Along with her mother, she had led efforts to free the youths. She said her activism made her an obvious target. Wallace, 29, was asleep in bed with her youngest child when her door was smashed down and she awoke to find a gun pressed to her head. A search of her home turned up no drugs. What was initially thought to be marijuana found on her kitchen table turned out to be broccoli stems from a meal the night before.

No matter that no drugs were found or that she was raising three small children in a town where she had lived her entire life. She was arrested and held on a $150,000 cash bond and her 1999 Mitsubishi Gallant was seized by police who held it in an impound lot at a fee of $12 a day, a cumulative amount that soon exceeded the value of the vehicle.

Samuel Howard was perhaps subjected to the most humiliating treatment. Sleeping naked in his bed when police broke down his door, he was tasered three times and guns were pointed at his three children. His home was damaged by flares fired into it and he was taken, still naked, to the town baseball field along with the other arrestees where he was forced to spend an hour without clothes until police finally brought him an orange jailhouse jumpsuit. A mechanic, he had four cars, two of which didn't run. All four were impounded along with about 50 other vehicles as "evidence," though officials have never produced any evidence despite attempts by defense attorneys to see videotaped evidence authorities claimed to have. Nor have the cars been returned to their owners. "They treated us like we was hardcore killers," Howard said. "The sheriff knows me. We went to school together. He knows I'm not a violent person."[3]

An online publication calling itself *Commonwealth for a Free Moral Society* had a slightly different take on events, saying there was calm and order throughout the neighborhood during the raid. It quoted Franklin as saying officers were prepared for the worst "but it was absolutely quiet. That shows you the caliber of people we put in jail today. The people in this community want their community back, and we gave it back to them today."

*Commonwealth* described the fire that damaged Howard's home as "a small fire" that started from a candle and which was "quickly contained." It said nothing about flares fired through his windows but did say Howard was tased because he "resisted arrest."[4]

No physical evidence of the alleged drug dealing was ever brought forth, but it didn't seem to matter. As Franklin hosted a barbecue the following afternoon in celebration of his successful raid, the words of District Attorney Reed Walters suddenly took on a new—and grim—meaning. Following the noose incident three years earlier, he had told Jena High black students who had the temerity to protest the nooses, "I can be your best friend or your worst enemy. With the stroke of a pen I can make your life miserable or ruin your life."[5]

Tina Jones, whose car was seized, said authorities built their cases on the word of snitches by threatening them with more serious charges if they did not cooperate. They were often paid off with small bribes like cell phones or hundred-dollar bills. If that failed, there were always the potential of threats and planted evidence, she said.[6]

Many members of Jena's black community believe the town's white power structure was seeking revenge for the noose incident and the ensuing negative publicity it brought down upon the town. They point out that the

## Chapter 25: Scott Franklin, LaSalle Parish

town is majority white but all but two of those arrested were black and the only arrestees in the local newspaper photographs were black.

Marcus Jones, father of Mychal Bell, was not one of those arrested. He expressed shock at the vast resources deployed in the raid. "Why did you need helicopters and military weapons?" he asked. "I could see it if you were going to arrest Noriega or the Mafia, but these were people with kids in their homes. The sheriff never had any violent run-ins with any of these people." He said he felt the entire campaign by Franklin was a gesture to assert control over the black community.

Howard echoed Jones when he said, "They know they're wrong. You can't tell me they don't know."[7]

Whether Franklin's militaristic-style raid was a legitimate effort to rid the community of drugs and dealers or retaliation against the black community for standing up against the racist symbolism of the noose incident at Jena High School is something only Franklin knows with certainty.

But the initial planning of the raid, coming as it did so soon after the Jena Six trials, is hard to overlook and more than a little coincidental—and troubling.

# 26
## Jack Strain: St. Tammany Parish

What began as a federal investigation into a work-release program ended on June 11, 2019, with the arrest of former St. Tammany Parish Sheriff Jack Strain on state charges of rape, incest and indecent behavior with a juvenile.

A St. Tammany Parish grand jury indicted Strain on two counts each of aggravated rape and aggravated incest and single counts of sexual battery and indecent behavior with a juvenile.

Two of his alleged victims were under the age of 12 and the alleged incidents date back as far as 1975, to when Strain himself was as young as 12, according to 22nd Judicial District Attorney Warren Montgomery. One of his victims claimed he was only six when Strain anally raped him.

At least four persons came forward to claim they were molested by Strain, one of whom said he was raped as late as June 2004. Strain, 56, was first elected sheriff in 1995, serving until his defeat by current Sheriff Randy Smith.

Strain was arrested at his home by state police and booked into his former jail where he was held in lieu of posting $400,000 bail. He faced the possibility of life in prison if convicted.

The federal investigation that precipitated his arrest by state authorities stemmed from Strain's privatization of the parish jail, which he turned over to two of his friends. Those two, Skip Keen and David Hanson, subsequently pleaded guilted in February 2019 to conspiracy to solicit bribes and to commit wire fraud.[1]

In 2013, the Slidell work release center was losing money with expenses up by a third. St. Tammany Parish Sheriff Jack Strain decided he needed to sell the 18-year-old facility to a private operator.

To make sure he would be able to unload it, he poured nearly half-a-million dollars into renovations of the center just a year before it was transferred to private operators. Sheriff's Department Maj. Clifford "Skip" Keen, who served as facilities manager for the sheriff's office, oversaw the renovation that included construction of a newer, larger kitchen. Partial renovations were performed by contractor Allen Tingle, who was paid $4,240 for his work.

Then, eschewing public bids on the proposed takeover, Strain signed a three-year contract with newly formed St. Tammany Workforce Solutions. One of the principals of the company was 21-year-old Jarret Keen, son of the aforementioned Maj. Skip Keen. Manager of St. Tammany Workforce Solutions, according to Louisiana Secretary of State corporate records, was Tingle. Brandy Hanson was also listed as a director for the company. She was a former sheriff's office employee and was described by the *New Orleans Advocate* as "the daughter of another member of Strain's inner circle."[2]

Strain told *The New Orleans Advocate* that he met with four potential operators but declined to identify them. None of them submitted a formal proposal to take over the facility. In fact, records would seem to suggest that Strain may have planned for St. Tammany Workforce Solutions all along. Secretary of State corporate records show that the company, which had no other business, filed its incorporation papers on March 23, 2013, less than two weeks before Strain indicated to a local newspaper that he was considering privatization of the center. The address given on the original incorporation papers was 141 Production Drive. That's the same address as the work release center. The address was changed to 201 Bunting Drive in Slidell on July 8, 2016.[3]

Under terms of the agreement with St. Tammany Workforce Solutions, the sheriff's office received $4,650 per month in rent plus $3.50 per day for each Louisiana Department of Corrections inmate. A Louisiana Legislative Auditor's report showed that the company had revenues in excess of $2 million in 2015 though it was not known how much of that amount was net revenue.

That rate was a bargain for the operators. Other private work-release operators in the state were paying upwards of $7,000 per month in rent, plus as much as $10 per day per inmate housed.

## Chapter 26: Jack Strain: St. Tammany Parish

Strain had earlier privatized another work-release center, this one located in Covington, near the parish jail. Like the Slidell facility, it was a sweetheart deal run by Northshore Workforce Solutions, owned in part by Strain's longtime campaign manager, Marlin Peachey, Jr. Northshore Workforce Solutions, unlike its counterpart in Slidell, bore all the costs of building its center.[4]

But that didn't guarantee success. Three inmates died there, two from drug use and a third in a trailer belonging to a company that used inmate labor. Another inmate was murdered while supposedly incarcerated, but had in fact, gone to his house in New Orleans. As bad as those deaths were, public-relations-wise, it was repeated escapes that proved to be the facility's death knell. There were nine alone in 2013, highest number in the state. Johnathan Leger walked off his work-release job in October 2013. He was subsequently booked on two counts of armed robbery, aggravated battery, and aggravated flight. Authorities said he stabbed one of his victims in the neck with a box cutter. One man filed a lawsuit against the sheriff's office and Northshore Workforce, claiming that Leger hit him with a car during his escape.[5]

A year later, there were three more escapes over only a few weeks' time. One of those was Christopher Ricker, who was captured in Tangipahoa Parish after police said he kidnapped his girlfriend and forced her to drive him to Hammond. Strain closed the facility in March 2014, curiously blaming "reckless journalism" for encouraging inmates to escape.[5]

Cracks had begun appearing in Strain's public image eight years earlier, however. In July 2006, less than a year after Hurricane Katrina devastated New Orleans, driving its residents to higher ground, it was Strain who let the poorer evacuees know they were no longer welcome on the Northshore, as St. Tammany Parish is known to residents of Orleans and Jefferson parishes. In an interview with a television reporter, Strain, obviously referring to young blacks, openly threatened racial profiling. "If you're going to walk the streets of St. Tammany Parish with dreadlocks and chee wee hairstyles, then you can expect to be getting a visit from a sheriff's deputy," he said.[6]

## Louisiana's Rogue Sheriffs

That probably shouldn't have surprised anyone, given the fact that former KKK leader David Duke years before had set down roots in St. Tammany Parish.

Nevertheless, it did prompt a lengthy letter to Strain by a Tulane alumnus writing in *The Black Commentator*, an African-American newspaper headquartered in Tarpon Springs, Florida. The essay was published on July 13, 2006, under the headline: "Little Man with a Gun in His Hand: An Open Letter to Sheriff Jack Strain, of St. Tammany Parish, Louisiana." Here are excerpts from that letter:

> "I always liked Slidell, even before Lucinda Williams sang about going there to 'look for (her) joy.' And my fond feelings for the town were rekindled recently when I discovered that Grayson Capps–with whom I went to Tulane in the late '80s, and who's quite the singer-songwriter himself–had written a song about it too.
>
> The way I see it, ya' gotta love any place that gets a song written about it–even Luckenbach, Texas. So, although I never enjoyed that interminably long drive across Lake Pontchartrain from New Orleans when I lived down there, on the few occasions when I made it to St. Tammany Parish, I always found the people to be nice. And considering that St. Tammany is the parish home to Abita Springs, from which place emanates some damned fine spring water, and even better beer, well, what's not to like?
>
> But today, I'm starting to wonder if maybe I should rethink my feelings towards your Parish; perhaps even the "nice people" thing. After all, those "nice people" elected you Sheriff, and yet there you were on TV recently, saying that you and your deputies weren't going to put up with any of the "trash" from New Orleans coming to St. Tammany in the wake of Katrina and its aftermath.

## Chapter 26: Jack Strain: St. Tammany Parish

I know you probably think you're just looking out for the citizens of your community. After all, you fashion yourself an important man, without whom everything would go to hell in a hand-basket. That shiny badge of yours, not to mention your gun, makes it official too: Jack Strain is a big man. Of course, Barney Fife had a badge and a gun, as did every member of the Keystone Kops, so, I suppose importance (to say nothing of competence) is in the eye of the beholder. And yes, I know those guys were fictional officers of the law, but it appears you have a soft spot for fiction, as we'll see here shortly, so keep reading.

What exactly did you mean, Sheriff Jack, when you said that anyone wearing dreadlocks or a 'Chee-Wee' haircut would be paid a visit by one of your deputies? (For those who don't know, a Chee-Wee is a regional snack, not unlike Cheetos.) Are certain hairstyles now seen as probable cause for a stop-and-search in St. Tammany? Under what creative interpretation of the Constitution–you know, that piece of paper that trumps whatever it is you think the law should be– do you figure such a policy is legal? Or do you just not care?

Putting aside legality for a second, perhaps I can just address you as a man, and a father. You see, I have two little girls: five and three. Among the many challenges involved with raising kids is trying to teach them not to say mean-spirited things about others. You know how kids are, right? Always pushing the envelope with such childish slurs as "poo-poo head" or "butt-face," or something they heard at pre-school, and which they don't realize to be hurtful until a parent sits them down and explains that whole Golden Rule thing. Maybe you've had this experience with your own kids: trying to get them to follow the old maxim, 'If you can't say something nice, don't say anything at all,' and then realizing–as my wife and I have–that it's a lesson you'll be re-teaching a lot, seeing as how once just isn't enough to make an impression. Kids are like that: in one ear and out the other.

But how much harder must it be for parents to teach their children proper behavior, and to teach them not to use hurtful words, when they have as adult role models, people like...well, people like you, Sheriff. People who refer to others of the human family as 'trash,' as you did on at least a half-dozen occasions in that interview. It's bad enough to ever call people by such a dehumanizing slur–after all, trash is what we take to the city incinerator and burn every week, or to the landfill to bury, so consider, for a second, the homicidal symbolism of your words–but to do so when you yourself have likely never met any of the persons for whom you reserved this verbal abuse makes it all the more vile.

You began by speaking of the 'trash' in New Orleans rather generically, leaving us all to wonder who you might be speaking of, not that we couldn't venture a guess. We know all the code words y'all have in places like St. Tammany for poor black people, after all. But then, just to make sure we hadn't misinterpreted, you clarified things, specifying that the trash in question were folks from the city's public housing projects, who you feared would be making the trek to Mandeville or some such place, in search of opportunities to ply their criminal trade, or new folks to victimize.

First, don't flatter yourself. The idea that the people of New Orleans really want to come to St. Tammany Parish–thereby trading in one of the most culturally vibrant and important cities in the history of the cosmos for a place where the opening of a new Chili's is cause for celebration–is more than a little silly. Please, remember where you live: a Parish whose most famous resident is David Duke; a Parish whose Republican Party Executive Committee several years ago unanimously voted Duke–the nation's most prominent

## Chapter 26: Jack Strain: St. Tammany Parish

Nazi–to be its chairperson. No, I don't think you need to worry about too many black folks seeking out such a place to live. Of course, if they did, the fact that you'd be more troubled by their presence than the presence of the nation's most prominent Nazi (and convicted criminal, seeing as how Duke recently spent time in jail for various and sundry forms of fraud) says a lot about you and the values you hold dear.

Secondly, while you take great pleasure in calling those who lived in New Orleans public housing before Katrina 'trash,' it should be noted that in some regards, they compare favorably to the folks in your own backyard. So, for example, consider that according to Census data, ten percent of your young people between 16-19 have apparently dropped out of school, which is actually higher than the percentage of dropouts among folks that age who lived in the B.W. Cooper Homes, or the old Desire projects in New Orleans, and roughly the same as the dropout rate for youth who resided in the St. Bernard development.

Of course, you wouldn't be the first person to negatively (and inaccurately) stereotype residents of public housing. It happens all the time, most often coming from people who have never set foot in the places about which they claim to know so much. I'm guessing that would be true for you, Sheriff Jack.

But I've been in those places where the 'trash,' as you put it, live, and you might be surprised at how wrong your preconceived notions are. I spent the better part of 15 months working with New Orleans public housing residents on various community initiatives in the mid-90s, and had the occasion to meet the kind of people you condemn. I've sat in their living rooms, and listened to them talk about their hopes, fears and dreams. I've heard them muster up more optimism in the face of crushing poverty than I could likely conjure–hell, more optimism than I have on a normal day now, even with all the privileges I've been afforded; and I've watched them demonstrate more character, in spite of all the odds stacked against them, than people in any other community I ever visited. Oh, and I can tell you this, without fear of contradiction: I saw far more drugs on my dorm floor at Tulane than I ever saw in the projects, to say nothing of problem drinking. I heard of far more sexual assaults at Tulane than in the housing developments when I was in both places–not that the former were as likely to be prosecuted, of course, or come to the attention of law enforcement at all, for that matter.

Truth is, if you look at New Orleans public housing, and examine some facts about the people who live there (or at least did before the flooding)–as opposed to consulting your own uninformed biases about the same–it's not hard to see that only an ignorant lout or a real asshole would call the residents of such places trash. Now don't get mad: since I'm fully prepared to let you figure out which of the terms fits you better, I haven't actually called you either, so I'm not in violation of that whole 'say something nice or don't say anything' rule that I so neatly promulgated a while back.

First off, about half the residents of New Orleans public housing prior to the flood were minors–they're kids, Sheriff. In the Iberville development, 42 percent were 12 years old or younger, and 20 percent were younger than five. In St. Bernard, a third were 12 or younger, and one in seven were under five years of age. In B.W. Cooper, the numbers were 36 percent 12 and younger, and 17.3 percent five or below. The same is true in the other projects. So, what this means is that as of the 2000 census, of the 15,000 or so residents of public housing (itself a very small percentage of the city's black folks, or even black poor), about 7500 were minors, perhaps 5500 or so were 12 or younger, and around 2500

## Chapter 26: Jack Strain: St. Tammany Parish

were infants or toddlers. So, these are a large number of the folks you just called trash. Children. I'm sure your momma and your pastor would both be proud.

Oh, and I'm sure you'll say you didn't mean them. Sorta like you said you didn't want to call anyone names, and then proceeded to call them trash and thugs, and make fun of their hairstyles by comparing them to fried cheese puffs. Sorta like you said you and your deputies didn't want to violate anyone's civil rights, right after you announced you'd be stopping anyone wearing their hair in one of two styles you know damned good and well are almost exclusively worn by black folks. Which means you can say whatever you like about your intentions, and I'll reserve the right to think you're lying.

So, you'll say you don't mean the kids, but rather, just their parents. They're the irresponsible ones, you'll insist. But in truth, you'd be wrong about the grown-ups too. So at least your ignorance is consistently woven throughout your commentary, and God knows, there's much to be said for consistency, Sheriff Jack.

Not that you're interested, but the facts are these: Contrary to conventional 'wisdom,' in most of the housing developments and their surrounding New Orleans neighborhoods, prior to Katrina, about six in ten households received income from paid employment, while only about one in four received income from government welfare programs. Even though the vast majority of residents in such places were officially poor, only a small percentage received public assistance in the form of cash support. In places like the old Desire and Florida projects, 61 and 69 percent of households, respectively, had at least one person in them who worked at a paid job; and in the case of Desire, only about five percent (or one in twenty households) received money from public assistance programs, or so-called welfare.

Although it's true that most adults in public housing don't work outside the home, when you exclude those who are elderly or disabled–two groups that make up more than a third of adults in most cases–it hardly seems fair to label the grown-ups in and around public housing as irresponsible. A third of all persons 16 or older in St. Bernard, for example, worked full-time–same thing in B.W. Cooper, or the Treme/Lafitte community, with a large number of the remainder working part-time, trying to help make ends meet. The clear majority of able-bodied adults in these places are either working or looking for work, contrary to popular belief. And the rest who don't work at a paying job, typically stay home so they can care for small children: the kind of thing that gets a mother labeled 'good' and responsible, so long as she's white and middle-class.

On a personal level, the strongest work ethic I ever witnessed was that of a resident of New Orleans public housing with whom I had the good fortune to work many years ago: a woman whose son was murdered while she and I were working at the same organization, but who nonetheless came in the very next day because, in spite of her grief, she had a job to do. I don't know about you Sheriff Jack, but I've called in sick because I was tired, and here was someone who felt it necessary to show up to work, even in the immediate aftermath of one of the greatest losses a mother can experience. Lazy? I don't think so. I'd be willing to bet you've got deputies or administrative staff out of the office today, right now, for less valid reasons than that. I'd bet you've missed plenty of days of work fighting the bad guys of Covington, for reasons that would seem quite pathetic compared to losing a child.

## Chapter 26: Jack Strain: St. Tammany Parish

And finally, Sheriff Jack, getting back to your comments in that interview, I really should point out that you've got some nerve sweating the so-called criminal element in New Orleans anyway. See, I hopped on your department's website today (and) I'm...trying to figure out what it is you have against people with dreadlocks, and I'll be damned if I didn't stumble across your Twenty Most Wanted list of alleged perps. And, nothing personal, but it looks to me as though you've got plenty of criminal types in St. Tammany, without having to worry about imported black New Orleanians. Funny though, only two of the twenty most wanted appear to have dreads, or any kind of particularly black haircut.

Yes sir, y'all got some real winners out there in St. Tammany, Mr. po-lice man. And some of 'em are bald, and some have short hair, and some look like former Boy Scouts, and some definitely don't, and some have facial hair, and then again, some are clean-shaven. But even the black folks, who seem to scare you the most, don't all look a certain way. A few are women, and none of the men look anything like Bob Marley, truth be told. Which leads one to conclude that your thinly-veiled racial profiling is not only racist, but rather stupid-ass law enforcement, seeing as how your twenty most wanted list seem to have more of a problem with receding hair lines than anything else.

I dunno, maybe you were just pandering to the David Duke types: folks who left Jefferson Parish (the original New Orleans white flight suburb) and moved to St. Tammany in recent years to get even farther away from black people. Or maybe you'd had one too many Abita Turbo Dogs before they stuck that camera in your face. Or maybe you weren't pandering, or plastered: maybe you're just a jackass (Ah, ah, I said maybe). But please, the next time you think about wasting several minutes of taxpayer-paid time in front of a news crew, remember that that's time you could be spending tracking down devil-tattooed white check-kiters, or serial drunk drivers."[7]

Jim Izrael, a writer for the Lexington (Kentucky) *Herald Leader*, was interviewed about Strain's rant on NPR. "The Katrina love fest is over," he said. "Sheriff Jack Strain...despises the migration of displaced New Orleanians so much, he started a kind of backwoods profiling campaign." He said Strain "just feels he has no other choice but to revert back to antebellum slave trapper type tactics, to bring peace back to his little hamlet. And I get it. Tammany is Mayberry, and Jack Strain is Andy Taylor. But Andy was never quite this ignorant."[8]

Old attitudes die hard, apparently. In May 2014, Belinda Parker-Brown, president and CEO of Louisiana United International, a Slidell-based civil rights organization, revealed the contents of 13 racially-charged emails sent and received by two of Strain's deputies. She obtained the emails through Louisiana's public records law and the *Huffington Post* had a story about them in April 2015, only six months before Strain would be up for re-election.

Parker-Brown said relations between African-Americans and law enforcement officers had further suffered because St. Tammany had one of the highest incarceration rates in a state that had the highest incarceration rate in the world. Known derisively as "St. Slammany, white officers shared (the emails) and no one was fired.

"Supervisors have discussed the matter individually with the two employees who forwarded some of the content," said Captain George Bonnett, a spokesman for the sheriff's office, in a letter to Parker-Brown. "The employees have been reminded of the importance of maintaining a character above reproach, both on and off the clock." Then, as if to mitigate the severity of the matter, Bonnett noted that the deputies involved used their personal email accounts to send the messages.[9]

Strain was challenged for re-election in 2015 by Slidell Police Chief Randy Smith. It proved to be a contentious campaign that featured efforts to obtain loyalty pledges from deputies, charges of ethics violations, and claims of preferential treatment by Strain's office of a complaint in a domestic dispute involving one of Strain's deputies.

## Chapter 26: Jack Strain: St. Tammany Parish

In the latter case, Deputy Jeremiah Abbott said his estranged wife ran over his foot with her car during a confrontation over custody of their children. His wife was arrested. Her boyfriend at the time called her in jail and a tape was made of their conversation during which the boyfriend discussed "burying his (Abbott's) body," which Abbott took as a threat against his life.

When the sheriff's office took no action on the incident—and refused to provide copies of the taped conversation to Abbott's attorney—Abbott was called to meet with Sheriff's Office Maj. Brad Hassert and recorded their conversation. The tape included Hassert questioning Abbott's loyalty to Strain. Hassert said on the tape that "you are not the first guy I've talked to about this and you won't be the last, but if you can still tell me you can support the sheriff, then we have no issue."

That conversation resulted in the filing of an ethics complaint by Concerned Citizens of St. Tammany (CCST), a public watchdog group formed to investigate ethics and criminal violations in St. Tammany Parish. Belinda Parker-Brown, representing the group Louisiana United International, and CCST spokesman Terry King held a joint press conference at which time they labeled Hassert's comments public salary extortion.

When he heard the tape, Hassert admitted that he took "some liberties I shouldn't have when I talked to Abbott" when he said during their conversation, "The sheriff asked me to talk to you." Recanting that statement, he said Strain never asked him to put pressure on anyone for the sheriff's support.

Hassert was also heard saying on the tape, "He's (Strain) not asking or telling you to leave…so can I tell him you aren't supporting Randy Smith for sheriff?"

For his part, Strain said he had never asked Hassert "or anyone else" to pressure deputies for their support. "I'm sure some of our deputies have voted against me and that's their right, but I'll be the first to say that I appreciate any of my supervisors who support me and this agency. If someone is disrupting this agency in any way, I appreciate any of our staff who are trying to address that."

Strain said the real motivation for the public attack on him was political and originated with the upcoming election.[10]

Strain's opponents must have been disheartened when the results of the October 24 first primary came in. Strain led a field of four with 27, 609 votes, or 45 percent of the vote, followed by Smith with 22,653 (37 percent). Scott Illing had 8,634 (14 percent) and in fourth place was Jennifer Werther with 1,948 (3 percent). Werther was a Libertarian while the others were Republicans.

Conventional wisdom says anytime an incumbent is forced into a runoff, he is in trouble. Still, Strain had come so close to an outright win in the first primary. With only 17 percent of the vote going to Illing and Werther, Smith, with 37 percent, would need virtually all of those outstanding 17 percent to pull off the upset.

But pull it off he did. On October 24, only 60,844 had turned out to vote, a turnout of just 38.3 percent. And this was an election for governor. With Democratic State Rep. John Bel Edwards pitted against U.S. Senator David Vitter in the November 21 runoff, things heated up pretty quickly. The national Democratic Party, which had not gotten involved in the election in a decidedly red state, suddenly saw one of their own leading the field and in a runoff with a U.S. Senator who had a sex scandal involving the D.C. Madam tied to him like an anchor. Just as suddenly, money that had been held back in the first primary was pumped into the Edwards campaign and people were paying attention.

For the second primary, 70,275 (44 percent) turned out to vote, an increase of 15.5 percent over the October 24 turnout. When the dust had settled, a Democrat was in the governor's office and there was a new sheriff in town. Smith pulled 36,616 votes (52 percent) to Strain's 33,659. Smith's vote total for the second primary was nearly 14,000 more than he received in October. Strain also picked up an additional 6,000 votes but it was not enough to carry him into a sixth consecutive term.[11]

---

Smith wasted no time setting about making changes in the department.

On the night he took the oath of office, he dispatched several deputies to enter the work release building in Slidell to take control of the center. What they discovered were missing security cameras and televisions and computers containing information about inmates gone, all removed by St. Tammany Workforce Solutions as its personnel walked out the door.

## Chapter 26: Jack Strain: St. Tammany Parish

While legal since the company had purchased the equipment, it made for a difficult transition for the new administration.

"Right after I was sworn in at midnight, we went over…and took it (the facility) over," Smith told a New Orleans television station. He said that after all the controversy about the parish work-release operations, he decided to take the program back in-house. "It's my responsibility. I'm the one that's held accountable for those inmates if they do something wrong and it's hard for me to trust someone from the outside to manage it the way it should be managed," he said.

Smith said he entered into negotiations with the operators about purchasing their computer system, their software and some of their vehicles but ultimately decided not to buy anything from them. "We started from scratch," he said.

He said that after some initial overhead expenses, he felt the center could generate "over a million dollars" in revenue that previously had gone into the pockets of Allen Tingle and the adult children of two of Strain's former top deputies.[12]

# 27
## Clay Higgins: St. Landry Parish
## [From Cajun John Wayne to Congress]

If ever there was a living caricature of the Barney Fife character from the old *Andy Griffith Show*, it would have to be Clay Higgins, aka the self-anointed "Cajun John Wayne," a Dirty Harry wannabe.

Originally a patrolman and a member of the Opelousas Police Department's SWAT team, Higgins, a former used car salesman, resigned from the OPD on May 18, 2007, in lieu of accepting disciplinary action from Police Chief Perry Gallow.

"Pfc. Clay Higgins used unnecessary force on a subject during the execution of a warrant and later gave false statements during an internal investigation. Although he later recanted his story and admitted to striking a suspect in handcuffs and later releasing him ..." read the minutes of the Opelousas Police Department's Discipline Review Board concerning the March 14, 2007, incident.

Among the actions that had been recommended by the review board:
- Demotion from Patrolman First Class to Patrolman;
- Reassignment to a patrol shift for more direct supervision and training;
- Immediate removal from the SWAT Team;
- 160 hours suspension from duty without pay.

Rather than be subjected to the disciplinary action, Higgins turned in his equipment and resigned, although his version of events varies somewhat with the official account.

The incident in question occurred, he said, when he and fellow SWAT Team members were guarding the perimeter of a drug bust and a car breached the perimeter. The driver claimed to have cash in the suspected drug house and wanted to retrieve it, according to Higgins. The man was detained and handcuffed, Higgins claimed, and threatened the officers and Higgins slapped a cigarette out of the man's mouth.

The man, who was subsequently released, filed a complaint and Higgins admittedly lied about slapping the man but later confessed to slapping him. While awaiting a determination of his punishment, he said he jokingly referred to Gallow as a peacock. He made the somewhat dubious claim that Gallow had someone recording his conversation and that Gallow threatened to disband the entire SWAT team. He said he approached his captain and said he was the one who called Gallow a peacock because he didn't want the entire team to suffer for something he'd said.

"I decided right then, on that day, that my career was over at OPD—that I would never, ever recover from this peacock thing. He was infuriated by it. So, because of that I went into the chief's office the following week and I turned in my badge and my gear and I resigned."[1]

That's not the way it happened, according to Captain Craig Thomas, who headed up Internal Affairs for the OPD. He said Higgins lied in saying that the driver of the vehicle, Andre Richard, committed a battery upon Higgins and that Higgins only came forward to tell the truth after learning that Sergeant Bill Ortego did not go along with the story told by Higgins and another officer. Ortego said that he, Higgins and a third officer were standing outside the home where the warrant was being executed when a young black man pulled up in a red vehicle, got out and approached the three officers, but did not breach a perimeter as claimed by Higgins because "there was no perimeter set up for Richard to see," Thomas said. "He was parked in the street."

When Higgins walked to the driver's side of the vehicle and started looking in the car through the open door, Richard attempted to close the door while Higgins was still standing in the doorway, at which time Higgins and the second officer threw Richard to the ground, Ortego wrote in his statement. Ortego made it clear that the driver had not placed his hands on Higgins before trying to close his car door.

Once the man was on the ground, Higgins asked for handcuffs and when the cuffs were on, Higgins grabbed him by the hair and told him to contact his lawyer, Ortego said, adding that the two officers began searching Richard's vehicle, which they did not have permission to do, and noted that Ortego himself and Lieutenant Craig Leblanc, who was also present, helped the man off the ground, at which time Richard told Higgins, "It's all right,

## Chapter 27: Clay Higgins: St. Landry Parish

everybody got to die someday." Higgins took it as an implied threat and it really pissed Higgins off, prompting him to remove the cuffs and push the man onto the car, then put his hand around his neck before slapping him in the face and telling him to leave, according to Ortego's statement. Higgins then pulled the cigarette out of Richard's mouth and pushed him toward his vehicle, Ortego said.[2]

Following his departure from the OPD, Higgins next showed up as a public information officer for the St. Landry Parish Sheriff's Office. His career there took an even more bizarre turn and established him as something of a pseudo folk hero in what he perceived as the mold of some kind of super cop, or better yet, the reincarnation of John Wayne himself. But his blatant—and oddly comical—self-parody bathed him more in the light of Deputy Fife than the Duke.

While employed by the SLP Sheriff's Office, Higgins took it upon himself to make a series of macho videos of himself in full battle garb and armed to the teeth. With a full contingent of law enforcement personnel, armaments and a police dog standing alertly in the background, Higgins embarked on a rant against thugs, gang members, and assorted criminals, promising them there was no safe haven for them as long as he was on the job.

The videos gained him instant notoriety on YouTube, garnering thousands of hits. That only encouraged Higgins to branch out and to begin offering commemorative cups, caps and T-shirts to an adoring public. Soon, he was appearing as a paid guest on talk shows, giving paid speeches and doing paid advertisements, all of which naturally, in today's media-dominated society, morphed into a TV reality show. Saying he had his reasons for preferring payment in cash, he charged $1500 for a television production, $1,000 for a radio production and $150 an hour in travel time and another $1,000 for a photo session.[3]

It also prompted swift action on the part of St. Landry Parish Sheriff Bobby Guidroz. After Higgins's forced resignation, Guidroz said, "Clay Higgins formed a personal business venture to raise money by selling mugs, T-shirts and other trinkets using department badge and uniform." Explaining that using the sheriff's office to promote his businesses was against departmental policy, Guidroz said, "I reined Higgins in." He said that Higgins needed to take his own advice to not be disrespectful and to "follow the law." Guidroz said he never authorized Higgins to appear on mugs, T-shirts or any other paraphernalia.[4]

The personal business to which Guidroz referred, Captain Higgins Gear Company, LLC, was incorporated on October 15, 2015, according to Louisiana Secretary of State records which show the company's agent to be Steven T. Ramos of Lafayette and officers to be Higgins, wife Rebecca Lee Higgins, and Garrett Andrew Ahrens who also served as an advisor to Higgins.

Guidroz related an incident in which Higgins requested extra body armor and an AR-15. He also asked to take the sheriff's department decals off his car because, Higgins said, "My wife is home alone a lot and I don't want them (those he had targeted in his videos) to see that I'm a policeman living in this area with the decals on my car."

Guidroz said he told Higgins, "No, and I'll tell you why: You put a target on 55 other deputies in this parish that have marked units. By calling these guys (gang members) out on the street, claiming to be a bad-ass, you put that target on them. Why should I grant you that request to unmark your car?"[5]

Guidroz also took issue with a statement made during testimony by Michael Cohen, former attorney for Donald Trump. "I've arrested several thousand men, and you remind me of many of them," he told Cohen in February 2019.[6] Higgins' claim of making "several thousand" arrests drew a snort of outrage from Guidroz. "I went back and checked the records of when he was employed here and I found exactly 51 arrests that he made. Fifty-one. I can document that," Guidroz added.[7]

As his supersized ego continued to grow, so, too, did his dream of a TV reality show in which he would out-Seagal actor Steven Seagal who at one time had his own TV reality cop show in which he did ride-alongs with the Jefferson Parish Sheriff's Department. Higgins, expanding on that theme, actually envisioned himself popping in on various police department SWAT teams around the country and inviting himself to raids where he would personally arrest perps and then exact confessions from them during on-camera interrogations. Left unexplained was just how he intended to convince local police departments to allow him to swoop in and claim the glory after what may have been months of investigation and surveillance on their part.[8]

## Chapter 27: Clay Higgins: St. Landry Parish

Only after he left the St. Landry Parish Sheriff's Office was it learned that Higgins had not paid federal income taxes for several years, and his salary there was being garnished by the IRS. Moreover, it was also learned belatedly that Higgins was being sued by one of his ex-wives for $100,000 after falling behind on child support payments a decade earlier.[9]

Higgins, who denied an accusation by another ex-wife (not the one who sued him for child support) that he put a gun to her head during an argument in 1991, landed on his feet, this time as a reserve deputy for Lafayette City Marshal Brian Pope who was himself indicted by a grand jury in August of 2016.

Meanwhile, Higgins was mounting an improbable run for U.S. Representative from Louisiana's Third Congressional District. He was seeking the seat previously held by Rep. Charles Boustany who ran—and lost in his race for the U.S. Senate seat vacated by the retiring David Vitter. Higgins, running as an unabashed supporter of Donald Trump, was pitted in the runoff against Scott Angelle, a member of the Louisiana Public Service Commission who finished third in a four-man race for Louisiana Governor in 2015. In the November primary, Angelle led with 29 percent of the vote to Higgins's 26 percent. But in the December 10 runoff, Higgins, with 77,671 votes (56 percent), swamped Angelle, who pulled but 60,762 (44 percent). After having lost two major races within a year's time, Angelle was likely through running for elective office though Trump later hired him to head up the federal Bureau of Safety and Environmental Enforcement.

Days before his runoff victory, Higgins was taped by ex-wife Rosemary Rothkamm-Hambrice as they discussed his delinquent child support payments. "...I really don't know how much we should talk about this on the phone," Higgins said. "I'm just learning really about campaign laws and shit, but there's going to be a lot of money floating around..." Higgins's attorney, Ted Anthony, said his client was simply attempting to tell Rothkamm-Hambrice that if he won, his $174,000 congressional salary would provide him the resources to resolve his delinquent child support payments.

Congressman Higgins, just as he had done as police officer and deputy sheriff Higgins, lost no time launching himself into more controversy. In office barely three months, he made headlines when, responding in April to an Isis attack in downtown London that left seven dead and 48 injured, he called for the mass extrajudicial killing of people even suspected of sympathizing with "radicalized" Islam.

"Not one penny of American treasure should be granted to any nation who harbors these heathen animals," he was quoted as saying in the online publication *ThinkProgress*. "Not a single radicalized Islamic suspect should be granted any measure of quarter. Hunt them, identify them, and kill them. Kill them all. For the sake of all that is good and righteous. Kill them all."

Without bothering to provide any guidelines as to how an Islamic sympathizer would be identified for extermination, he went on to describe the conflict as a war between Christendom and "Islamic horror."[10]

Three months later, he was at it again. Traveling to Germany for no other reason than to be seen in the company of Trump on the President's visit there, Higgins paid a visit to Auschwitz, the concentration camp where hundreds of thousands of Jews were murdered by Germany's Nazi regime during World War II, Higgins videotaped himself inside the facility, taking the occasion to go political, saying, "This is why homeland security must be squared away, why our military must be invincible."

A sign outside the Auschwitz gas chambers clearly says, "You are in a building where the SS murdered thousands of people. Please maintain silence here: Remember their suffering and show respect for their memory."

The video prompted an immediate reaction from the Auschwitz Memorial and Museum. "Everyone has the right to personal reflections. However, inside a former gas chamber, there should be mournful silence. It's not a stage."[11]

# 28

## Rodney Arbuckle: DeSoto Parish

DeSoto Parish Sheriff Rodney Arbuckle abruptly stepped down in March 2018 after 18 years in office, claiming concerns over health problems experienced by a grandchild.

But lingering problems in his office stemming from a 2014 state audit combined with additional criticism anticipated in a pending audit could have been a contributing factor in his decision to suddenly retire.

A former DeSoto Parish sheriff's deputy may have violated state law by using his office to run background checks for a company in which he owned a major interest, according to an investigative audit report by the Legislative Auditor's office in Baton Rouge.

But the attorney for Sheriff Arbuckle says Robert Davidson, the former deputy did nothing wrong.

His company, Lagniappe and Castillo Research and Investigations, ran 41,574 background checks through the sheriff's office during an 11-month period between April 1, 2012, and February 28, 2013, the report says.[1]

The report also noted that three DeSoto Parish Sheriff's Office (DPSO) employees were paid nearly $2,000 by Lagniappe and Castillo Research and Investigations for running the background checks between January 2011 and May 2013, duties they would normally perform as part of their jobs with the sheriff's office.

The company charged its customers $12 for each background report and paid the sheriff's office $3 per report. That represents an income of more than $498,800 and a profit of more than $372,000 for owners Davidson and Allan Neal Castillo over the 11-month period.

Davidson, retired chief investigator for the DeSoto Parish Sheriff's Office, is 50 percent owner of Lagniappe and Castillo and the company's address is the same as Davidson's residence, according to records provided by the Louisiana Secretary of State.[2]

Davidson was employed by DeSoto Parish Sheriff's Office from 1980 until his retirement in May of 2013. Besides being listed by the Secretary of State as 50 percent owner, he also is listed as the registered agent of the company.[3]

Arbuckle, through his legal counsel, defended the practice, saying that Davidson did not own a "controlling interest" in the company and that he did not "participate" in the transactions because he was employed in the criminal investigation division of the sheriff's office and the background checks were performed by the civil administrative division. "The criminal investigation division is both physically and functionally separate and apart from the civil administrative division," he said. "Thus, he did not 'participate' as defined by the Code of Ethics…"[4]

Arbuckle also claimed that the three DPSO employees ran the background checks for which they were paid by Lagniappe and Castillo on holidays and weekends, adding that state law does not prohibit deputies from being paid by a non-public source for off-duty work.

State law requires that employers obtain criminal background checks prior to making an offer to employ or contract with a non-licensed person. Background checks are run through the Louisiana State Police Internet Background Check System database.

The obvious question becomes: could there conceivably have been a need for 41,574 background checks over an 11-month period in a rural parish of only 27,000 residents, including children? If not, for what purposes were these background checks done, what information was contained in them, and to whom were they sold? The sheer volume of background searches raised a Fourth Amendment issue over unreasonable searches and seizures.

One other question still unanswered is whether or not Sheriff Arbuckle received any of the proceeds from the transactions other than the $3 per report charged by the sheriff's office.

Employers are charged a fee of $26 per background check requested through Louisiana State Police. Authorized agents approved by LSP are also charged $26 for each report but until July 1, 2013, LSP did not charge a fee to local law enforcement agencies. To circumvent the $26 charge for each report, Lagniappe and Castillo simply routed its requests through the

## Chapter 28: Rodney Arbuckle: DeSoto Parish

DPSO, which was not charged for the reports. For that privilege, the company paid the sheriff's office $3 while charging clients a cut-rate fee of $12 for each reported generated through the DPSO, the audit report said.[5]

State Police records indicate that during the 11-month period from April 1, 2012 through Feb. 28, 2013, all local law enforcement agencies statewide combined to run 91,074 background checks. Of that number, 65,174 (72 percent) were ordered by the DeSoto Parish Sheriff's Office. The 41,574 ordered by Lagniappe and Castillo represented 63.8 percent of the total run by DPSO. Arbuckle said his office averaged 200-300 background checks per day.

"During the audit period, Mr. Davidson's company paid DPSO more than $124,000 ($124,722) for information that we understand his company sold to private clients for nearly half a million dollars," ($498,888) the audit says. "Because Mr. Davidson entered into transactions with the DPSO in which he had a personal, substantial economic interest, he may have violated the state's ethics laws."[6]

Arbuckle's attorney James R. Sterritt of Cook, Yancey, King & Galloway of Shreveport argued that because Davidson, with 50 percent ownership, did not own a "controlling interest" in the company, he committed no wrongdoing.[7]

Sterritt's legal interpretation notwithstanding, Louisiana Revised Statute 42:1102(8) clearly defines controlling interest as "any ownership in any legal entity…which exceeds 25 percent of that legal entity."[8]

The audit report also cites a state statute which "prohibits public servants from participating in transactions involving the governmental entity (sheriff's office) with any legal entity in which the public servant (Deputy Davidson) exercises control *or owns an interest in excess of 25 percent* (emphasis added) and who by reason thereof is in a position to affect directly the economic interests of such public servant."

Thus, the report says, "former DPSO Chief Investigator Robert Davidson's 50 percent interest in Lagniappe and Castillo was a controlling interest which may have prohibited Lagniappe and Castillo from entering into transactions with the DPSO."[9]

The audit also cites yet another state statute [R.S. 42:1111(C)(1)(a)] which "prohibits public servants from receiving anything of economic value for any service from a nonpublic source that is similar to the work being done for the public employer."[10]

The audit report said that since the three employees' jobs "were to run background checks for the DPSO, this relationship may have violated the state's ethics law." The report added that the "vast majority" of the reports "appear to have been performed during on-duty hours, thus contradicting Arbuckle's contention that the work was done on weekends and on holidays.

The audit report also dismissed Arbuckle's examples of off-duty deputies working for private concerns such as providing security for businesses. "The instant case differs from the instances cited by Sheriff Arbuckle in that, here, the deputies were performing the same—not similar—services that they are paid to perform in their on-duty jobs."

The audit report, signed by Legislative Auditor Daryl Purpera, ended with a recommendation that Arbuckle seek *further* legal guidance (emphasis added).

"We recommend that the DPSO consult with legal counsel and the Louisiana Board of Ethics on the legality of these relationships.

"The DPSO should also adopt detailed ethics policies and procedures, including requiring all employees to complete the annual ethics training in accordance with (state statute) and prohibiting employees from contracting with the DPSO," it said.[11]

A copy of the audit letter was sent to the Board of Ethics.

Sterritt, meanwhile, insisted that "no one involved understood there to be an ethical violation or that there was a potential for a violation. Further, Mr. Davidson has retired and is no longer employed by the DPSO. Accordingly, the relationship in question and the potential for a conflict have terminated."[12]

LACE is an acronym for Local Agency Compensation Enforcement whereby the local district attorney's office pays the salaries of law enforcement officers to beef up traffic patrol for the parish. The LACE program was hit with problems in two State Police troops earlier when it was learned that troopers were reporting hours worked on LACE detail that were not actually work.

The same problem existed in DeSoto Parish. In that case, it was sheriff's deputies who fudged the numbers on their timesheets, and three of Arbuckle's deputies subsequently left under a cloud. An investigative audit by the Legislative Auditor's Office was expected to be critical of the LACE program and possibly other areas of operation.

## Chapter 28: Rodney Arbuckle: DeSoto Parish

Then there is Arbuckle's annual budget which reflects revenues of $12 million, which was more than double the $5 million of next-door neighbor Sabine Parish, which has a population of 24,000—only slightly fewer than DeSoto.

Arbuckle's office had expenditures of more than $14 million for the fiscal year ending June 30, 2017. That was $3 million move than the $11 million spent by the sheriff's office in Natchitoches Parish, which has a population of 40,000—and a university. It is also more than triple the $5 million spent by the Sabine Parish sheriff for the same year.

So, just what did Arbuckle spend all that $14 million on? For starters, the bulk of that amount, *$11 million,* to be precise, went for salaries. It appears that Arbuckle hired deputies almost indiscriminately. Arbuckle himself was the second-highest paid sheriff in the state (only the Beauregard Parish sheriff made more). His department's salary figures compare with salary expenditures of less than $4 million for Sabine and $8 million for Natchitoches.

# 29

## Joseph Reed Bueche: Pointe Coupee Parish

Joseph Reed Bueche, 51, was a ten-year veteran with the Pointe Coupee Parish Sheriff's Office when he was arrested in August 2013 following a drug investigation.

Pointe Coupee is a largely rural parish located an hour northwest of Baton Rouge and across the Mississippi River from historic St. Francisville in West Feliciana Parish.

Sheriff Bud Torres said Bueche was arrested and charged with two counts of malfeasance in office and was fired immediately following his arrest. He said his office had received numerous complaints that Bueche was involved in "illicit drug sales."

Once an internal investigation showed there was credible evidence to support the allegations, the State Police Criminal Investigation Unit was notified and state police in turn determined there was probable cause to execute a search warrant on Bueche's home.

"Sgt. Bueche was held in high regard in the community," Torres said. "There is nothing worse than a cop that goes bad and violates the trust of the community."[1]

# 30
## Willy Martin: St. James Parish

St. James Parish Sheriff Willy Martin doesn't concern himself with nepotism. He apparently will hire *anyone* who bothers to apply for employment as a deputy even at the risk of jeopardizing criminal cases that make it to a courtroom.

Martin hired two deputies who had been fired by neighboring parish sheriffs' offices—one of those just nine months following his arrest and firing for committing perjury in courtroom testimony in a 2014 drug case he worked.

Cody Malkiewiez even disclosed on his application for the St. James position that he was terminated from the St. John the Baptist Parish Sheriff's Department. He completed a pre-trial diversion program and the charges against him were dismissed by the St. John the Baptist district attorney, according to a New Orleans television station.

The St. James sheriff also hired Yule Pouchie in August 2016 after he had been fired as a correctional officer by the Jefferson Parish Sheriff's Office. Pouchie was fired in May 2015 after several disciplinary actions were imposed against him. Those actions included "multiple suspensions," according to WVUE-TV reporter Kimberly Curth.[1]

Martin, contacted by WVUE, said Malkiewiez was capable as a commissioned patrol deputy and that there had been no complaints about his work. Martin added that Pouchie was a deputy for only a short period before being reassigned to corrections. That reassignment came after further disciplinary problems with his new employer. He was caught sleeping in his patrol car while assigned to monitor traffic during flooding. He also was observed drinking off duty just prior to reporting to work a detail and then he was disciplined for inadequately searching a suspect prior to booking which resulted in contraband being brought into the parish jail. Finally, he handcuffed a driver during a routine traffic stop.²

Rafael Goyeneche, president of the New Orleans Metropolitan Crime Commission, wasn't as easy to convince of the propriety of the hires, however. "Here are two instances where individuals with checkered pasts were dismissed from other law enforcement agencies, yet both…resulted in hires by the St. James Sheriff's Office," he said, adding that he felt Martin owed "an explanation to the public as to what criteria he used" in hiring the two.

Goyeneche, in addition to stressing the importance of Malkiewiez's integrity, also expressed concern about his potential involvement in any criminal cases. "…If he ever has to appear in court in connection with an arrest or giving testimony in a case, the sheriff needs to disclose (his personnel record) to the district attorney…and the district attorney has an ethical obligation to turn that over to the defense because the officer's integrity and truthfulness are relevant in any case that he would appear as a witness in to testify," he said.³

Goyeneche said every case in which Malkiewiez might be involved "is tainted by his prior arrest for lying under oath." He added that the possible ramifications "could potentially cost the agency that hired him millions of dollars in a civil judgment, so it's critically important for law enforcement to do extensive background checks to make sure that they're not taking another agency's problems and bringing (them) into their organization."

He said rehiring officers with problematic backgrounds is nothing new in Louisiana. "This has been historically a problem area for law enforcement," going back for decades. "As long as I have been here, there have been instances where law enforcement employees have been fired by one agency and rehired by another agency. Not only does it undermine public confidence in law enforcement, it could be potentially a very big financial burden if misconduct results in civil judgments against a sheriff's office or a municipal police department for hiring someone with a problematic background," Goyeneche said.⁴

# 31

## Greg Champagne: St. Charles Parish

In 2016, St. Charles Parish Sheriff Greg Champagne served as President of the National Sheriffs' Association. It was in that capacity that he made an on-site visit to the Dakota Access Pipeline construction site in North Dakota in November of that year and issued a glowing report on the performance of law enforcement officials at the site while generally characterizing protestors as thugs and miscreants.

But three years earlier, it was Champagne who is said to have attempted to influence state police to alter an accident report so as not to reflect badly on his department and one of his deputies who was killed in a high-speed accident. The alleged attempt may have been to mitigate legal liability for his department as much as to assuage criticism of his deputy's actions.[1]

On August 4, 2013, Deputy Jeff Watson, responding to a call for backup from another deputy, was driving at an estimated speed of 90 miles per hour on a two-lane road in the St. Charles Parish town of Luling. Watson, 41, was driving in a northward direction when a pickup truck driven by Dallas Veillon attempted a left turn in front of the speeding deputy and was broadsided by Watson.

The State Police report indicated that even though Watson was responding to an emergency, he failed to regard the safety of others. The report, citing a surveillance video from a nearby store, said the deputy did not activate his emergency lights or sirens until less than a second before the collision. Moreover, he was not wearing his seatbelt. "Driver 1 (Watson) was found to be in violation of LRS 14:39/Negligent injuring due to the injuries sustained by Driver 3 in the crash," the report said.[2]

Driver three was Arthur Tregre, 80, of Hahnville, who was driving a Ford Expedition. He was struck by Watson after Watson had first struck

Veillon. Tregre was critically injured in the accident. Veillon was determined to have a blood alcohol level of .10. A BAC content of .08 is considered intoxicated in Louisiana. A parish grand jury later charged Veillon with first-offense drunk driving. The grand jury had considered a charge of negligent homicide but declined to return an indictment for that charge.[3]

Lloyd Grafton, retired from the Bureau of Alcohol, Tobacco and Firearms and who now serves as an expert witness in cases involving excessive force and other violations by law enforcement officials, said that Champagne attempted to influence the investigating State Trooper's supervisor to soften the critical language in the report on Watson's accident. "State Police refused to change the language of the report despite pressure from the sheriff," Grafton said.[4]

In 2016, Champagne visited Standing Rock, North Dakota, where he observed for himself the protests over the construction of the Dakota Access Pipeline near the Sioux Reservation. On Nov. 1, 2016, he used the occasion of his visit to post a lengthy 1,000-word critique of both the protestors and the national media that had been covering the controversial project. Here is that post from the National Sheriffs' Association Web page:

> I was extremely privileged in the last several days to have the opportunity to travel to North Dakota as President of the National Sheriffs' Association to see firsthand the protest and the response thereto to the Dakota Access Pipeline Project near the Standing Rock Sioux Reservation about 25 miles south of Bismarck.
>
> I learned first that the pipeline project, which has been in the works for several years, will traverse four states including North Dakota, South Dakota, Iowa and Illinois carrying crude oil. I was surprised to learn that a natural gas pipeline is already underground on the same right of way. The DAP has received all federal approvals over several years and, litigation which attempted to stop it in the federal courts has been resolved. Despite this project being very "federal" in nature and clearly in interstate commerce, the Obama

## Chapter 31: Greg Champagne: St. Charles Parish

administration has refused to provide any law enforcement or other support to North Dakota state and local law enforcement that has placed them in the position of having to enforce the rule of law. As usual, law enforcement is put between the rock and hard place due to various political agendas.

Based upon sensational news reports, I had the wrong impression that this pipeline was to run directly through the Standing Rock Reservation and would disturb ancient burial grounds of the Sioux Tribes. The argument has evolved now that this pipeline will jeopardize the water supply of the Missouri River (despite the fact that the pipeline will pass under other rivers including the Mississippi throughout its entire route).

Also, the Cannonball River which runs throughout the Standing Rock Reservation is actually "upstream" from the pipeline crossing. This false narrative has understandably generated a great deal of sympathy and support from many quarters for the Standing Rock Sioux People.

I quickly learned and saw for myself that this was untrue.
The pipeline passes about two miles north of the reservation and years of archeological study uncovered no significant native historical sites. It is difficult to believe that a single modern pipeline would be more environmentally risky than transporting crude oil by rail or truck through the same territory.

The Dakota Access Pipeline is 95% complete and the construction work near Standing Rock is the last phase which will tie the pipeline together. It is a 3.7 Billion Dollar Project. This past Thursday, October 27th, steps were taken the morning before I arrived which evicted protestors from private property directly in the path of the pipeline. This

## Louisiana's Rogue Sheriffs

"northern" camp was erected just days before and the occupants had been warned repeatedly for several days that their presence there was unlawful and that eviction was imminent.

These warnings went unheeded. Despite the statements coming from the media and protesters that they were completely peaceful and prayerful, it has been a fact that more militant protestors (terrorists) have destroyed property and physically beaten employees of the company in recent weeks. I personally witnessed and photographed what I estimate to be at least a half of a million dollars in damage to bulldozers and excavators.

I further learned that many protestors other than Native American groups have descended upon the area such as anarchists and eco-terrorists who are hell bent on committing violence and damage. The police presence in the area to protect farmers, ranchers and other private property interests have been costing the state of North Dakota millions of dollars.

The Sheriffs of several states have contributed manpower over the last several weeks to help preserve order and protect property. On October 27th, law enforcement evicted the trespassers form the north camp on private property about three miles north of the Cannonball River. While pleading with the trespassers for a peaceful move, law enforcement officers were met with Molotov cocktails and various missiles such as rocks and logs being thrown at them causing numerous injuries to the officers.

The only discharge of a firearm occurred when a protestor fired at the line of officers. Miraculously, none were hit by the bullets. When the protestors were moved south of the bridge, two trucks used to blockade the roadway were set on fire by

## Chapter 31: Greg Champagne: St. Charles Parish

the protestors. This action now has very possibly jeopardized the integrity of that bridge. News accounts ironically then decried the use of defensive equipment such as "riot gear" and armored vehicles by law enforcement.

Many media sites reported only that "heavy-handed" police tactics were used upon the protestors who were only praying and "peacefully" protesting. These same outlets failed to mention the shooting, Molotov cocktails, and extensive property and equipment damage produced by some of the protestors. The protestors even cut fences and attempted to induce a domesticated buffalo herd to stampede through the area. The owners of the herd, whom I spoke with personally indicated that at least a dozen of their buffalo were killed by protestors.

The next morning, I was present as law enforcement leaders including Sheriff Paul Laney met with leaders of the tribe. The tribal representatives lamented the violent and destructive behavior of "outsiders" who had come in only to commit violence. They indicated that they would encourage these violent agitators to leave the camp and protest.

While the entire situation seemed to be de-escalating upon my departure on Sunday October 30th, it remains to be seen if the violence and illegal acts are truly over.

I must commend the professionalism and patience of law enforcement officers under the leadership of sheriffs such as Cass County Sheriff and National Sheriffs' Association Board member Paul Laney, Morton County Sheriff Kyle Kirchmeier, and Burleigh County Sheriff Paul Heinert. The North Dakota State Police as well as several area Police Departments also played essential roles.

The operation evicting trespassers, some of which became violent was carried out with professionalism and restraint despite liberal press stories to the contrary. I must also commend the numerous sheriffs' office throughout the multi-state area including NSA Executive Committee Member Rich Stanek of Hennepin County, Minnesota who sent personnel to assist with protecting lives and property.

I certainly feel empathy for the Native American peoples of America and especially the Sioux due to the treatment they received at the hands of the U.S. Government in the latter part of the 19th Century. These Native American Cultures are and should be a proud people for whom we should all have concern. However, the law and facts simply do not weigh in their favor in this case from everything I've seen. This project went through an extensive approval process over many years and court challenges in Federal Court have failed to be successful.

We are a nation of laws. Emotion and empathy cannot carry the day. It just seems that opposition to this pipeline is not reasonably based upon legitimate environmental concerns. Energy independence has been one of the major goals of this country for decades. In my home state of Louisiana, we are surrounded by gas and oil pipelines and safely so. In another ironic twist, it is widely known that the Standing Rock Tribal Chairman owns a convenience store and gasoline station on the reservation.

It's time for everyone to move on in reference to The Dakota Access Pipeline and stop putting further strain on the citizens and law enforcement officers of North Dakota and surrounding states.

Greg Champagne, President<br>National Sheriffs' Association[5]

That prompted an immediate rebuke from Monique Verdin of the United Houma Nation of Louisiana and Cherri Foytlin, State Director of Bold Louisiana. "After hearing the derogatory and

## Chapter 31: Greg Champagne: St. Charles Parish

untrue comments made by Sheriff Greg Champagne about Water Protectors at Standing Rock on WWL-TV, Bold Louisiana Director Cherri Foytlin and Monique Verdin, a citizen of United Houma Nation, sent this letter in response to Sheriff Champagne, who also serves as President of the National Sheriffs' Association:

Dear Sir,

We write to you today concerning your recounting of your recent visit to North Dakota, published on November 27 to the WWLTV website, as President of the National Sheriff's Association.

We too have been to Standing Rock, yet our experiences appear to have been very different than yours. While there, and at adjacent resistance camps, we have seen and participated in only prayerful ceremony and actions - all of which included prayers for yourself, the other officers and the families of all involved.

If you are looking as to who has engaged in acts of war, sir, it might be best to see who came for one. A simple Internet search will produce countless images of unarmed Water Protectors being confronted by military-grade weaponry pointed at them by law enforcement.

The several key points that you left out of your assessment require bearing to the public in a way that travels beyond your extreme bias and obvious misunderstanding of both the issue and of the local Louisiana landscape as well.

For instance, you neglected to mention that the Army Corps of Engineers – a U.S. federal agency under the Department of Defense – has ordered a halt to any construction of the Dakota Access Pipeline under the Missouri River until a deeper environmental review can be completed.

## Louisiana's Rogue Sheriffs

Additionally, in your response, you infer that it is only the Missouri River where water protectors have their concern. I assure you, strong opposition to this pipeline can be found all along the route, particularly at the Mississippi River as well.

With reference to your assertion that the Standing Rock Sioux Tribe has no claim to the lands that the Dakota Access Pipeline disturbs, you show a complete and utter disregard to both history and the Constitution of the United States, which openly declares that treaty law is the law of the land.

Under the 1868 Fort Laramie Treaty between the U.S. and the Great Sioux Nation, Article 11, the tribe not only retains off-reservation hunting rights to the area, but also under article 12, "no cession of land would be valid unless approved by three-fourths of the adult males." Yet, in an act of continuing land theft, the U.S. government has never obtained that consent, an issue the U.S. Supreme Court has addressed, stating, "A more ripe and rank case of dishonorable dealings will never, in all probability, be found in our history."

You also mentioned sacred sites and burial grounds in your writings, yet you failed to discuss the fact that on September 3 of this year, only hours after Standing Rock Sioux legal representation filed evidence in court that documented a culturally significant site in direct line of the pipeline route, Energy Transfer sent bulldozers to destroy the location. Paid company mercenaries - armed with dogs and pepper spray - were used to shield this egregious and cowardly act, which ended with peaceful protectors being assaulted and bitten.

It is funny to us how you can, as you say, photograph and document "at least half a million dollars in damage to bulldozers and excavators," yet not one department or DAPL

## Chapter 31: Greg Champagne: St. Charles Parish

security force has been able to snap a photo of the alleged Molotov cocktails or "various missiles, such as rocks and logs" being thrown.

Nor have you - or any rancher or department - been able to produce a single photo or physical evidence of even one carcass of any so-called "dozens of buffalo" you claim have been killed by protectors. A person would think after 200 years or so, these false allegations would change or evolve in some way.

Regarding your claim that the tribe did not participate or engage in discussions much earlier in the process of approving DAPL, your rumination is unfounded. The Standing Rock Sioux Tribal Council went on record back in 2012, and again in 2014, as standing in opposition to this pipeline crossing the Missouri River.

So you see, sir, the argument has always been about the water and protecting it for the millions of Americans who depend upon it for drinking and thus for life.

Yet of all the ignorant and misguided remarks in your accounting, I take the most extreme offense to the false idea and narrative that the environment and people of the state in which you and I both reside have not suffered largely, due to the disproportionate number of pipelines below our feet.

By your assertion, the opposition to the pipeline "is not reasonably based upon legitimate environmental concerns," yet since 2010, there have been over 3,300 leaks or ruptures of crude oil or other hazardous liquids from pipelines in the United States. These incidents have not only released toxic chemicals into soil, water, and air, but have also killed 80 people, injured 389 more, and collectively cost $2.8 billion in damages.

Louisiana is not excluded from these pipeline disasters. Since 1996, there have been 391 significant pipeline spills or leaks in Louisiana, spilling 216,166 barrels of hazardous liquids, including crude oil, refined petroleum products, propane, ethane, etc. In just crude oil alone, there were 208 reported leaks or spills, resulting in 124,861 barrels released.

The most recent oil spill from a pipeline in Louisiana was last September, in which over 5,300 gallons of crude oil was discharged, and 200 birds were oiled.

In late July of this year, there were three pipeline spills in ten days. These are not uncommon incidents. In fact, the National Response Center receives approximately 1,500 oil spill notifications for Louisiana each year. This represents approximately 20 percent of all spills occurring in the United States.

Supplementary to your concern for our "energy independence," it might be noted that Dakota Access parent company Energy Transfer is also building the Bayou Bridge Pipeline here in Louisiana.

The Bayou Bridge Pipeline that will cross 11 parishes in our state, displace 600 acres of wetlands, cross 700 bodies of water, and endanger life and livelihoods of fisherfolk in the Atchafalaya Basin. The end point for this sister pipeline to Dakota Access is being constructed with the singular goal of Energy Transfer and its partners receiving opportunity for the best refining cost for their product, before exporting through our ports to foreign countries across the globe. Both the Dakota Access and the Bayou Bridge Pipelines are for the profit of this corporation only.

However, we will agree with you on one thing with regard to your report. "Facts do not weigh in favor" of the tribe or

## Chapter 31: Greg Champagne: St. Charles Parish

the water protectors, or the State of Louisiana - but only when you refuse to see them.

Further, we stand with you when you say that it is "time for everyone to move on in reference to the Dakota Access Pipeline and stop putting further strain on the citizens and law enforcement officers."

It is time to end both the Dakota Access and the Bayou Bridge pipelines.

Sincerely,

Monique Verdin
Citizen of the United Houma Nation

Cherri Foytlin
Louisiana Resident
State Director of Bold Louisiana[6]

# 32

## Louis Ackal: Iberia Parish

Twenty-two-year-old Victor White III was stopped by Iberia Parish deputies on March 3, 2014. The deputies said marijuana and cocaine were found on White and he was placed in a sheriff's department patrol car, his hands cuffed behind his back. While cuffed, deputies said, he somehow managed to get a gun and "committed suicide" by shooting himself in the back.[1]

A coroner's report released five months later, however, said White shot himself in the chest, a feat that would seem to defy the laws of physics. That White's hands were never tested for gunpowder residue only served to cast further doubt on the official version of events. Still, the parish coroner, Dr. Carl Ditch insisted White's death was a suicide.[2]

W. Lloyd Grafton, an expert retained by the White family, weighed in on the evidence in an interview for this book. He said the entry wound was more to the right side than frontal area and that the bullet exited from White's left side. "There is no way he could have shot himself the way they (officials) described it, with his hands cuffed behind his back," Grafton said.[3]

On May 19, 2015, U.S. Rep. Cedric Richmond of Louisiana's Second Congressional District, wrote a gut-wrenching three-page letter to then-U.S. Attorney General Loretta Lynch in which he requested an investigation into mistreatment to the deaths of eight people who were in the custody of the Iberia Parish Sheriff's Office.

Richmond also asked that the U.S. Justice Department look into other incidents of beatings and the violations of prisoners' civil rights, including at least ten cases of civil lawsuits which resulted in settlements totaling more than $1 million.

Richmond, the only Democrat among Louisiana's eight-person congressional delegation (two senators and six representatives) does not represent Iberia Parish, nor was Iberia Parish in his district at the time he penned his letter to Lynch. He represents Louisiana's gerrymandered Second Congressional District which includes all or parts of the parishes of Orleans, St. Charles, St. John the Baptist, St. James, Ascension, Assumption, Iberville, and East and West Baton Rouge.

Iberia Parish is in Louisiana's Third Congressional District, represented by Dr. Charles Boustany until 2016 when he attempted to move up but lost his bid for the U.S. Senate seat held by retiring David Vitter. Also included in Boustany's district was his home parish of Jefferson Davis where the murders of eight prostitutes over a four-year period, beginning in 2005, remain unsolved.

But where Republican Boustany did not appear overly concerned, Richmond was. Here is the text of his letter:

> It is with great concern that I write to request an investigation into alleged civil rights violations (by) members of the Iberia Parish Sheriff's Office (IPSO). Since 2005, at least eight people have died in the custody of the IPSO—in its jail or after an arrest—according to records compiled by the *Baton Rouge Advocate*. Seven of those who died were inmates. At least two of those seven suffered from mental illness. These figures are troubling, but it is unclear whether they actually paint a complete picture of what has gone on at IPSO. According to Iberia Parish Sheriff Louis Ackal, the IPSO does not keep records of how many inmates or arrestees have died in its custody. This makes it difficult to know with any certainty how many people have actually died in IPSO custody.
> 
> In addition to the numerous incidents that have ended tragically, there are several indications that IPSO has committed many more violations in recent years. According to records provided by the IPSO and the Louisiana Sheriffs' Association, which insures the Sheriff's Office, the office has settled civil suits with at least 10 plaintiffs since 2008 paying out roughly $1.1 million in damages. By comparison,

## Chapter 32: Louis Ackal: Iberia Parish

the Lafayette Parish Sheriff's Office's lawsuit settlement costs since 2008 are about half those for Iberia Parish despite having a population about three times its (Iberia Parish's) size and (despite) a Sheriff's Office that employs almost three times as many officers. The suits include complaints of excessive force, improper medical care of inmates, and inmate deaths, sexual assault and harassment, and wrongful termination

The following list highlights some of the incidents alleged to have occurred at IPSO over the past 10 years:

- In 2005, a former inmate alleged that deputies beat him so badly when he was booked into jail that he had to spend two weeks in a hospital.
- In 2008, a man alleged that a deputy beat him so badly during an arrest that he coughed up blood and then a muzzle was put over his mouth. The man later settled a suit with the Sheriff's Office for $50,000.
- In 2009, Michael Jones, a 43-year-old man who suffered from bipolar disorder and schizophrenia, died in the jail after an altercation with then-Warden Frank Ellis and then-lieutenant Wesley Hayes. This year, a judge ruled that two Sheriff's Office employees were responsible for Jones' death. The judgment in the case totaled $61,000.
- In 2009, former inmate Curtis Ozenne alleged that officers began a contraband sweep by forcing him to remain in the "Muslim praying position" for nearly three hours. Mr. Ozenne alleged he was kicked in the mouth multiple times, threatened with police dogs and then his head was shaved. In his complaint, Mr. Ozenne also alleged that Sheriff Ackal threatened him with a dog and watched as an officer struck him with a baton for smiling. Mr.

Ozenne's suit against the Sheriff's Office was later settled for $15,000.

- In 2009, Robert Sonnier, a 62-year-old mentally ill man, died as the result of a fatal blow delivered by an IPSO Deputy in the course of a physical altercation. After Mr. Sonnier was unable to receive a psychological evaluation authorized by his wife, he was left in a wheelchair to stew in his own waste for several hours. He eventually became agitated which led to altercations with Deputies that resulted in Sonnier being pepper sprayed twice and eventually leading to the fatal blow.
- In 2012, Marcus Robicheaux, an inmate at Iberia Parish Jail, was pulled from a wall and thrown to the ground as IPSO correctional officers ran a contraband sweep. A deputy's dog then attacked Mr. Robicheaux, biting his legs, arms and torso, as the deputy stomped and kicked the prone inmate. The whole three-minute incident was captured on video from the jail's surveillance cameras.
- In 2014, Victor White III died as the result of a fatal gunshot wound while handcuffed in the backseat of an IPSO car. The sheriff's deputies who arrested Mr. Victor (sic) alleged that he wouldn't leave the car and became "uncooperative." They say he pulled out a handgun, while his hands were cuffed behind his back, and shot himself in the back. However, the full coroner's report indicated that Mr. White had died from a single shot to his right chest, contradicting the initial police statement that he had shot himself in the back.

Recent unrest in communities across the country have shed light on the fact that many people feel they have been

## Chapter 32: Louis Ackal: Iberia Parish

unfairly targeted by police and forced to live their lives under the threat of an oppressive regime. The rule our law enforcement officers fill is too important to the function of our society to allow this dynamic to go unchecked. It is incumbent upon us all to step in and intervene for the people we serve whenever it appears that their rights have been abridged in any way. There is perhaps no institution better suited to serve as that intervening force than the U.S. Department of Justice. For that reason, I am asking you to launch a full investigation into the IPSO to uncover what, if any, civil rights violations the citizens of Iberia Parish and the inmates at Iberia Parish Jail have been subject(ed) to over the course of the last decade.

I ask that you respond to this inquiry no later than June 5, 2015. ...I look forward to your prompt reply.[3]

Donald Broussard of New Iberia can attest to the dangers of crossing a vengeful sheriff like Ackal. On July 8, 2016, Broussard was rear-ended by a hit-and-run driver In Lafayette Parish who minutes later collided head-on with an 18-wheeler in adjacent Iberia Parish and was killed. Yet it was Broussard who was indicted on a charge of manslaughter by an Iberia Parish grand jury on March 19, 2017, just nine days before the seven deputies were sentenced.

So just how did Broussard find himself in Ackal's crosshairs? On July 1, a week before the auto accident, Broussard committed the unpardonable sin when he became the impetus behind a recall of Iberia Parish Sheriff Louis Ackal.

Broussard, an African-American, was one of the organizers of The Justice for Victor White III Foundation which filed a petition on July 1 to force a recall election. White was the 22-year-old who died of a gunshot wound while in the back seat of a sheriff deputy's patrol car in March 2014. The official report said the gunshot was self-inflicted. The coroner's report said he was shot in the front with the bullet entering his right chest and exiting under his left armpit. White's hands were cuffed behind his back at the time.

It was into that hostile territory that Broussard unwisely ventured with his recall effort.

A story in the March 19, 2017, *Daily Iberian* read, "A New Iberia man who was instrumental in the drive to recall Iberia Parish Sheriff Louis Ackal last year has been indicted for manslaughter in the aftermath of an alleged road rage incident that left a Bossier City man deal in July."[4]

Here's the chronology of events:

Moments before the fatal crash, Rakeem Blakes, 24, rear-ended a Cadillac driven by Broussard at the corner of Ambassador Caffery Parkway and U.S. 90 in Lafayette Parish. Broussard said he followed Blakes when Blakes fled the scene after Broussard had approached his car but denied that he chased Blakes. "The guy hit me," Broussard said. "I got within 20 feet of him so I could get his license plate number. I gave it (the license number) to the (911) dispatcher and they told me to fall back, so I fell back." Broussard said reports that he had a gun were ridiculous. "I don't even own a gun, he said. "I told the State Police they could search my car. They just handed me my license and let me go on my way."[5]

Broussard said Blakes was driving erratically, causing a hazard for other drivers.

Iberia Parish District Attorney Bo Duhé said the case involving Broussard was turned over to his office for review in November following completion of the LSP investigation. In what has to be one of the most convoluted reviews of the investigation, Assistant District Attorney Janet Perrodin presented the case and the grand jury returned a true bill indicting Broussard for manslaughter and "aggravated obstruction of a highway," which led to Blakes' death.

Unexplained in this bizarre episode was how Broussard created an "aggravated obstruction" when it was Blakes who rear-ended him and subsequently fled the scene. Duhé, in some fancy verbal footwork, said state law allows a manslaughter charge to be brought when an offender "is engaged in the perpetration of any intentional misdemeanor directly affecting the person. Aggravated obstruction of a highway is the performance of any act on a highway where human life may be endangered," he said.[6]

By those definitions, virtually anyone could be arrested, jailed, tried and convicted at just about any time. That, of course, is not likely. This was

## Chapter 32: Louis Ackal: Iberia Parish

a scenario tailored just for Broussard who had the temerity to take on a powerful sheriff whose proclivity to extract revenge against those who would dare stand up to his authority was already well-established.

Broussard, for his part, vowed to fight the "malicious and unwarranted" prosecution. "I welcome their witch-hunt. The truth will come out at trial. They like to keep niggers in their place in Iberia Parish because most of the time, that's what they're used to dealing with. But they're dealing with an educated black man who has never been, nor will I ever be, scared to speak truth to power—especially in instances when those in power abuse that power. They picked the wrong one to go to war with."[7]

Broussard's bond on the manslaughter charge was set at $75,000 and bond for the aggravated obstruction charge was set at $10,000. Only the most naïve observer would discount a good-ol'-boy, back scratchin' network between two powerful local officials like a sheriff and a district attorney. The recall effort eventually failed for a lack of sufficient signatures and Ackal was acquitted of all criminal charges, leaving him to exact revenge on all who had crossed him. A long memory and the propensity to call in favors create the perfect formula for revenge when a ruthless sheriff can tweak the system to do his bidding.

**Controversy from the start**

For a small community, Iberia Parish, population 74,000, has more than its share of problems with Sheriff Louis Ackal. Ackal was first elected sheriff in 2007 and took office in July 2008. Less than a year later, he was neck-deep in the first case of prisoner abuse to surface during his tenure when Michael Jones died in his custody. That was five years before the death of Victor White III.

On February 13, 2009, officers from the Abbeville Police Department in Vermilion Parish were called to a residence in the pre-dawn hours on a complaint Michael Jones was causing a disturbance at his mother's home.

Officers said he was shown a Taser in order to convince him to comply with their orders for him to calm down and put on his clothes. The Taser, they said, was not used and Jones was arrested for battery on an officer and for resisting arrest. Taken to Abbeville General Hospital, he was examined, cleared for incarceration and transported to Iberia Parish

Correctional Center as per a contract between the Abbeville Police Department and the center.

He was booked into the correction center at 6:48 a.m. Six hours later he was dead. The fatal sequence of events began when Jones began yelling and removing his clothing while in a holding cell. When officers opened his cell door, he bolted past them but was quickly apprehended since there was no place for him to run. During a brief struggle, he bit one of the officers. After cuffing and shackling Jones, his body was dragged by officers back to his cell where he was left lying on his stomach.[8]

Lloyd Grafton is a veteran of 21 years as a special agent for the Justice Department's U.S. Bureau of Narcotics and Dangerous Drugs and with the U.S. Treasury as a special agent for the Bureau of Alcohol, Tobacco and Firearms. Today, he serves as an expert witness in cases involving alleged excessive force by law enforcement. He was retained by the attorney for the family of Michael Jones.

In his report of September 28, 2009, he said he felt that Jones needed medical assistance from his first encounter with officers at his mother's home. He had been in treatment for alcohol abuse and addiction prior to the incident and Grafton said his behavior was that of a man who appeared to be experiencing alcohol withdrawal symptoms. "After Michael Jones was cuffed with his hands behind his back and his legs were shackled, there was a lack of care for his physical well-being," he wrote in his report.[9]

No sheriff's office personnel admitted an awareness that Jones had stopped breathing. "To conclude that proper law enforcement techniques were used by Warden (Frank) Ellis and Lieutenant Wesley Hayes, one would have to completely disregard the presence and statements of the inmates who were there when the incident occurred," Grafton wrote. He said that after reviewing inmate statements, it appeared that Jones was subjected to a choke hold which was said to have lasted about five minutes and which produced "choking sounds" from Jones.[10]

"His face turned blue, he urinated on himself and he went limp," Grafton's report says. "When Jones was dragged to his final resting place in a holding cell, he was further described as foaming from the mouth and appearing dead."

Grafton offered withering criticism of deputies. "Michael Jones was not going far. He was housed in a lockup facility," he said. "One cannot

## Chapter 32: Louis Ackal: Iberia Parish

justify a five-minute choke hold on an inmate under the conditions that existed here. One thing was agreed upon by all interviewed and that was the fact that no CPR or any resuscitation techniques were used by employees of this facility in any effort to save Michael Jones's life."[11]

When detention center nurse Stephanie Celestine commented, "He's not breathing and there is no heartbeat," a second nurse asked her if anyone was doing CPR on Jones, Celestine responded, "Yeah, the ambulance is on the way," Grafton's report said.[12]

In a three-page supplement report dated October 26, 2009, Grafton said, "Many inmates refused to be interviewed or (to) make any statements." That is understandable as will be shown in a later chapter about a federal investigation into inmate abuse by Iberia Parish Sheriff's Department deputies. Grafton's supplemental report cited interviews with five inmates, each of whom described witnessing deputies choking Jones. One inmate, Edward Anderson, said he saw deputies choking Jones. "A heavyset white female guard was like, 'Get up and stop pissing on yourself,'" he said. "They later dragged him out of the booth, leaving blood puddles trailing the victim—obviously of murder."[13]

Another inmate, Tarik David, said he saw Jones was foaming at the mouth. "I didn't want to watch anymore so (I) walked back to my rack and laid down."[14]

Albert Jones, III, gave a two-page written report in which he described Jones as "being choked out, head plunged to the cement."[15]

Grafton called the department's actions "objectively unreasonable and indifferent to the well-being of Michael Jones. Michael Jones...was the victim of excessive force and had his rights violated by those sworn to protect and serve.[16]

Apparently, Lynch took Richmond's letter to heart. In March 2016, ten months after his letter, Ackal and one of his top deputies, Lieutenant Colonel Gerald Savoy, were indicted by a federal grand jury on charges of conspiracy and civil rights violations over the alleged multiple beatings of detainees in the jail's chapel where there were no security cameras.

The indictment said it was the "plan and purpose of the conspiracy that IPSO officers and supervisors would punish and retaliate against inmates and pretrial detainees by taking them to the chapel of the (Iberia

Parish Jail), where there were no video surveillance cameras, to unlawfully assault them."

Ackal remained defiant in the face of the indictments. "In spite of recent allegations made against me, I am confident I will be vindicated. I also speak on the behalf of my current employees when saying I am positive they are dedicated to protecting the citizens of Iberia Parish.

"For my entire professional career, I have had faith in our judicial system. I continue to believe in our system and that history will show I have always stood on the side of good," he said.[17]

Facing a maximum sentence of 10 years in prison for each of the civil rights violations, as well as a potential $250,000 fine for each count, a trial was scheduled in the federal courthouse in nearby Lafayette. But when the judge appeared impaired at the trial, she was removed and the trial transferred to Shreveport.

Sheriff's office personnel witnessing the assaults agreed not to intervene, according to the indictment. In one reported instance, Ackal was accused of telling Deputy Byron Benjamin LaSalle to "take care" of an inmate, identified as C.O. LaSalle, along with nine other deputies, pleaded guilty to abusing the prisoners.[18]

One inmate would be beaten for an alleged offense and if he blamed another inmate, the second inmate would also be beaten with no apparent effort being made to ascertain who was telling the truth. In at least one case, a second inmate beaten over another's accusation (after the first had been similarly beaten) blamed a third who was then brought in and beaten like the others, the indictment said.[19]

In another case, when it was learned that an inmate was in jail as an accused sex offender, a deputy held his baton between his legs as if it were his penis and forced it down the inmate's throat, causing him to gag.[20]

In spite of the gravity of the charges against him Ackal, incredibly, was acquitted in what was described as "a dramatic turn." Meanwhile, more than 100 criminal cases involving those deputies have been tossed as a result of the investigation of the sheriff's office, which stretched back to 2008 during Ackal's first term of office.[21]

Former Deputy Jason Comeaux said after deputies got drunk at a party, they wanted to find someone to beat up so they targeted two young black men, ages 16 and 21. Ackal was later furious—not over the beatings,

## Chapter 32: Louis Ackal: Iberia Parish

but over the fact the deputies were caught and a written report made, Comeaux testified.[22]

Black employees of the sheriff's office said Ackal treated them well but other evidence painted Ackal as anti-black and anti-Semitic.

Prior to his trial, the sheriff was secretly recorded as he made threats against federal prosecutor Mark Blumberg, including threats to kill him, court filings revealed. Court transcripts show Ackal threatening to shoot the prosecutor, who was a special litigation counsel in the Justice Department's Civil Rights Division in Washington, D.C.

Recounting a conversation in which Ackal said he was told by an unidentified person, presumably from the Justice Department, that he could help the government: "'You know these people, you can give them to us,'" he quoted the person as saying. "I said, 'the only thing I'm gonna give you, fucking shoot you right between your goddamn Jewish eyes, look-like-an-opossum bastard,'" Ackal also called Blumberg a "sorry, son-of-a-bitch Jew bastard in Washington."

Victor White, Jr., father of Victor White, III. who died of the gunshot wound while handcuffed in the back of a sheriff's department patrol car in 2014, said he felt anger as he watched Ackal spit tobacco juice into a cup in the courtroom during testimony in his trial. White said trial testimony "validated everything that he was hiding and the things that we knew." He said he and his wife drove from their home in Alexandria, 100 miles from the trial in Shreveport so he could "look at him (Ackal) face-to-face and let them say they didn't do those types of things."

But upon hearing the verdict he could only feel sick.

Ackal was tried and acquitted but when you've got retired federal judge and family member Fred Haik helping with the defense, you tend to land on your feet.   For his part, Ackal claimed he was "totally exonerated," accusing those who testified against him as lying "about the whole thing."

He said the investigation of his office ferreted out bad lawmen from his agency who, he said, hurt "innocent people." He added that he was going back to New Iberia "and make sure my house is very clean." He said deputies' testimony shook him "to the core. I guess it's because I'm very nice."[23]

211

Ackal's defense attorney, John McLindon, said no one ever testified that Ackal personally laid a hand on anyone. He said the abuses described were the deeds of members of the sheriff's department's narcotics unit gone rogue.[24]

Seven of Ackal's former deputies received sentences in U.S. District Court in Lafayette on March 28, 2017. Each of the seven had testified in Ackal's trial four months earlier. The sentences ranged from 87 months in federal prison for Chief Deputy Gerald "Bubba" Savoy[11] and 54 months for Byron Benjamin LaSalle and Bret Broussard to six months for former canine handler Robert Burns who pleaded to a single count of deprivation or rights for his failure to intervene when fellow deputies beat inmate Anthony Daye in August 2011 in the parish jail chapel.[25]

Federal Judge Donald E. Walter, who said he never liked sentencing those who appeared before him in court, told the deputies that they were "the worst. So many law enforcement officials are out there risking their lives for little pay. All I can say is you had lousy leadership," he said. "How sad this is for all concerned."[26]

The sad saga of Louis Ackal would be bad enough if that was the end of the story but sadly, it is not.

In March 2018, Ackal quietly settled a federal lawsuit brought by the family of Victor White III—almost exactly four years after his March 3, 2014, shooting death while in the custody of deputies. As has become more and more common in such cases, terms of the settlement were sealed and White's family was prohibited by a confidentiality clause from disclosing the settlement amount, believed to be about $600,000.

In an interview with the author, White's father, Victor White, Jr., said he was unhappy with the judge's order that terms of the settlement not be disclosed. "The judge says we can't talk about the settlement amount, but I believe the people of Iberia Parish have a right to know how much the sheriff department's actions cost them," he said.[27]

The Victor White case was not the only case in which Iberia Parish Sheriff Louis Ackal had to make substantial payouts.

Christopher Butler sued after he was beaten while handcuffed by a deputy Cody Laperouse in 2013. Ackal fired Laperouse who promptly went to work as an officer for the St. Martinville Police Department. Ackal's office paid out $350,000 in that case.

## Chapter 32: Louis Ackal: Iberia Parish

Ackal also paid out $175,000 to the family of 16-year-old Daquentin Thompson who hanged himself while being held in Iberia Parish's adult jail in 2014.

In a case that displayed the ugly side of Ackal's idea of justice, the sheriff instructed two of his deputies to "take care of" Howard Trosclair after Ackal had been told Trosclair assaulted one of his (Ackal's) relatives, according to appeal documents filed by deputy David Hines with the U.S. Fifth Circuit Court of Appeals. When Trosclair was arrested, the court records say he was "compliant and followed the officers' commands." Hines nevertheless used his knee to strike Trosclair "several times in the side" and struck him "two to three times" with his baton in the back of his legs. Hines continued to knee Trosclair in the abdomen or groin even after he was restrained. Hines then filed a false police report to cover up the wrongful assault, the appeal record says.

That episode cost the sheriff's office $275,000.[28]

Additionally, Ackal's office is the only sheriff's office in Louisiana to make use of a special Louisiana Sheriffs' Law Enforcement Program (LSLEP) set up to pay sexual harassment and discrimination claims—and he had to use the program twice.

The Iberia Parish Sheriff's Department paid more than $400,000 to the plaintiff in a 2015 lawsuit filed by a female deputy who claimed that Ackal did nothing to stop retaliation from Bert Berry, chief of the criminal department, who "egregiously" harassed her for ten months.

The other complaint was filed by three female employees in 2009. They claimed that chief deputy Toby Hebert sexually harassed them. Their claims were eventually settled for $7,500 each.[29]

In 2004, the New Iberia Police Department was dissolved and law enforcement within the city limits was taken over by the sheriff's department (the department was reinstated on July 1, 2018 after 14 years of inactivity). Ackal became sheriff in 2008 and since that time, not a single homicide has been solved and in 2015, none occurred, according to FBI crime data.[33]

And that is precisely the problem: Reporting is voluntary and homicides are simply not reported by the Iberia Parish Sheriff's Department. And the sloppy reporting practices only contribute to continued killings, according to Thomas Hargrove who runs the non-profit Murder Accountability Project.[30]

He called the sheriff's office's reporting record "God-awful...the worst reporting I've ever heard. First of all, you haven't a clue whether murders are being solved. This is literally a matter of life and death."

In December 2004, Nelson Landry, Jr., left home in a new car and never returned. A missing person report was filed but when his car was found two days later, the sheriff's office had no record of the missing person report. Landry's body was not found in February 2005 and his murder remains unsolved after nearly 14 years.

On December 4, 2015, Terry Delahoussaye, Sr., was shot in his vehicle in an apparent robbery-murder. Gold jewelry he was wearing and a "significant amount" of money he had in his wallet were missing. After nearly three years, the investigation into his death appears to have hit a dead end. "Ackal did not do his job," said Delahoussaye's brother, Ricky. "They were too busy looking for drugs on him while he was lying there fighting for his life."

"If you call and say, 'There's a drug deal going on,' they'll come right away. But if you call and say, 'Someone's dying at the end of the street,' they'll be here in 40 minutes, an hour," he said. "It feels like they're just saying, 'Let the niggers kill the niggers. It's a black-on-black crime, so who cares?' When a white guy gets shot, they treat it differently. Yeah, I'm pissed off and I'm going to stay pissed. I used to think my brother was in the wrong place at the wrong time. Now, my opinion is different."

Both Landry and Delahoussaye were African-American.

"African-American murders are much less likely to be cleared than any other kind of murder," Hargrove said while acknowledging that because they are more likely to be drug- and gang-related, they are statistically more difficult to solve. "But that doesn't begin to explain the depth of the racial divide. We are not providing sufficient resources to African-American murders," he said.[31]

Community activist Robbie Bethel-Carrier said blacks are reluctant to talk to the sheriff's department because it "has proven not to be a friend of the community. When the head of your department (Ackal) says it's okay to call the residents monkeys, it's okay to turn a dog loose on somebody,

## Chapter 32: Louis Ackal: Iberia Parish

it's okay to shove a stick down their throat to sexually violate them—who would talk to them?"

Althea Augustine, who lost a young daughter and an elderly mother to stray bullets, said if Ackal only demonstrated that he cared, "it'd go a long way."

Along with the breakdown in relations between the sheriff's department and the residents of New Iberia it was contracted, the absence of an accurate FBI reporting system, the public is kept in the dark about community safety. That, said Hargrove, lowers public accountability and hinders criminology research.[32]

Ackal's problems continued into 2019 when his office agreed to a $2.5 million settlement to bring to an end a lawsuit filed by Derrick Sellers who was beaten senseless by deputies in 2013. Another $275,000 was paid to Marcus Robicheaux, the prisoner who was subjected to police dog attacks as he lay face-down during a jail shakedown in 2012.

Sellers, a former U.S. Marine from Abbeville once ran 15 miles a week but today cannot even pick up trach without falling. His left cheekbone was broken up to his eye socket, causing the eyeball to shift outward. He was left crawling across the floor of his cell following the beating. He wears darkened frames cupped around the sides, like racehorse blinkers, in order to train his focus. He wears a lanyard around his neck which holds a device that pulses electric current to his cranium through a pair of wires clipped to his earlobes. He wears a back brace because of three ruptured discs. He no longer can drive a car or ride a bicycle. "I have a tricycle," he said.[33]

What's even worse is the deputy who inflicted the most damage, Eric Blanchard, is still employed by the sheriff's office.[34]

The LSLEP has since terminated the Iberia Parish Sheriff's Office from participating in the insurance pool because of the mounting number of lawsuits against the department.[35]

A multitude of lawsuit judgments and settlements has cost the department almost $6 million, an average of about $50,000 for every month of Ackal's ten years in office.[36]

# 33
## Mike Couvillon: Vermilion Parish

The sheriff, dating all the way back to the year 1066 in England, is, by definition, the local tax collector in addition to his law enforcement duties.[1]

As such, the duties of Mike Couvillon came in direct conflict with his duties as Sheriff of Vermilion Parish when he bid and won the purchase of a home for about half its assessed value at a sheriff's sale in 2014.[2]

A Vermilion Parish homeowner lost her home when her mortgage payment doubled from $350 to $700 and her home, assessed at $106,000, was put up for sheriff's sale in February 2014. Couvillon submitted the winning bid of $58,000 on the home which was next door to his brother's home.

"The sheriff gaining out of the sheriff's sale, it just doesn't seem right," said homeowner Michelle McNabb. "It should be unethical."[3]

As a matter fact, it wasn't right and it wasn't ethical. Louisiana Revised Statute 42:1113(A) specifically prohibits public servants from entering into contracts and transactions with the agencies they serve.[4]

Couvillon, of course, denied any wrongdoing. But Pearson Cross, head of the Political Science Department of the University of Louisiana Lafayette had a different opinion. "This is a case of corruption," he said. "It seems at the face of it, to be a gross violation of the law, specifically, the Code of Ethics for the State of Louisiana, that says no employee, no sheriff's employee, can bid at a sheriff's sale."[5]

When reporters for a Lafayette television station asked Couvillon how his situation differed from what the code of ethics spelled out, he replied, "I'd like you to request the opinion, or the answer from my attorney, Ike Funderburk."

Funderburk, ostensibly a man with at least a passing familiarity with the law, said the transaction was between the mortgage company and the highest bidder. "The sheriff's department is merely acting as an agent," he said.[6]

Three separate opinions by the State Ethics Board and a Legislative Auditor's report all agreed with Cross, Funderburk's legal counsel notwithstanding.

In 1983, the Ethics Commission was chaired by Louisiana Tech University English professor Robert C. Snyder. The commission, which also included as a member Louisiana AFL-CIO President Victor Bussie, ruled that the acquisition of movable and immovable property by bid at public sales conducted by the sheriff's office constituted a transaction which is under the supervision or jurisdiction of the sheriff. "It therefore follows and is the commission's opinion that … the code prohibits an employee of the office of Civil Sheriff from bid(ding) on or enter(ing) into any contract or subcontract or other transaction which is under the supervision of jurisdiction" of the sheriff, "including specifically those transactions involving the disposition at public sales of movable and immovable property.

"Similarly, in parishes in which there is no civil sheriff and (in cases when) such sales are under the supervision and jurisdiction of the sheriff's office, the same prohibition applies to all employees of the division of the sheriff's office that handles these sales."[7]

Likewise, a 1997 opinion by the ethics board said that the purchase of vehicles by Webster Parish Sheriff Royce McMahon and four of his deputies violated Section 1113A by the purchase of vehicles and cattle panels at an auction conducted by McMahon's office.

McMahon bought a 1989 truck for $5,000 and cattle panels for $300. His four deputies purchased a truck, three cars, and two trailers totaling $4,500 at the auction held at the Webster Parish penal farm.[8]

In that case, McMahon returned the items that were auctioned for a full refund when the impropriety was brought to his attention and he was fined $500 for the purchases at the April 18, 1996 auction. The board could have imposed a fine of up to $10,000 for the violation. The four deputies were absolved of blame when it was learned that McMahon had erroneously

## Chapter 33: Mike Couvillon: Vermilion Parish

advised them that they could purchase the items without any legal ramifications.⁹

A state audit of the Vermilion Parish Sheriff's Office for the fiscal year ended June 30, 2016, noted that "The Sheriff, under the advice of his two attorneys, may have violated LA RS.42:1113A by entering into a transaction to purchase a foreclosed house at a sheriff's sale conducted by Vermilion Parish Sheriff's Office" and recommended that Couvillon "consult with legal counsel to resolve the ethic charges that were filed."⁹

A third State Ethics Commission opinion, in the form of a December 16, 2016, consent order, imposed a fine of $2,500 on Couvillon.¹⁰ That meant, of course, that by violating the state ethics laws, he still managed to obtain a home assessed at $106,000 for $58,000.

Following the purchase of the home and the initial story and during the course of the Ethics Commission's consideration of the complaint against him, Couvillon was re-elected to his fourth consecutive term as sheriff in October 2015 with 79 percent of the vote.¹¹

# 34
## Jack Stephens: St. Bernard Parish

In early 2015, the head of the Metropolitan Crime Commission (MCC) in New Orleans said his organization might undertake a study of the St. Bernard Parish criminal justice system. And while Rafael Goyeneche, III, head of the citizens' organization dedicated to exposing public corruption, said the purpose of such a study would be to "raise the level of accountability and efficiency in the criminal justice system," he stopped short of making any direct reference to shady deals involving then-Sheriff Jack Stephens following the disastrous BP Deepwater Horizon rig explosion and ensuing oil spill in the Gulf of Mexico.

St. Bernard, situated below New Orleans and along the eastern bank of the Mississippi River in the toe of the Louisiana boot, was the site of the historic Battle of New Orleans in 1814. Andrew Jackson defeated the British with a ragtag force of Tennessee volunteers with help from pirate Jean Lafitte several weeks after a peace treaty had been signed ending the War of 1812. What the British could not do nearly 200 years earlier, Hurricane Katrina accomplished in 2005.

Obliterated by Katrina, its population was nearly halved as thousands of victims simply decided not to return. Fire protection, mosquito control and garbage collection ceased when the parish's tax base dried up. Five years later, disaster would strike again with the April 20, 2010 BP Deepwater Horizon spill that wiped out the parish's shrimping and fishing industry.

This time, the most damage was inflicted not by nature or a massive oil spill, but by politically-connected locals who put their own enrichment before the general welfare of their fellow citizens—and at considerable expense to BP. And St. Bernard Parish Sheriff Stephens was right in the thick of all the financial exploitation.

## Louisiana's Rogue Sheriffs

Local companies with connections to the parish power structure reaped profitable cleanup contracts and then charged BP for every conceivable expense. The prime cleanup contractor, which had no oil-spill experience to go with its history of bad debts, submitted bills with little or no documentation. A subcontractor charged BP more than $15,000 per month to rent a generator that usually cost only $1,500 a month. And a firm owned in part by Sheriff Stephens charged more than $1 million per month for land it had been renting for less than $1,700 per month.

While there was money to be had, the bulk of the cash influx flowed to companies and individuals who had the right connections to the parish power structure, including the son of Jefferson Parish Chief Deputy Sheriff Craig Taffaro, Parish President Craig Taffaro, Jr., who doled out jobs and contracts to personal friends, political cronies and relatives.[1]

Amigo Enterprises Inc., which for years leased land to one of the busiest marinas in the parish, got in at the outset. BP based the cleanup operation at the marina at an astronomical cost. Amigo had previously leased the land for less than $1,700 a month from the Arlene & Joseph Meraux Charitable Foundation Inc. BP, in turn, was billed for more than $1.1 million a month.

Amigo wasn't just any company. One of the owners was 26-year sheriff Jack Stephens, who, it happens, also sat on the board of the Meraux Foundation. According to the most recent ethics form Stephens filed with the state, he earned more than $100,000 from Amigo the year before the BP spill.[2]

Stephens's cousin, Anthony Fernandez Jr., formerly worked as Stephens' chief deputy and was one of Stephens's two partners in Amigo. Fernandez said BP paid less than the $1 million a month in rent to Amigo claimed by critics.

Fernandez also got substantial revenue from BP for another company, Parish Oilfield Services LLC. Parish Oilfield hired off-duty sheriff's deputies to provide security for the spill.[3]

The sheriff's office signed an eviction notice for BP on August 31 because BP had not paid some $3 million in rent to Amigo. The message on the eviction notice was terse: "Landlord wants possession of his property."

## Chapter 34: Jack Stephens: St. Bernard Parish

Not said was notification that the sheriff's company was the landlord. BP paid Amigo and the work on the cleanup resumed.[4]

Goyeneche speaking at a St. Bernard Parish Chamber of Commerce luncheon said any study would be similar to those done in Orleans and Jefferson parishes by the MCC, the non-profit public watchdog established nearly seven decades before to hold public officials and employees accountable for corrupt, unethical, and wasteful practices. He said any such research undertaken would be for the purpose of raising "the level of accountability and efficiency in the criminal justice system."

He said a comprehensive study would be "a way of determining how well the criminal justice system is doing. It introduces transparency to the system, identifies strengths and weaknesses that can be made stronger. The number of arrests being made doesn't mean anything until you know the outcomes. The objective is to convert felony arrests to felony convictions" rather than seeing felony arrests reduced to misdemeanors, he said.[5]

Unfortunately, the study proposed by Goyeneche never took place. "We never received the funding for it," he explained nearly three years later.

Goyeneche's words in January 2015, however, may well have been prophetic. Less than seven months after that address, on August 4, 2015, St. Bernard deputy sheriff Jarrod Gourgues was indicted for felony theft, perjury and three counts of malfeasance in office for allegedly receiving pay while on duty for the sheriff's office and at the same time collecting pay for work as the parish's road director. He also was accused of accepting more than $10,000 from a parish IT contractor, ParaTech, according to the indictment. His perjury count was for lying to a grand jury.[6]

Additionally, he was charged with two malfeasance counts which stemmed from his being a defacto co-owner of a lawn care and debris removal company that had a contract with the parish. Parish employees are barred by law from doing business with the parish, said a spokesman for the Louisiana attorney general's office. Gourgues was accused of accepting about $50,000 through the lawn care business and from the owner of a parish waste and recycling contractor.[7]

Eleven months later, a parish judge threw out all five counts of the indictment in a decision that only served to enhance the image of a parish which, like Plaquemines, its neighbor across the Mississippi River, pretty much does as it pleases, conflicts of interests and ethics—and the law itself—be damned.

Thirty-Fourth Judicial District Judge Jeanne Juneau granted a motion by Gourgues to quash the five-count indictment because the sheriff's office had provided copies of two subpoenas to a New Orleans television station. The copies had been provided in response to a formal public records request by WWL-TV. Juneau, in her ruling, said the station reported on the grand jury investigation the day before the actual indictment. And that, she said, violated the prohibition against disclosure of secret grand jury materials, thereby exerting "prejudice and influence on members of the grand jury."[8]

"Malfeasance is very difficult to prove. Law enforcement agencies do a good job of investigating others' criminal activity but don't do as well policing themselves, as we have seen with the Louisiana State Police and the problems it has experienced," Goyeneche said, referring to a number of scandals that rocked State Police under the nine-year leadership of former Superintendent Mike Edmonson. "Police agencies have internal affairs departments that investigate their own and they don't always do as thorough a job as we would like."[9]

In December 2013, four sheriff's deputies were indicted for violating the civil rights of an inmate who died in the parish prison in 2014. The indictment charged that Captain Andre Dominick, Corporal Timothy Williams, and Deputies Debra Becnel and Lisa Vaccarella each knew that 19-year-old Nimali Henry had serious medical conditions. They willfully failed to provide her with necessary medical attention despite claims by family members that they repeatedly tried to tell authorities about her health issues.

As a result of the lack of medical attention, Henry died at the St. Bernard Parish Prison on April 1, 2014, after being deprived of medical treatment for kidney and thyroid disease, and congestive heart failure. During her ten days in parish prison, she was found unresponsive on the floor of her cell and later died. The indictment also charged each of the defendants with making a false statement to the FBI.[10]

Stephens, at the completion of his seventh term, did not seek reelection in 2011, ending the second-longest tenure of any St. Bernard Parish Sheriff after 28 years. He said he decided against seeking an eighth

## Chapter 34: Jack Stephens: St. Bernard Parish

term because of increased scrutiny and a growing bureaucracy following Hurricane Katrina. Mostly, though, he said, he had "seen it all."[11]

# 35

## Austin Daniel: West Feliciana Parish

Standard procedure for law enforcement in reported rapes calls for a sexual assault exam, more commonly known as a "rape kit," which includes, in addition to fluids to be sampled for DNA, the victim's statement, descriptions of any signs of violence such as bruises or scratches, and an evaluation by a specially-trained nurse.

In the case of a woman in West Feliciana Parish who claimed she was raped twice by an assistant warden at the Louisiana State Prison at Angola, that protocol was not followed by Sheriff Austin Daniel or District Attorney Sam D'Aquilla. And because a parish grand jury was never provided the sexual assault forensic examination and report, the accused, Barrett Boeker, was never charged.

The 23-year-old woman, a nursing student, told authorities she was raped at the home of Boeker. She was staying at the Boeker home—a Louisiana taxpayer-supported home on the grounds of the state penitentiary—on November 30, 2016, because she is Boeker's wife's first cousin and she had been forced from her own home by the floods that struck South Louisiana in August 2016. She returned to the Boeker house three days later, on December 3, she said, because she thought she would be safe with Boeker's wife present at the house even though his wife had passed out from drinking that first night. Instead, she says she was again raped by Boeker.[1]

In the woman's case, she took the initiative to go to a Baton Rouge hospital for a sexual assault evaluation but the results remained with the East Baton Rouge Parish coroner's office for nearly three months—until a week *after* the grand jury decision to not charge Boeker—and nearly three months after the test was conducted, because incredulously, neither Daniel nor D'Aquilla ever requested the report. Only after news media called attention to authorities' neglect in obtaining the kit and examination, was the kit finally retrieved.

Why? Because Boeker, who the lawsuit said had previously raped his sister-in-law, who it said was believed to have sexually assaulted a number of inmates at the state penitentiary, and who had been the subject of numerous Prison Litigation Reform Act claims, while admitting the two had sex, said it was consensual.[2] That, apparently, was good enough for Daniel and D'Aquilla.

But it wasn't good enough for the woman who, in accusing the sheriff and DA of conspiring to protect her alleged assailant from prosecution, filed suit in federal district court in Baton Rouge against Daniel, D'Aquilla, Boeker and West Feliciana Parish. The two, she said, "had a duty to diligently investigate the allegations and to collect the rape kit, submit it to the crime lab for examination, and review it and the sexual assault examination as part of their own investigation." Instead of protecting her rights as the victim of a violent crime, they "engaged in a course of conduct" that violated her rights by willfully refusing to do their jobs and instead, colluded to give preferential treatment to Boeker the woman's lawsuit said.[3]

Nor was it good enough for Racheal Hebert, president and CEO of Sexual Trauma Awareness & Response (STAR). She said the kit was critical and the best evidence a prosecutor can have in order to prove sexual assault. The fact that it was not reviewed, she said, "is not only shocking, it's also unbelievable," leading her to call the entire matter a "mishandling in this case."[4]

Sue Bernie, retired East Baton Rouge Parish assistant district attorney who prosecuted sex crimes for three decades, was of the same opinion. "If there's a rape exam done, I can't imagine not looking at the sexual assault exam," she said. "You'd always want to see that." She said even in cases where consent is the primary issue, as claimed by Boeker, it is still protocol for a DA's office to review the rest of the rape exam report for evidence of violence and injuries. "That would be one of the first things I would want to see, the rape exam report," Bernie said.[5]

D'Aquilla had trouble keeping his own story straight. He first said the kit wasn't needed because both the victim and the perpetrator admitted that sexual intercourse had occurred the night of the incident. He said the

## Chapter 35: Austin Daniel: West Feliciana Parish

main issue in the case was consent, which could not be tested by the evidence included in the kit. He said even if there were photos of bruising or other evidence in the rape kit, he still did not feel it would have made a difference in his prosecution.

But then, appearing to backtrack, he said his office had called the East Baton Rouge Parish coroner to request the kit on several occasions, but he was unable to confirm how or when those contacts were made.

East Baton Rouge Parish Coroner Beau Clark, however, vehemently denied any such attempt on D'Aquilla's part. He said he checked to see if his office had received inquiries from the DA's office and that it had not. He added that it is the responsibility of the authorities in West Feliciana Parish to retrieve the kit and not that of his office to deliver it.

Daniel, for his part, refused to answer any questions about why his office did not follow up on retrieving the kit and evaluation during its investigation of the rape claim, saying any comment could impact future proceedings. His office also denied a public records request to view the investigative file of the case on those same grounds.[6]

Three months later, in June 2017, however, he did admit that the process of obtaining the rape kit and evaluation "should have been done more timely (sic)." He said, "Once the grand jury came back with a no-true bill, I didn't think it was a great big hurry. I thought it was a moot issue, but evidently it wasn't."[7]

The victim said she had been asking the DA and the West Feliciana Parish Sheriff's Office about the kit and evaluation "since the very beginning. "I just felt like I did it all for nothing and it didn't matter. What was the point of going through all that and then not to even look at or consider...it?"

She said she wanted the kit sent to state police "because this is my right as a woman, a young, educated woman. I wanted to expose the truth about what happened to me."[8]

She says in her lawsuit that Austin and D'Aquilla "had a duty" to investigate the allegations and to collect the rape kit, submit it to the crime lab for examination, and review it and the sexual assault examination "as part of their own investigation."

Instead, she says, the sheriff's office "did not have a policy requiring rape kits and sexual assault examinations to be picked up and reviewed or sent to the state crime lab for testing."[9]

The woman who says she was raped managed to record a face-to-face conversation with Daniel which she provided to a Baton Rouge TV station:

**Woman:** "Why did you find it unnecessary to bring my rape kit from the beginning to get tested?"

**Daniel:** "I can't answer that."

**Woman:** I don't know if you know what's in a rape kit, but it's not just DNA. There are pictures of my naked body with bruises. I find it offensive in 2017 that y'all did not do your job or duty. Who made the decision to not send detectives to go get it?"

**Daniel:** I don't know what the answer to that is."[9]

In addition to damages, her lawsuit asked that the court "within 60 days" provide for a written policy providing for the sheriff's office and the DA's office "to collect and review rape kits and sexual assault examinations, send them to the crime lab for testing and present them as evidence in grand jury proceedings."

The petition also asks the court to require that the sheriff's and DA's offices implement a plan for the policies, training all members of each office on the written policy, and to provide training for all members of each office on sexual assault awareness.[11]

# 36
## Wayne Morein, Eddie Soileau: Evangeline Parish Sheriff's Office and Ville Platte Police Department

The Civil Rights Division of the U.S. Justice Department delivered a stunning blow to the Evangeline Parish Sheriff's Office and the Ville Platte Police Department in a late 2016 scathing report that may leave the door open to a flood of lawsuits against and criminal prosecution of the two departments for civil rights infringements through unconstitutional incarceration, intimidation and extortion.

The report's findings also cast a cloud of legal doubt that could potentially taint an undetermined number of past criminal convictions that resulted from such practices.

In a blockbuster report dated Dec. 19, the Justice Department said in something of an understatement that a "thorough investigation" by the Justice Department concluded "that there is reasonable cause to believe that both the Ville Platte, Louisiana Police Department (VPPD) and the Evangeline Parish Sheriff's Office (EPSO) have engaged in a pattern or practice of unconstitutional conduct" that dates back "as far as anyone (at either department) can remember."

The 17-page report went on to say, "Both VPPD and EPSO have arrested and held people in jail—without obtaining a warrant and without probable cause to believe that the detained individuals had committed a crime—in violation of the Fourth Amendment to the Constitution. We have additional concerns that these unconstitutional holds have led to coerced confessions and improper criminal convictions. These findings reflect the results of an investigation into both agencies, which have engaged in nearly identical practices within overlapping jurisdictional boundaries."[1]

The arrests, called "investigative holds," were used routinely by both VPPD and EPSO as a part of their criminal investigations during which threats of continued wrongful incarceration were employed to induce arrestees to provide information. Authorities also threatened their family members and potential witnesses, the report said.

"The arrests include individuals suspected (without sufficient evidence) of committing crimes, as well as their family members and potential witnesses," it said.

Other violations cited by the report included claims that individuals improperly arrested were:
- Strip-searched;
- Placed in holding cells without beds, toilets, or showers;
- Denied communication with family members and loved ones;
- Commonly detained for 72 hours or more without being provided an opportunity to contest their arrest and detention;
- Held and questioned until they either provide information or the law enforcement agency determines that they do not have information related to a crime.

The report further said there were "concerns that some people may have confessed to crimes or provided information sought by EPSO and VPPD detectives, apparently to end this secret and indefinite confinement."

It said that the practice is "routine at EPSO and VPPD" and that both agencies acknowledged that they used holds to investigate criminal activity for as long as anyone at the agency can remember. The number of holds used in recent years is "staggering."

"Between 2012 and 2014, for example," it said, "EPSO initiated over 200 arrests where the only documented reason for arrest was an investigative hold. In that same period, VPPD used the practice more than 700 times. The number of holds by EPSO and VPPD is likely even higher; both agencies use such rudimentary arrest documentation systems that the total number of arrests for investigative hold purposes is likely underreported."

Following the onset of its investigation in April 2015, "leadership of VPPD, EPSO and the City of Ville Platte admitted that the holds are unconstitutional" and have taken steps to begin eliminating their use, the

## Chapter 36: Wayne Morein, Eddie Soileau: EPSO and VPPD

report says, adding that still more work "remains to be done." The agencies' policies, procedures, training, and data collection and accountability systems "must ensure that investigative holds are eliminated permanently," it said, adding that local officials "must work to repair community trust, because many people may still be justifiably reluctant to provide information to law enforcement for fear that doing so could subject them to an unconstitutional detention."

The report was the culmination of an investigation of a cross-section of community residents, some of whom were subjected to the investigative holds.

"To gain additional information, we spoke with former FBI investigators and officials at the Louisiana State Office of the Inspector General who have interacted with Ville Platte and Evangeline Parish residents during their own investigations," the report said. "Finally, we reviewed thousands of pages of documents, including City Jail booking logs, Parish Jail booking cards, and other records; probable cause affidavits; policy and procedure manuals; and more. This review highlighted that both EPSO and VPPD lack a consistent and detailed process for recording and tracking information about arrests, detentions, and interrogations."

The Justice Department concluded that it found "reasonable cause to believe that both EPSO and VPPD engage in a pattern or practice of violating the Fourth Amendment by arresting and detaining individuals without probable cause. Moreover, we have serious concerns that these agencies use holds to obtain coerced statements that taint the criminal convictions of the unlawfully detained individuals.

"This pattern or practice is widespread and longstanding throughout both agencies. Between January 2012 and December 2014, EPSO—an agency with four detectives that polices a jurisdiction populated by only 33,000 residents—listed "investigative hold" as the sole basis for over 200 arrests. During the same time period, VPPD arrested individuals on investigative holds more than 700 times while policing a jurisdiction of only 7,300—10 percent of the city's entire population. At least 30 of VPPD's investigative hold arrests were of juveniles. The investigative hold practice violates the Fourth Amendment to the United States Constitution, which guarantees the right to be free from unreasonable searches and seizures, including arrests. The United States is authorized to address a pattern or practice of Fourth Amendment violations under 42 U.S.C. § 14141, which grants the Department of Justice authority to bring suit for equitable and declaratory relief when a "governmental authority . . . engage[s] in a pattern or practice of conduct by law enforcement officers . . . that deprives persons of rights, privileges, or immunities secured or protected by the Constitution or laws of the United States." 42 U.S.C. § 14141. A pattern or practice exists where violations are repeated rather than isolated."

Detectives from both agencies violated individuals' Fourth Amendment when, "lacking probable cause, they instructed officers to 'pick up' an individual and 'bring him in' for questioning rather than making an 'arrest,'" the report's narrative said. "Indeed, there can be little doubt that the Fourth Amendment's probable cause requirement applies where suspects are involuntarily taken to the police station. This practice subjects individuals to arrest and detention without cause and erodes the community trust that is critical to effective law enforcement in Evangeline Parish and Ville Platte."

The investigative holds are made "without a warrant, without any showing that the testimony is essential and that obtaining it via subpoena is impracticable, and without any attempt to obtain prior judicial approval," the report says.

"EPSO and VPPD officers have used unlawful investigative holds as a regular part of criminal investigations for more than two decades. Most holds operate as follows:

- When a detective at either agency wants to question someone in connection with an ongoing criminal investigation, the detective instructs a patrol officer to find that individual in the community and bring him or her in for questioning.
- The patrol officer commands the individual to ride in a patrol vehicle to either the City or Parish jail, where pursuant to the jail's standard procedures, jail personnel strip-search the individual and place him or her in a holding cell (sometimes referred to as "the bullpen" at the Parish Jail) until a detective is available to conduct questioning.
- At the City Jail, there are two holding cells; both are equipped with a hard metal bench, and nothing else. Neither holding cell at the City Jail has a mattress, running water, shower, or toilet in the cell.

## Chapter 36: Wayne Morein, Eddie Soileau: EPSO and VPPD

- The Parish Jail is similar; the "bullpen" is equipped with only a long metal bench, and the walls are made of metal grating. EPSO detectives and deputies refer to the process of detaining a person in the "bullpen" for questioning as "putting them on ice."
- Investigative holds initiated by VPPD often last for 72 hours—and sometimes significantly longer—forcing detainees to spend multiple nights sleeping on a concrete floor or metal bench. Indeed, VPPD's booking logs indicate that, from 2012-2014, several dozen investigative holds extended for at least a full week. During this time, VPPD exerts control over the detainees' liberty: The detained person is not permitted to make phone calls to let family or employers know where they are, and have access to bathrooms and showers only when taken into the jail's general population area.
- Similarly, EPSO's investigative holds often last for three full days. During that time, detainees are forced to sleep on the Parish Jail's concrete floor. One EPSO deputy reported that he saw someone held without a warrant or a probable cause determination for more than six days.
- As with VPPD, EPSO also controls the detainee's liberty. EPSO does not permit detainees who are "on hold" to make phone calls to let family or employers know their whereabouts. Indeed, we were told that certain detectives have threatened EPSO jail officers (referred to as "jailers" in the Parish Jail) with retaliation if the officers allowed detainees to make phone calls. One EPSO jail officer described an incident in which an EPSO detective reprimanded him after the jail officer provided toothpaste and other personal supplies to a person locked in the holding cell.

These investigative holds are not even ostensibly supported by probable cause. Both EPSO and VPPD detectives acknowledged that they use investigative holds where they lack sufficient evidence to make an arrest, but instead have a "hunch" or "feeling" that a person may be involved in criminal activity. One VPPD officer noted that they use investigative holds specifically where the officer needs more time to develop evidence to support a lawful arrest. Similarly, an EPSO detective described using investigative holds when he had "a pretty good feeling" or a "gut instinct" that a certain individual was connected to a crime.

The report indicated that officers at both agencies admitted that they use the time that a person is "on hold" to develop their case, either by gathering evidence or by convincing the detainee to confess. One EPSO detective told investigators that he experimented with investigative holds by testing whether a crime wave subsides while a particular person is in jail. He explained that if the crimes continue during the hold, the presumably innocent person is released but if the crimes cease during the detention, the detective investigates the person further.

VPPD officers explained that holds assist their investigations by inducing people to talk to investigators and by allowing detectives to gather evidence while the individual they suspect is in custody and cannot communicate with people on the outside. Moreover, both agencies confirmed that they used holds to detain individuals whom they did not suspect of involvement in criminal activity, but who instead had the misfortune of being related to suspects, may have witnessed crimes, or otherwise might have knowledge of criminal activity.[2]

Incredulously, Ville Platte Police Chief Neal Lartigue professed not to know the indiscriminate use of the investigative holds may have been in violation of the Fourth Amendment which requires authorities to have probable cause to detain citizens.[3]

In an ominous warning of the perils of investigative holds, the report said, "The willingness of officers in both agencies to arrest and detain individuals who are merely possible witnesses in criminal investigations means that literally anyone in Evangeline Parish or Ville Platte could be arrested and placed 'on hold' at any time."[4]

The Louisiana Attorney General was tasked with the job of reminding Evangeline Sheriff Eddie Soileau of his constitutional duties as the parish's chief law enforcement officer. Soileau had requested a legal opinion as to whether or not he was required to enforce the law. He said in his request that budgetary shortfalls had left him with insufficient staff to carry out its functions his office's functions as tax collector, process server, and law enforcement office.

The Attorney General's opinion replied that the sheriff's duties are spelled out in the Louisiana Constitution, which says the sheriff "shall be

## Chapter 36: Wayne Morein, Eddie Soileau: EPSO and VPPD

the chief law enforcement officer in the parish..." The opinion further pointed out that the duties are reiterated in state statute which says, "Each sheriff shall be keeper of the public jail and his parish shall preserve the peace and apprehend public offenders."

The opinion concluded by saying, "No law provides a sheriff discretion in which duties to exercise and no advisory opinion can absolve any sheriff of the legal duties of office as the chief law enforcement officer tasked with keeping peace and making arrests. Accordingly, despite the discretion available to sheriffs regarding how to execute certain official duties, it is our opinion that no public official may choose to shrug a yoke his office bears by Constitutional decree."[5]

# 37

## Jerry Larpenter: Terrebonne Parish

Terrebonne Parish Sheriff Jerry Larpenter apparently never read the First Amendment. Neither, it seems, has 32nd Judicial District Court Judge Randal Bethancourt. Nor does it seem that either ever checked into the constitutional status of Louisiana's criminal defamation statute.

Larpenter made national news on August 2, 2016, when he sent a posse of six deputies to the home of a suspected blogger and hauled away two laptop computers because the blogger said bad things about the sheriff. Somehow, six men to confiscate two laptop computers approaches overkill, but perhaps that's the way things are done in Terrebonne Parish. After all, the laws that apply to the rest of us don't seem to hold much water with Larpenter and Bethancourt.[1]

The blogger, a Houma police officer, posted critical observations about Larpenter, Parish President (and former State Rep.) Gordon Dove, Dove's business partner Tony Alford, who landed a huge benefits package brokerage contract for Larpenter's office, and their jointly-owned trucking firm. Also thrown into the mix were Dove's former legislative assistant Debbie Ortego who was given a $79.000-a-year job as Dove's new officer manager, Debbie's husband Dana who was Dove's Risk Manager, and Dana's nephew Parish Attorney Joe Waitz, III (District Attorney Joe Waitz Jr.'s son), Sheriff Larpenter's wife Priscilla who enjoyed a six-figure job as manager of Tony Alford's office, and Jackie Dove, who is married to Assistant District Attorney Sye Broussard. There were a few other names in the organizational flow chart compiled by the publisher of the Internet blog, since taken down, but it gets complicated and somewhat confusing after that.

The gist of the story was that certain connected entities evaded their responsibility to pay nearly $400,000 in parish taxes and that local officials committed malfeasance by not pursuing the collection of the delinquent taxes. Those same officials, it said, were guilty of nepotism, committed ethics violations, and violated environmental regulations.

In 2014, it was learned that Dove and his trucking company got into trouble with the environmental watchdogs in Montana who, unlike their counterparts in Louisiana, tend to do their jobs with no consideration given to oil company political contributions and highly paid oil and gas lobbyists milling around the State Capitol's rotunda with steak restaurant vouchers for famished legislators.[2]

The blogger, Wayne Anderson, who had worked as a Terrebonne Parish sheriff's deputy before going to work for the Houma Police Department, had documents and links to documents to support claims in his post and yet all that apparently made no difference to the two officials who went after him with a vengeance.

Overlooked by Sheriff Larpenter was the guarantee under the First Amendment of the U.S. Constitution of Anderson's right to free speech. Even more astonishing was that Bethancourt, supposedly something of a legal scholar by virtue of his position as a judge, went along with the sheriff's scheme.

Relying upon an obscure state criminal defamation statute[3] designed to discourage freedom of speech and enacted during the last term of former Gov. John McKeithen (1964-1972), Bethancourt said he had to stay within the "four corners" of the warrant and affidavit and that he was unable to discern if Alford was a public official (under the landmark U.S. Supreme Court case *Sullivan v. New York Times* which ruled that for a public official to claim libel, he must prove not only malicious intent but "reckless disregard for the truth")—despite Alford's status as a member of a local levee district. Louisiana's criminal defamation statute, he said, is "pretty broad" and that he would have to have a "look-see" at what was contained on the computers that might have defamatory statements on them.

The only problem with the judge's interpretation of the state's "pretty broad" defamation statute is that it is non-existent. David Ardoin, Anderson's attorney, correctly pointed out that Bethancourt made a mistake in approving the warrant to raid his client's home because in 1981, the second year of former Gov. Dave Treen's term of office, the defamation statute was declared unconstitutional.[4]

## Chapter 37: Jerry Larpenter: Terrebonne Parish

Since the law was held unconstitutional, it would seem that neither Judge Bethancourt nor the sheriff—nor anyone else, for that matter—had any right to have a "look-see" at what was contained on Anderson's computers. That, simply put, constituted an invasion of privacy.

Former Governor Edwin Edwards not only remembered the ruling when asked about it on the eve of his 89th birthday but added that "It sounds to me like the sheriff has some very serious legal problems. I would love to be that blogger's attorney in that civil litigation."[5]

Sheriff Larpenter and Judge Bethancourt greatly overstepped their authority—so much so that the local newspaper, the *Houma Daily Courier*, took a big risk in alienating the local power structure when it took the sheriff to task in a sharply worded August 7 editorial.[6] The paper, however, stopped short of condemning Judge Bethancourt for going along with the sheriff's strongarm tactics.

Just a cursory read of the blogpost made it abundantly clear that there were some cozy—too cozy—relationships that bordered on political incest in Terrebonne Parish. A lot of power was vested in the hands of so few people as to impede a workable system of checks and balances. Those few controlled the expenditure of millions upon millions of public dollars with no oversight. Under such conditions, greed invariably becomes the motivating factor that drives virtually every action.

And it is the citizens who are the ultimate losers.

Local media are subject to economic realities. They can be—and quite often are—squeezed by those in power so that any real investigative reporting is tempered by whatever financial pressure (read: advertising revenue) can be applied by those with the most to lose.

Fortunately, the story did not end there. After a federal judge dressed down Bethancourt and Larpenter by familiarizing them with the First Amendment and ordered that Anderson's computers be returned, Anderson and wife Jennifer promptly filed suit against Larpenter, Dove, the Terrebonne Parish government, the Terrebonne Levee District and Alford. Alford and the levee district were dismissed but Dove settled for about $50,000 and Larpenter settled for another $200,000.

Anderson told a New Orleans television station, "I think the sheriff finally learned that he can't bully people and violate people's constitutional rights. In our case, he stepped on the wrong people's constitutional rights because we knew our rights. Hopefully, he thinks twice the next time he gets his feelings hurt."[7]

Larpenter, still smarting over the decision, would later turn on the judge who helped him to pull off the illegal raid. His dust-up with Bethancourt was over the provision of security in the parish courthouse—which he refused to provide despite laws on the books that clearly said that is part of his job.

Larpenter demanded more pay for doing so and the judges said no dice. That standoff more or less backed the judges into a corner by forcing them to retain private security and municipal police officers.

Following the dispute over additional security vs. additional pay, Larpenter took photographs of inmates being transported to court and being held in holding cells until being called for their hearings and arraignments. Armed with the photographs, Larpenter called the State Fire Marshal down on the court, apparently for the overcrowded conditions in the cells.

The State Fire Marshal, like the State Superintendent of Police is a position filled by appointment of the governor and no governor would dare make such an appointment without the blessings of the Louisiana Sheriffs' Association. The sheriffs' association dictates to every governor who shall fill the positions of Secretary of the Department of Public Safety and Corrections, State Fire Marshal and State Superintendent of Police. Accordingly, Larpenter felt sufficiently confident to call in the major players on the judges—major players that his association props up.

Down and dirty politics at the local level? Absolutely, and normally, that would be a lethal weapon given the formidable alliance of the sheriffs' association, Secretary of Public Safety, State Superintendent of Police and State Fire Marshal. Those are the predominant law enforcement agencies of the state. One generally doesn't cross swords with that kind of political muscle.

Larpenter, feeling he had the upper hand, then went to the local press with his brainstorm for a great cost-cutting measure: video arraignments. But that was only a temporary setback as the judges came back with their own "gotcha." First, they issued an order banning all video arraignments, thereby forcing Larpenter to bear the costs of transporting more than 150 prisoners for hearings.

## Chapter 37: Jerry Larpenter: Terrebonne Parish

Then, Judge David Arceneaux signed an order in which he struck through language requiring the warden of Dixon Correctional Institute in East Feliciana Parish, 120 miles north of Houma, to transport a prisoner from that facility to Houma and back. Judge Arceneaux then wrote in longhand, "Terrebonne Parish Sheriff to transport from Dixon Correctional Institute," adding that Larpenter was to deposit $1,500 for the cost of transporting the prisoner.

Larpenter told Bethancourt that it was the judge's fault that he, Larpenter, had to pay monetary damages to the Andersons, forgetting, apparently, that it was he, not the judge, who asked for the search warrant in the first place. Larpenter must have also forgotten for the moment that he didn't have to pay a dime of the judgement—or his attorney bills. Those were covered by his office's liability insurance policy.

And just as with the raid on the Andersons was ruled unconstitutional, Larpenter's refusal to provide courthouse security appeared to be at loggerheads with what the law said his duties are. State statutes leave little wiggle room when they say:

- *"Court criers are to be provided by the sheriff of each parish to each district judge."*
- *"The crier of a court (notice this is not restricted to Orleans) shall attend all sessions thereof, under the direction of the judge shall open and close court at each session, and **maintain order and decorum in the court room**, and shall perform such other duties as are assigned to him by law, the court, or the sheriff."* (emphasis added)
- *"Each sheriff or deputy shall attend every court that is held in his parish..."*
- *"Security in the courthouse is the responsibility of governing authority (Gordon Dove), but an agreement may be made between the parish officers and the building to share the expenses."*
- *"The principal functions of the criminal sheriff are that of being keeper of parish jail and executive officer of the Criminal District Court."*

And then there is Opinion 12-0187 of the Louisiana Attorney General's office dated Feb. 7, 2013, which said in part: "...security provided in the courthouse is the responsibility of the parish governing authority under this statutory regime..." and that "...the governing body of the parish shall pay to the sheriff or his deputies attending upon the sessions of their respective courts of appeal and district courts..."[8]

In another matter involving apparent legal violations, public records requests were made of Larpenter in August 2017 for records of purchases made from businesses owned by two of his deputies, purchases that would constitute a violation of state ethics laws governing public employees doing business with agencies for whom they work.

A 1995 opinion by the State Ethics Commission addresses that scenario. It said that the owner of Fire Apparatus Specialties, who also serves as Assistant Fire Chief of the Third District Volunteer Fire Department in Jefferson Parish, purchased equipment from his company on behalf of the fire department in violation of state ethics laws.[9]

In all, there are more than 80 opinions by the Ethics Commission that address various schemes in which agency heads or employees sold goods and/or services to their agencies—all of which are violations of the law.

In Terrebonne Parish, Brent Hidalgo and Douglas Chauvin, Jr. were sheriff's deputies who, concurrent with their employment as deputies, also owned side businesses. Hidalgo operated Promotek, LLC, a screen printing and embroidery company in Houma that sold specialty items like shirts, caps and mugs with company and organization names imprinted on the product and Chauvin owned First Circuit, LLC, an electrician firm in Bourg, Louisiana.[10]

Reports were received by the news media that the sheriff's department purchased all its shirts, with logos of the department, from Hidalgo's firm and that Chauvin's electrical company had performed work for the sheriff's department despite prohibitions of employees or their immediate family members from doing business with an agency that employed them.

A public records request for any payments made to the two firms or to Hidalgo or Chauvin directly resulted in a response from Larpenter that said in part, "...this office has never paid anything to Brent Hidalgo or any

## Chapter 37: Jerry Larpenter: Terrebonne Parish

of his family members, representatives or employees or Douglas or Doug Chauvin or any of his family members, representatives or employees."

But one of Larpenter's deputies says said the department was "back-dooring" the purchases—at least insofar as Hidalgo was concerned. The deputy, who for obvious reasons was not identified, said that Larpenter's deputies were required to personally purchase any shirts they are required to wear and that they are directed to Hidalgo as the vendor and that Hidalgo handles all such transactions.

That's a gray area. A 2011 Board of Ethics opinion said the owner of a specialty company who also was a member of the Covington City Council *"would not be prohibited from selling products with the city logo, through his company, to city employees so long as the city employee pays for such products with his or her personal funds."*[11]

The key word is *directed*, as "directed to Brent Hidalgo." It would seem as long as the purchases are 100 percent voluntary, Hidalgo and Larpenter would have no problem with Hidalgo's selling shirts to deputies. But if the unidentified deputy was accurate in saying they are *directed* to purchase from Hidalgo, then that would seem to be an implied contract between Hidalgo and Larpenter.

---

Then there is the story of the "Mysterious X" that first catapulted Larpenter into the Sheriff's Office in 1987. At the beginning of April of that year, Charlton P. Rozands was still the sheriff, but at that particular point in time, he was:
- Under federal indictment;
- Dying of cancer.

Rozands and his two sons, along with Chief of Detectives Aubrey Authement and deputy Elmore Songe were all indicted on charges ranging from malfeasance in office, improper removal of weapons from the sheriff's office, unauthorized and illegal personal use of weapons being held as evidence, and the disposal of weapons being held as evidence but which had been in Authement's possession.[12]

The sheriff's cancer was so advanced, in fact, that he was said to have been heavily medicated on morphine and thus, unable to perform the simplest of tasks—even as simple as signing his name. Rozands died on April 19. Six days before his death, on April 13, Larpenter supposedly signed the required oath of office as Rozands' Chief Criminal Deputy. On the second page of that document, in the left-hand margin, is the signature, "C.P. Rozands, Sheriff."[13]

Except it's not Rozands' signature. A comparison of that signature with a document actually signed by Rozands makes that clearly evident. Several people who were in positions to know said that Rozands would have been physically unable to sign anything because of the advanced stages of his cancer and because he was heavily medicated with morphine. What is not clear is who actually did sign his name.

In fact, at some point prior to Larpenter's signing his oath of office, a meeting was reportedly held to discuss a successor. Said to have been at that meeting were Rozands' wife Mae, his two sons, and Houma attorney William F. Dodd, legal counsel for the sheriff's office and son of a former Louisiana state politician and Earl Long contemporary. The year was 1987, and at the time, state law allowed an official's widow to assume his seat but Mrs. Rozands let it be known she wasn't interested in the job. Nor were either of their sons. The choices were quickly eliminated until there was only Larpenter who, when asked, said he would take the job.

The affidavit was quickly drafted, presumably by Dodd, that named Larpenter as Chief Criminal Deputy, which would make him next in line for the office of sheriff. But to make the appointment official, Rozands was required to sign it. Despite being described as being in no condition to do so, he supposedly signed the document with an "X."

But did he? One person close to the series of events said, "I don't think Rozands would have waited until he was that sick to appoint Jerry Larpenter. They were close, but I think if Rozands had wanted Larpenter as his Chief Criminal Deputy, he would have appointed him while he was well enough to know what he was doing."[14]

Besides the job promotion and salary boost that came with Larpenter's ascension into the sheriff's chair, it also gave him the decided advantage of running as an incumbent in the next regular election only months away in October. In that election, the incumbency proved beneficial, all right. Larpenter, running against eight opponents, got a whopping 44 per cent of the vote, a full 30 points more than his closest

## Chapter 37: Jerry Larpenter: Terrebonne Parish

competitor, who got 14 percent. In the November runoff, he received 69 per cent of the vote to win his first of seven terms, interrupted only by his unsuccessful run for Parish President in 2007.

Each one of his elections were won by wide margins and he ran unopposed in 2015. But the details of how he went from obscure deputy to sheriff for those few months in 1987 remain murky and clouded with questions of whether Rozands actually scrawled that "X" or it was done by someone in his name.

---

Finally, there are the unanswered questions that persist, three decades after his death, concerning Rozands' heavy-handed control over local bars, gambling and prostitution—and rumors of his ties to organized crime during his tenure as Terrebonne's chief law enforcement officer.

Now a municipal judge, a man who worked for Rozands as an 18-year-old deputy while attending college shared some revealing stories about Rozands. During his tenure with the Terrebonne Parish Sheriff's Office, the young deputy witnessed some interesting practices, which included, among other things, Rozands' insistence that bar owners in the parish keep an eight-by-ten photo of him hanging over their bars' cash registers.

Whenever a parish bar owner applied for a liquor license or a renewal, he was provided along with his license, a photo of the sheriff. He was instructed to hang it in a conspicuous location, preferably over the bar. The bars were regularly checked by deputies for compliance and if it was found that the photo was not where is was supposed to be, Rozands would promptly pull the bar's license and order it closed.

But an even more disturbing revelation was that of Rozands' office making regular payoffs to New Orleans Mafia boss Carlos Marcello. "Carlos controlled the pinball machines and all the pool tables in Terrebonne Parish," said the former deputy. "They were owned by Lafourche Novelty Company but Carlos controlled the entire coast from Texas to Florida at that time. All the bars had to have their cigarette machines from CNL Cigarettes. CNL ran the bookie business in the parish, along with prostitution and pinball.

"A.B. Pereira was the bag man for Marcello. Everyone called him Abe. He would pick up the payoff money from the bars and of course,

Rozands was getting a take for himself. A man named George Saadi put Rozands and Marcello together. All the sheriff department uniforms had to come from Saadi Haberdashery. "

The former deputy said every Wednesday, a briefcase full of cash would be placed in the trunk of a sheriff's department vehicle which would then be driven to Mosca's Restaurant in Westwego in Jefferson Parish. "The driver of the sheriff's car would park next to one of Marcello's Cadillacs in the parking lot. Marcello got all his Cadillacs from Pontchartrain Cadillac and sheriff got his from Cournoyer Cadillac in Houma."

Inside the restaurant, keys would be exchanged and one of Marcello's men would go to the cars and open the trunks. "The full bag of money would be taken out of the sheriff's vehicle and placed in the trunk of Marcello's car. An empty briefcase would be taken from the Marcello car and placed in the trunk of the sheriff's car. Back inside the restaurant, the keys would swap hands again."

A naïve kid at the time, the deputy had not even started law school. "Looking back, there was so much going on in that office, it would curl your hair," he said.[15]

# 38
## Litigation: The Costs of Bad Sheriffing

Louisiana sheriffs have paid out a combined minimum of $6.1 million in settlements and judgments since 2015, according to records provided by the Louisiana Sheriffs' Law Enforcement Program (LSLEP).

Iberia Parish Sheriff Louis Ackal has paid out at least $3 million of that, or almost 40 percent of the total for all sheriffs. That's just from 2015. Ackal has been in office for ten years and his office has paid out an average of $25,000 in legal judgments for every month he has been in office.

Two other parish sheriffs' departments, Jackson ($650,000) and Morehouse ($503,000) were a distant second and third, respectively, behind Iberia. Together, the three parishes were responsible for about $4 million in payouts for damages and wrongful deaths, or about 59 percent of the total for all 45 parishes that participate in LSLEP.

Besides the $6 million-plus in judgments that were paid out, seven law firms also ran up another $1.2 million in legal fees defending the various lawsuits against sheriffs. That amount represents more than 83 percent of the total legal fees paid to all firms.

Pursuant to a public records request, LSLEP, through Usry & Weeks, provided reports that showed file names, claimant names, attorneys who handled the files, the amounts paid in attorney fees, and settlement/judgment amounts. The amounts paid out were divided into "corridor" (deductible), indemnity, and excess carrier payments. Excess payments are generally paid out by a second insurance company that covers claims in excess of a certain amount covered by LSLEP's primary insurer.[1]

There were seven payments made by the LSLEP excess carrier, records show. They range from a low of $15,000 in a case involving two payouts to a plaintiff by the West Baton Rouge Parish Sheriff's Office (the other payment was for $100,000 and was listed as an "indemnity" payment) to what is believed to be a payment of at least $600,000 in Iberia Parish in the case of the shooting death of a handcuffed Victor White, III.

The actual amount of that payment is unclear because in the case of Shandell Bradley v. the Iberia Parish Sheriff's Office, the amounts of the settlement payments were ordered sealed by the presiding judge—the only payments among the records provided that were redacted. That was the case in which White was shot in the chest while in custody of sheriff's deputies. The coroner somehow managed to rule that White had gotten hold of a weapon and somehow managed to shoot himself in the chest—while his hands were cuffed behind his back.

In an interview with the author, White's father, Victor White, Jr., said he was unhappy with the judge's order that terms of the settlement not be disclosed. "The judge says we can't talk about the settlement amount, but I believe the people of Iberia Parish have a right to know how much the sheriff department's actions cost them," he said. The Victor White case was not the only case in which Iberia Parish Sheriff Louis Ackal had to make substantial payouts.[2]

Christopher Butler sued after he was beaten while handcuffed by a deputy Cody Laperouse in 2013. Ackal fired Laperouse who promptly went to work as an officer for the St. Martinville Police Department. Ackal's office paid out $350,000 in that case. Ackal also paid out $175,000 to the family of 16-year-old Daquentin Thompson who hanged himself while being held in Iberia Parish's adult jail in 2014.[3]

In a case that displayed the ugly side of Ackal's idea of justice, the sheriff instructed two of his deputies to "take care of" Howard Trosclair after Ackal had been told Trosclair assaulted one of his (Ackal's) relatives, according to appeal documents filed by deputy David Hines with the U.S. Fifth Circuit Court of Appeals. When Trosclair was arrested, the court records say he was "compliant and followed the officers' commands." Hines nevertheless used his knee to strike Trosclair "several times in the side" and struck him "two to three times" with his baton in the back of his legs. Hines continued to knee Trosclair in the abdomen or groin even after he was restrained. Hines then filed a false police report to cover up the wrongful assault, the appeal record says. That episode cost LSLEP $275,000.[4]

## Chapter 38: Litigation: The Costs of Bad Sheriffing

LSLEP paid out half-a-million dollars on behalf of the Morehouse Parish Sheriff's Office in connection with the death of 18-year-old Edwin Battaglia while he was in a holding cell.[5]

Perhaps the strangest judgment was the $600,000 payout to vacuum cleaner sales representatives in Jackson Parish in 2013. It seems that a group of door-to-door salespeople had close encounters with Jackson Parish sheriff's deputies despite their having a permit to solicit door-to-door. Deputy Gerald Palmer told the sales reps, "We're not too keen on door-to-door salesmen in this parish, so you probably gonna run into a lot of problems. You're probably better off to go to another parish, according to my sheriff (Andy Brown)," according to court documents. Court documents quoted other examples of intimidation by deputies in efforts to discourage the sales reps.[6]

The Alexandria law firm of Provosty, Sadler & Delaunay billed $247,000 for defending 33 lawsuits against sheriffs' offices in Allen, Grant, Iberia and Rapides parishes, records show.

The Chalmette law firm of Gutierrez & Hand was a close second with $237,000 in billings for defending twenty lawsuits against the St. Bernard Parish Sheriff's Office.

Other top-billing firms included:
- Cook, Yancey, King & Galloway of Shreveport—$191,390 for defending 26 cases in the parishes of Claiborne, DeSoto, and Webster;
- Hall, Lestage & Landreneau of Deridder—$149,745 for representing Allen, Beauregard, Rapides, and Vernon parishes in 36 litigation cases;
- Homer Ed Barousse of Crowley—$135,400 for representation in the defense of litigation in 11 cases in Acadia Parish;
- The Dodd Law Firm of Houma—$132,000 for the defense of ten cases in East Feliciana and Iberia parishes;
- Borne, Wilkes & Rabalais—$112,800 for defending ten cases in Acadia and Iberia parishes.[7]

Not all lawsuits were filed against Ackal by prisoners. Laurie Segura was an administrative assistant for the sheriff's office who obtained a settlement of $409,000 for sexual harassment by Bert Berry, chief of the

Criminal Department whose action included rubbing his hands and crotch against her body, sneaking up behind her and kissing her, making inappropriate inquiries about her sex life, discussed fantasies of having sex with her, simulating sex in her presence and trying to get her to engage in phone sex. She said in her lawsuit that he ignored her repeated requests to leave her alone and when she complained, she experienced retaliation.[8]

    Besides having to settle her claim, Ackal got an added bonus when Segura testified against him in federal criminal charges brought against him for a multitude of offenses.

# The Others
## (Non-Sheriff Law Enforcement Officers)

# 39

## George D'Artois: City of Shreveport

In terms of pure corruption, greed and unrepentant reprisals against anyone who might stand in his way, the saga of former Shreveport Commissioner of Public Safety George D'Artois stands alone. His story underscores the undeniable argument that unrestrained autonomy on the part of law enforcement can ultimately lead only to a bad ending for everyone involved.

D'Artois served as a deputy under Caddo Parish Sheriff J. Howell Flournoy from 1952 until his resignation in 1962 to run for Public Service Commissioner under Shreveport's city commission form of government, a five-member body that exercised combined executive and legislative functions for the city with the mayor serving as the commissioner of administration. D'Artois, a Democrat, upset two-term incumbent J. Earl Downs. He was re-elected in 1966, 1970 and 1974. Far more power was enjoyed by commissioners, each of whom ran his own fiefdom, than under the mayor-council form of government which was established with the 1978 elections when single-member legislative city council districts and an executive mayor were elected.[1]

As public safety commissioner, D'Artois frequently lectured in Baton Rouge at the LSU Law Enforcement Institute and at the Southwestern Legal Foundation at Southern Methodist University in Dallas. He was cited by the National Police Officers Association of America in 1973 for outstanding work in law enforcement.[2]

But all was not what it appeared to be. When several hundred thousand dollars earmarked for financing a synchronized traffic system by D'Artois's department disappeared in 1968, none of the Shreveport commissioners could ever account for it. Mayor Calhoun Allen was dismissive, speculating in a somewhat cavalier manner that the money was used for other "needed projects."[3]

Before the murder of advertising executive Jim Leslie engulfed D'Artois, he was said to have been involved in another, much quieter scandal. A black female civil rights worker named Ann Brewster died from a gunshot wound to the head. The police report, written in 1964, two years after D'Artois was first elected, said she had committed suicide by shooting herself in the head with a .38 special.

Local activist Dr. Artis Cash was skeptical. "The gun was in her right hand, but her trigger finger still on the trigger," he said. "If you blow your head off the recoil itself is going to kick the gun out of your hand." He is convinced Brewster was murdered.

D'Artois was known in the black community to do "night creeps," Cash said. "What we mean by a night creep is that he would come into the black community and mess with black women even though in the daylight hours he was putting his foot on our neck."

The "foot on the neck" claim, however, is subject to interpretation. D'Artois pandered to both whites and blacks by on one hand, telling the White Citizens Council that he had stepped up patrols in the black communities while on the other hand, he allowed black nightclubs to remain open long after hours while running gambling rooms.

Cash believes that D'Artois was responsible for the death of Ann Brewster. "There was a whispering campaign going on that this woman was killed by her lover and the lover was George D'Artois," he said.[4]

Even as D'Artois was running not only the Department of Public Safety, but the entire city of Shreveport "with an iron fist" without the niceties of a velvet glove, New Orleans organized crime boss Carlos Marcello was making regular visits to Shreveport.[5]

The 1970 election served as a wake-up call for D'Artois. Though he received 59.8 percent of the vote in defeating Republican William Kimball, the election was too close for D'Artois who was accustomed to polling much higher numbers against token opposition. For his 1974 re-election campaign, he hired advertising executive Jim Leslie who had previously

## Chapter 39: George D'Artois: City of Shreveport

worked as a reporter for *The Shreveport Times*. It would prove to be a fateful move for both men. Following his easy victory, D'Artois, in a crass and arrogant gesture, paid Leslie for his work on the campaign with a check drawn on city funds. Leslie returned the check and asked that he be paid from D'Artois's campaign funds. Instead, D'Artois told Leslie to keep the city check and to keep the matter between the two of them. Leslie again returned the check, along with a threat to go public if he was not paid properly. From that point forward, Leslie was a marked man.[6]

Leslie subsequently contracted with the Louisiana Association of Business and Industry (LABI) to spearhead its push for passage of the hotly contested right to work bill pending before the Louisiana Legislature. The bill, thanks largely to Leslie's work, narrowly passed the legislature. He joined other proponents of the bill to celebrate the victory into the early morning hours of July 9, 1976. As he exited from his car after parking in the parking lot of the Prince Murat Hotel on Nicholson Drive about two a.m., he was killed instantly by a blast from a 12-gauge shotgun fired from behind a wooden fence. He was less than four months shy of his October 27 birthday. He was 38.[7]

There had been a labor-related killing at a Lake Charles petrochemical plant only a few weeks before, which those in the labor movement feel helped grease the wheels to passage of the right to work bill, so the immediate speculation was that Leslie's killing also was attributable to the high voltage emotions on the part of organized labor that accompanied the right to work movement. That theory was quickly dismissed and all eyes turned toward Shreveport and the fallout from the ongoing D'Artois-Leslie dispute over a $3,500 city check.[8]

On August 6, 1976, less than a month after Leslie's murder, Douglas Gonzales, judge for the 19th Judicial District in Baton Rouge, issued a warrant charging D'Artois for his alleged part in the killing. Though he was soon released for lack of evidence, D'Artois was forced to resign from office.[9]

Two months later, on October 13, D'Artois was ordered by John F. Fant, judge for the 1st Judicial District in Shreveport, to appear in court on October 13 to face charges of theft of $300,000 and intimidation of witnesses for a grand jury investigating him. D'Artois's attorneys told the judge their client, who was suffering from heart disease, was too ill to appear in court.[10]

The slide in D'Artois's fortunes continued in April 1977. He was arrested a second time in the Leslie murder. Barricaded in his home, he typed a note declaring his innocence.[11]

Later that month, 1st Judicial District Court Judge William Fleniken ordered him to stand trial for felony theft of $30,000 in municipal funds which D'Artois said was paid to informants. His attorneys questioned how he could stand trial in light of his deteriorating heart condition to which Fleniken instructed prosecutors to have doctors and medical equipment in place during the trial which had been postponed several times already.[12]

D'Artois died during heart surgery ten months later in San Antonio. The allegations against him, including any part he may have played in Leslie's murder, were never resolved.[13]

That was not the end of the story, however. An associate of D'Artois, a man named Rusty Griffith, was eventually identified as the trigger man, the man who killed Leslie. But before he could face trial, he was himself assassinated on October 15 or 16, three months and a week after Leslie was murdered. He was apparently lured to the Three Rivers Wildlife Management Area in Concordia Parish. As he stood next to a car unknowingly talking to his killers, he peered into the back seat through an open window. He was hit in the face by a blast from a 12-gauge shotgun fired first from only three feet away and a second from about eight feet away.[14]

Shreveport political consultant Elliott Stonecipher called D'Artois "the most powerful ever public official [in Shreveport] ... who dragged the citizenry through the deep ditch of a corruption scandal which forever stained our city." He wrote that after Leslie twice refused the city check from D'Artois and threatened to go public, D'Artois "went to work looking for someone to kill him." He said D'Artois solicited the hit from Shreveport police officers, a city department head and at least one "professional" killer "well-known to law enforcement."[15]

## Chapter 39: George D'Artois: City of Shreveport

In the spring of 1976, months before the Leslie murder, Shreveport Police Chief T.P. Kelley and Captain Sam Burns approached *The Shreveport Times*, at the time still privately-owned by the Ewing family, on a furtive mission to get the newspaper to investigate public corruption which was spreading like a cancer under D'Artois, Stonecipher wrote, adding that both the informal Dixie Mafia and the real Mafia operated with impunity in Shreveport. The two law enforcement officers shared the belief with many others that D'Artois had too much power, that he ran both Mayor Calhoun Allen and the city itself.[16]

*The Times*, under the watchful eye of Executive Editor Raymond McDaniel, assigned a four-member "Enterprise Team" of reporters led by one of the paper's more capable reporters, Marsha Schuler. The reporters' first story broke like a bombshell over Shreveport on April 25, 1976.

"An incomparable frenzy of local and state news coverage yielded some outstanding journalism about what had happened to us," Stonecipher wrote. "Only three weeks after *The Times*' opening barrage, Caddo Parish District Attorney John Richardson handed his concurrent criminal investigation over to Louisiana Attorney General William Guste.[17]

The Caddo Parish grand jury first met on June 6. One month and three days later, Leslie was dead. Three months and one week after that, his accused killer was dead.

# 40

## John Guandolo, Keith Phillips, Ekko Barnhill

> *I fell into a burning ring of fire*
> *I went down, down, down*
> *and the flames went higher*
> *And it burns, burns, burns,*
> *the ring of fire.*
> ---Ring of Fire: composed by June Carter and Merle Kilgore

Lest one think that malfeasance, malicious arrest and prosecution and other illegal acts are restricted to local sheriffs and shady state troopers, it's important to know federal officials are not exempt from going rogue.

John Guandolo is a disgraced FBI agent who was fired after sleeping with a confidential source and then trying to keep it, well, confidential. Actually, Lori Mody, Guandolo's paramour, was the FBI's star witness in its case against then-Democratic Congressman William Jefferson.[1]

Mody was wired to secretly record conversations with Jefferson and Guandolo was her handler—in more ways than one—who drove her to her meetings with the congressman. Guandolo's expertise was in counterterrorism, which made him an odd choice to become Mody's handler.[2]

After her meetings with Jefferson, at which Mody also delivered cash to him, she and Guandolo apparently would go undercover again—literally.

His indiscretions nearly wrecked the government's case against Jefferson who was ultimately convicted. Guandolo was, of course, summarily fired from his FBI job.

It is his background in counterterrorism, coupled with his apparent obsession with Islamic terrorism, that led to Guandolo's next career move after it was determined he was not a good fit for the FBI.

He now runs an outfit called *Understand the Threat* (UTT) and travels around the country charging big bucks for law enforcement types to hear him warn of the threat of an Islamic attack looming behind every telephone pole in much the same manner as Wisconsin Sen. Joe McCarthy made his name in the 1950s by threatening to out perceived communists from the State Department, Hollywood, newspapers and any other organization that caught his eye.[3]

In February 2017, Guandolo took his presentation to Hammond, Louisiana, where he gave a closed-door presentation to prosecutors and law enforcement officials—most likely consisting of deputies from Gov. John Bel Edwards' brother, Sheriff Daniel Edwards.[4]

## UTT 3-Day Law Enforcement Program
## FEB 21-22 in Louisiana

UTT will conduct its 3-Day "Understanding and Investigating the Jihadi Threat" in Hammond, Louisiana February 21-22. There is no cost for attendees. Only law enforcement officers, prosecutors, analysts, and related personnel permitted. National Guard and first responders welcome!

For more information and to register email us at Register@UnderstandingtheThreat.com

That Guandolo is still able to train law enforcement following his disgraced firing by the FBI should be a red flag for all law enforcement agencies. Nevertheless, his relentless pursuit of jihadists continues unabated.

From Hammond, he moved on to the historic Hotel Bentley in Alexandria, according to an advertisement on the Louisiana Tactical Police Officers' Association's (LTPOA) Web page.

## Chapter 40: John Guandolo, Keith Phillips, Ekko Barnhill

The advertisement said the three-day event "will blend overt anti-Muslim bigotry with tactics on investigating the alleged jihadi and Muslim Brotherhood threat in Louisiana.[5]

Some of the scheduled highlights included:

- Going over scenarios on how local law enforcement can "identify and pursue" so-called jihadis' (sic) in local jurisdictions (you'd think whoever wrote this would learn to spell jihadist);
- Cover "training scenarios" on how to "investigate known Muslim Brotherhood entities in their areas;"
- Breaking off into "Investigative Teams" and running through "a number of training scenarios, discussions, and exercises" on how to "investigate known Muslim Brotherhood entities in their areas;"
- "Instruction on doctrinal Sharia (Islamic Law)" and "how jihadis (sic) use Sharia in furtherance of their operations;
- Run "through the process of building affidavits, discuss how to educate local city/district attorneys on this threat, and will be given resources to take with them to further their education."[6]

While he goes all over the country spreading his message, he has been shut down in a few of his appearances.

The Rapides Parish event was to be the third UTT training seminar held in Louisiana in the span of only a few months. In September 2016, it was the St. Charles Parish Sheriff hosting the event followed by similar seminars hosted by the Tangipahoa Parish District Attorney in Hammond and the Rapides DA in Alexandria.[7]

The question is if the sessions are being held because Louisiana is a hotspot for Islamic terrorist activity or whether Louisiana officials are just saps for giving taxpayer money to a fast-talking fear monger and disgraced former member of the law enforcement community selling his message of fear to…the law enforcement community.

> *I know a thing or two,*
> *I learned from you*
> *I really learned a lot, really learned a lot*
> *Love is like a flame, it burns you when it's hot*
>
> ---*Love Hurts*: composed by Felice and Boudleaux Bryant

Former FBI agent John Guandolo's sexual overdrive almost torpedoed the government's 2009 case against former U.S. Rep. William Jefferson of New Orleans by sleeping with the confidential informant he was assigned to handle but it wasn't a precedent.

A decade earlier, Dallas EPA investigator Keith Phillips and Louisiana FBI agent Ekko Barnhill kept a bogus investigation and prosecution of a Louisiana businessman going for five years so that they could satisfy their mutual sexual urges.

And all it cost the federal government was $1.7 million to settle the lawsuit brought by Opelousas used oil processing plant manager Hubert Vidrine.[8]

Phillips received an unusually light sentence of five months in federal detention, another five months of home confinement and ordered to undergo two years of supervised release and to pay $8,000 in fines. Barnhill, for her part, is no longer with the FBI and now helps run a family farm in Arkansas.[9]

There are scores of low-income inmates who couldn't afford adequate legal representation who are serving far longer stretches in the Louisiana State Penitentiary at Angola for possession of a few ounces of pot. And they didn't subject anyone to malicious investigation, indictment, prosecution and arrest the way Phillips and Barnhill did—just so Phillips could make regular trips from Dallas to Lafayette to continue his extra-marital affair with Barnhill.

U.S. District Judge Richard Haik cited Phillips' military service and 20 years as a civil servant as his reason for not imposing a longer sentence. Haik retired in 2016 just in time to help serve as a defense attorney for family member and Iberia Parish Sheriff Louis Ackal who was indicted for violating prisoners' civil rights.

## Chapter 40: John Guandolo, Keith Phillips, Ekko Barnhill

Leslie Minora, writing for the *Dallas Observer* in 2011, wrote that Barnhill testified in Vidrine's civil lawsuit in federal court that she and Phillips, who was married, began a sexual relationship while assigned to the case. The affair, which lasted from 1996 until early 2001, resulted in repeated trips to Lafayette by Phillips under the auspices of continuing his investigation, thereby providing the opportunity for their affaire de coeur to continue unabated.[10]

It all began innocently enough as an investigation into waste storage methods at the refinery and plant manager Hubert Vidrine, Minora wrote. But over time, Phillips and Barnhill began their secret affair as they worked together on the case. In order to extend the relationship, Phillip began to string together a series of lies, half-truths, false findings, twisted facts, and omissions, according to Louisiana Judge Rebecca Doherty, who presided over Vidrine's civil trial against the EPA.[11]

> *I'd lie for you and that's the truth*
> *Do anything you asked me to*
> *I'd even sell my soul for you*
> *I'd do it all for you*
>
> ---*I'd Lie for You*: composed by Diane Warren

Judge Doherty said in her decision:
"The evidence strongly indicated Agent Phillips deliberately used his investigation and prosecution of Hubert Vidrine to foster, further, facilitate and cloak his extra-marital affair with Agent Barnhill, and perhaps, to exert improper influence over the manner in which she investigated and reported upon this case."

She ruled that in the course of Phillips's investigation, "He reported a series of twisted facts and false findings, which eventually resulted in Vidrine's indictment. He was arrested, locked up, and released on bond in 1999 only to have the charges voluntarily dismissed by the government four years later." Judge Doherty wrote in her decision that if the investigators had delivered thorough and truthful findings, "Hubert Vidrine would not have been indicted."

During the investigation and prosecution, Barnhill, who was single, lived in South Louisiana, the judge noted. "Phillips, who was married, lived in Dallas with his wife. Prior to and at trial, plaintiffs' counsel consistently argued Agent Phillips used the Vidrine investigation as a cover, excuse and opportunity to facilitate his illicit affair with Agent Barnhill and to hide the affair from his wife. Plaintiffs consistently argued Keith Phillips manufactured a case, both in law and fact, against Hubert Vidrine, and carefully fed the (Assistant US Attorney) and his supervisors only the information which would further that end and perpetuate the case, all to promote access to Agent Barnhill and perpetuate and conceal their illicit affair. Regrettably, the Court agrees with plaintiffs: this inappropriate and unprofessional behavior likely was, at least in part (if not in whole) a motivation for Agent Phillips' continued pursuit of Hubert Vidrine, without probable cause, and certainly with a complete and total reckless disregard of Hubert Vidrine's rights."[12]

# 41
## Lafayette City Marshal Brian Pope

*[Lamar White is a tenacious political watchdog who covers Louisiana politics in his Web blog, Bayou Brief. A disappearing breed, he is an investigative reporter who has broken several major stories about elected and appointed officials in the Bayou State. The following story about Brian Pope, the city marshal of Lafayette, Louisiana, was first published on his blog on January 31, 2018. Pope in addition to his legal problems, hired Clay Higgins after Higgins was fired by St. Landry Parish Sheriff Bobby Guidroz and just before his successful campaign for Congress. White has graciously allowed his story to be reprinted in this book in its entirety.]*

On the morning of Dec. 16, 2017, the highest-paid elected official in Acadiana bundled up in a gray sweater and a pair of black gloves. It was 50 degrees, but in Louisiana, especially when it is damp outside, 50 can sometimes feel like it's freezing. Brian Pope, the city marshal of Lafayette, needed warm clothes, because on that Saturday, he would be working outdoors, picking up trash and litter along the side of the road.

This was not a selfless act of public service or a staged photo-op for a political campaign, though the news cameras were definitely there.

Brian Pope was being punished.

He makes nearly $100,000 a year more than the governor by pocketing fees to which, according to the state attorney general's office, he is not legally entitled.

He was sentenced to house arrest and forced to spend six figures for violating public records laws.

He was the target of a recall petition that received 3,000 more people who signed a petition to remove him from office than the number who voted for him in the first place. Yet, because of laws designed to protect the currency and power of incumbency, it still wasn't enough to trigger a recall election.

The day after the recall failed, he had the co-chairman of the effort arrested for writing hot checks, worth less than $200 total, checks written more than twenty years before.

Moreover, according to multiple sources, there is compelling circumstantial evidence that he was behind the recent arrests of a former police officer and his wife, an attorney who had, only days prior, filed a public records request with his office.

Now, he is facing seven felony counts, including two for perjury and five for malfeasance in office; the case is scheduled to go to trial in late February.

In a state that has always suffered from a surplus of corrupt politicians, the story of Brian Pope stands out as extraordinarily shameless and, at times, both comically and dangerously inept.

Sure, other politicians have been more corrupt. After all, former New Orleans mayor Ray Nagin is currently sitting in a jail cell in Oakdale, at the same federal prison once home to former governor Edwin Edwards and, until recently, former congressman William Jefferson.

But Brian Pope is somehow more brazen and yet not nearly as sophisticated.

Chances are that if you're not from Acadiana, you've probably never heard of him, and if you are from Acadiana, you're probably tired of hearing about him.

During the past two weeks, *The Bayou Brief* spoke extensively with those who know the story best, some of whom requested anonymity for fear of retaliation. We attempted to reach out to Pope through his office and have yet to receive a response. When we followed him on social media, on which he is active daily, he blocked our accounts within minutes.

My colleagues and friends in the Acadiana media were not surprised. For several years, I was a regular freelance writer and contributor at *The Independent*, Lafayette's late, great alt-monthly news publication, and for Pope, that is where the story begins.

On (its) website, under a page titled "News & Events," Brian Pope's office asserts it is "(c)ommitted to creating a culture of service, diversity and transparency."

## Chapter 41: Lafayette City Marshal Brian Pope

There are a grand total of three stories on the page: A reminder about a crime prevention fair, a notification about a public hearing, and a photo of Clay Higgins wearing the uniform of a deputy city marshal, above the caption, "Lafayette City Marshal (sic) would like to present our newest Reserve Deputy Clay Higgins in his Official Uniform."

It's objectively weird.

Pope's decision to honor Higgins with a ceremonial title allowed the so-called "Cajun John Wayne," who had resigned from the St. Landry Sheriff's Office in a swirl of controversy, the ability to campaign for U.S. Congress while still wearing the uniform of a law enforcement officer, even if it was really just a costume. (In 2015, Pope gave Shaquille O'Neal the same title, which Shaq had already received years before, under the previous city marshal).

The page, which promises a "culture" of "transparency," is a perfect metaphor for what has plagued Pope: There's only one actual "news" story- an announcement that his office had apparently used its resources to bolster a political candidate.

Oh, and fittingly, it hasn't been updated in nearly two years.

Indeed, Pope's use of his office's resources to help a friend's campaign is the exact reason he is staring at seven felony indictments right now.

On Oct. 7, 2015 and in the middle of a heated race for Lafayette Parish sheriff, Brian Pope held a bizarre press conference at the city marshal's office, in which he accused candidate Mark Garber, a Lafayette lawyer, "of inviting undocumented immigrants into the United States to file workman's compensation claims without fear of deportation," according to Christian Mader of *The Independent*.

Garber, who eventually won the race, had committed the unpardonable sin of appearing in an interview on Honduran television two years prior, during which he spoke about the American values of due process and *habeas corpus* and advised immigrants to seek legal counsel if they suffer a workplace injury. It was imminently reasonable and legally sound analysis and advice, a defense of the rule of law, but to Pope, it was a nefarious conspiracy.

His press conference seemed less like official government business and much more like a campaign stunt designed to benefit the other candidate in the race, Pope's friend and Scott, Louisiana, police chief Chad Leger, and the team at *The Independent* immediately suspected collusion between Leger's campaign and Pope's public office. The very next day, they filed a public records request seeking any and all e-mail correspondence between the two.

A week later, Pope's lawyer, Charles K. Middleton, denied the request in a rambling and unwittingly incriminating letter, asserting, among other things, that the city marshal could not search through his own e-mails because he was, ironically enough, on vacation in Mexico, that the only responsive e-mail Pope had sent was a media advisory, and that any other e-mails on the subject were "private."

But most troublingly, Middleton, an attorney who specializes in DUI cases (and who was indicted last year for lying to a grand jury about a motion he filed to unseal Garber's divorce settlement), argued, as a "theoretical point," that even if there were additional records, Pope would not have to release them because Garber, in speaking about legal rights to a Honduras television news program, had potentially committed a federal crime.

# Chapter 41: Lafayette City Marshal Brian Pope

FOR IMMEDIATE RELEASE

October 7, 2015
10:30 AM

FOR MORE INFORMATION CONTACT

Brian Pope, Lafayette City Marshal
(337) 291-8723
bpope@lafayettela.gov

**Sheriff Candidate Mark Garber Encouraged Illegal Immigrants to Come to Louisiana.**

*Lafayette City Marshal Brian Pope Calls on Sheriff Candidate Mark Garber to Repudiate His 'Irresponsible' Statements, Made on Television in Honduras.*

Lafayette City Marshal Brian Pope is calling on Sheriff Candidate Mark Garber to repudiate his statements, made in a 2013 interview on Honduras HCH Television, in which Garber encourages illegal immigrants to come to Louisiana, reassuring them that if they are hurt, they can file worker's compensation claims with the help of a "qualified attorney", "without fear of being deported."

Garber is a Worker's Compensation Attorney whose two-man firm specializes in serving Spanish speaking clients.

Pope is concerned about the increasing difficulty of dealing with illegal immigrants who commit crimes in Lafayette Parish, and current Sheriff Department policies that prevent making arrests.

In 2013, Garber traveled to Honduras to "get the word out" that illegals can safely come to Louisiana, file claims against local businesses for work injuries, and not worry about being deported.

> "Making your living as a Workmen's Compensation lawyer who specializes in Spanish speaking clients is one thing, but to actually travel to Central America and do a television interview to "get the word out" that illegal immigrants can come to Louisiana, and file worker's compensation claims without fear of being deported is entirely another. It's irresponsible" said Lafayette City Marshal Brian Pope.
>
> "Imagine. A candidate for Sheriff of Lafayette Parish, actually filing worker's compensation claims for illegal immigrants, while protecting them from deportation. That's just shocking." Pope said. "Flying to Honduras to drum up business? Disgusting." Pope continued.
>
> "We already have a serious challenge in that the current Sheriff refuses to let the Marshal's office arrest illegal immigrants accused of misdemeanor crimes or to track them. We have over 1,000 open warrants and pending charges that we are prevented from addressing.

# Louisiana's Rogue Sheriffs

Mr. Pope is presently out of the country on a previously scheduled family trip and will be back a week from next Monday and at that time he will search his computer for these press conference replies and if they are indeed responsive he will turn them over immediately. He is the custodian of the Marshal's Office documents as is customary with status of Marshal.

Lastly, as a theoretical point in connection with Attorney General Opinion 13-0141, if my client had any emails whether sent or received in connection with containing the key phrases, particularly, "Garber, Neustrom, immigration, workers compensation, or illegal alien, " since September 1, 2015, it is our position they would be exempt from production as evidencing the promotion and condoning of criminal actions of "illegal status" foreigners' presence and residence in our parish. No doubt it is illegal activity by the promoters or condoners of such illegal activity while being a parish law enforcement official or member of the Louisiana Bar Association. It's obvious that it's illegal for a sheriff, police chief, or marshal to condone and/or promote any illegal activity and therefore, such illegal acts of promoting and condoning illegal foreigners to reside in Lafayette Parish illegally or fail to detain illegal foreigners caught by law enforcement, would more than likely become the subject of a criminal investigation by the Federal Government. As for lawyers, if we either tacitly or expressly promote illegal activity i.e. promoting illegal foreigners presence in our parish, state or country "who might get hurt on the job here to file workers compensation claims and not be deported here in Lafayette" would certainly sooner or later lead to an investigation by The Office of Disciplinary Counsel for the Louisiana State Bar Association and a criminal investigation by the local arm of the Federal Government, whether, Attorney General, Immigration Department or ICE.

The Marshal's Office wishes to cooperate with any reasonable and discoverable records requests made on it by the press and to maintain transparency and fair dealings with the press and public. I'll be happy to visit with you about these issues. I will be out of town starting next Thursday morning and back the following Monday afternoon for these purposes.

## Chapter 41: Lafayette City Marshal Brian Pope

Apparently, Pope and his lawyer believed it was a crime for someone to speak through a Spanish translator about the U.S. Constitution.

The city marshal's office has one primary responsibility: They are tasked, by law, with executing orders and warrants issued by the Lafayette city court. During his press conference, Pope claimed that there were at least 661 illegal immigrants in Lafayette with outstanding warrants. "But it was 'fake news,'" wrote Gary McGoffin, who represented *The Independent*. "Under oath... in a video trial deposition, (Pope) could not identify a single warrant for a single illegal alien, much less 661 — regardless of whether they were Hispanic/Spanish, white, black, Asian, Indian or 'other.'"

Armed with Pope's phony numbers, Louisiana attorney general Jeff Landry pilloried Lafayette as a "sanctuary city" and lobbied like-minded state legislators to pass a bill that would have stripped funding from the city. The legislation failed. Soon thereafter, Lafayette was quietly removed from an unofficial list of sanctuary cities in a way that allowed Landry to save face and, perhaps ironically, was due almost entirely to the advocacy of their newly-elected sheriff, Mark Garber.

*The Independent* decided to file suit against Brian Pope, and eventually, though not without some wild twists and turns, they won one of the biggest public records cases in state history and, only weeks before they closed their doors, the most coveted award from the Louisiana Press Association.

Three years after *The Independent* filed its first record request, their case against Pope now appears stronger than ever, and they have not relented, despite the fact that they are no longer in business.

In late December of last year, during a probation revocation hearing, the judge assigned to the case, Jules Edwards, told Pope, "Much of your conduct is mystifying." The whole thing, the judge lamented, was a "very tortured experience."

Brian Pope, the judge seemed to be implying, was his own worst enemy. It was solid advice, and it's astonishing that the city marshal hasn't done the sensible and dignified thing and simply resigned from office. Instead, he appears to have doubled-down on his most destructive impulses: Using his public office to exact personal revenge against his political opponents.

If he had recognized the embarrassment he was causing his community, Aimee Robinson would have never organized a recall campaign against him. All told, more than 21,000 Lafayette voters signed up to recall Pope, Robinson told *The Bayou Brief,* and although Pope, in 2014, had received slightly more than 18,000 votes in his first and only election, Robinson was still nearly 4,000 signatures shy of triggering a recall election.

"We struggled to get African-Americans to sign on," Robinson said, "but not because they didn't support what we were doing." Robinson, who is white, was repeatedly warned that Pope, as city marshal, could potentially use the petition as a weapon against his opponents.

For those who recognize the racial inequities in the American judicial system and are statistically more likely to be targeted by law enforcement, it is imminently sensible to avoid affixing your name to a petition against the man responsible for executing arrest warrants, because that petition could easily be turned into a database and every name on it could become a person of interest.

"On the same day a drive to recall Lafayette City Marshal Brian Pope ended unsuccessfully, the co-chairman of the movement was arrested by the City Marshal's Office on twenty-year-old misdemeanor charges," *The Daily Advertiser* reported last month. "Steven Britt Wilkerson of Lafayette was arrested Monday on a 1997 Lafayette City Court warrant for four counts of issuing worthless checks, according to a city court administrator."

There is no way to actually prosecute Wilkerson for allegedly writing bad checks as a college student; in his case, the statute of limitations expired 18 years ago. This was political retribution, plain and simple, and it is stifling and dangerous and an unapologetically gleeful abuse of power. "Warrants of arrest do not expire until they are executed," Pope told *The Daily Advertiser*.

Immediately after Wilkerson's arrest, Robinson shredded the one and only copy of the recall petition. There were only two names that were officially associated with the effort to oust Brian Pope, Aimee Robinson and Steven Wilkerson, and one of them had just been arrested on specious charges. If Pope were in possession of a list of all 21,000 of his opponents,

## Chapter 41: Lafayette City Marshal Brian Pope

she realized, then he could do exactly what she had been warned he would do: Weaponize the recall petition against its signatories.

Last week, Pope's lawyer, Brett Grayson, requested subpoenas against Robinson and Wilkerson in order to compel the production of the entire original petition. Grayson argued he needed the full petition to facilitate jury selection, which is absurd considering that he could easily ask potential jurors, "Have you ever signed a recall petition against any politician?"

Robinson's instincts were right. "It's unfortunate because I have destroyed those (documents)," she said at the time.

Some argue that the recall petition, although it was ultimately unsuccessful and entirely grassroots (raising a total of $600 in donations), was still a public record, and that its destruction may be a civil violation. I doubt a court would ever take up that case.

But, for many, it would be poetic justice if the closing chapters of the saga of Brian Pope included a few felony convictions and the illegal but noble destruction of a public record that he desperately wanted.

# 42

## Jason Kinch, Corey Jackson: Lafayette Parish

"Need to frame someone in Louisiana and send them away to prison for a long time?" asked *Waste and Corruption News*, an internet blog that tracks corruption at all levels nationally. "For the bargain price of $100,000, you can get not just a Louisiana State Trooper but a Sheriff's Deputy as well and they will plant whatever evidence you want to help frame someone."[1]

When Bryan Knight was arrested for narcotics possession in Lafayette by the Lafayette Metro Narcotics Task Force in June 2014, it set off a series of events that culminated in not only the exoneration of Bryan Knight, but the arrest of Knight's brother, an employee of Knight Oil Tools, a Lafayette Parish sheriff's deputy and a Louisiana state trooper on racketeering charges.

It wasn't until nine months later, in March 2015, that investigators confirmed that the magnetic cases recovered from the undercarriage of Bryan Knight's car were purchased by Knight Oil Tools employee Russell Manual, who answered directly to Bryan Knight's brother, company CEO Mark Knight.

Through comparisons of the unique characteristics of the cases recovered at the time of Bryan Knight's arrest (cases which are made specifically to contain GPS tracking devices), investigators were able to ascertain that they were identical to those purchased by Knight Oil Tools.[2]

Bryan Knight was arrested on June 4, 2014, after Lafayette Metro Narcotics Task Force agents, acting on an anonymous tip, found the containers which held illegal narcotics.

The comparison of the containers, along with other e-mails and text messages, to and from Russell Manual's cell phone revealed that Manual was a participant in a scheme to plant drugs on Bryan Knight's vehicle and then call law enforcement to set up the arrest of Bryan Knight. Investigators further learned that two law enforcement officers were brought into the plot to arrange Bryan Knight's unlawful arrest.[3]

According to court documents, two law enforcement officers were consulted to arrange for the stop and arrest of Bryan Knight: Jason Kinch, a Lafayette Parish Sheriff's Deputy, and Corey Jackson, a Louisiana State Trooper.

Kinch and Jackson were consulted to provide specific information intended to enhance the possibilities of Bryan Knight's unlawful arrest. Through statements from Russell Manual, documents say Mark Knight did pay or arrange payment in excess of $100,000 in cash and gifts directly or indirectly to Kinch, Jackson and Manual in exchange for committing conspiracy.[4]

Kinch was taken into custody and booked into the Lafayette Parish Correctional Center. He was placed on administrative leave without pay pending an Internal Affairs investigation.

Jackson was subsequently placed under arrest by Troopers at Troop I Headquarters in Lafayette on April 11, 2015. He was transported to the Lafayette Parish Correctional Center where he was booked on the arrest warrant for racketeering.

Bond for each was set at $100,000 by the 15th Judicial District Court.

Warrants were issued for the arrest of Mark Knight on the charge of racketeering and for Russell Manual on the charges of Criminal Conspiracy, Possession of Cocaine, Possession of Lortab, Possession of Methadone, Extortion and Intimidating a Witness.[5]

"We don't know his whereabouts," Lafayette Parish Sheriff Office Chief Deputy Maj. Art LeBreton told the *Lafayette Advertiser* on April 4 when asked about Mark Knight, who was said to have resigned from his position as CEO and president of Knight Oil Tools in January, although he remains chairman of the company's board of directors. All charges against Bryan Knight were dropped.[6]

By April 14, however, Mark Knight had turned himself in. It was not yet immediately known why Mark Knight wanted to frame his brother, but LeBreton told the *Acadiana Advocate* the motive was financial.

"Many of the employees are shocked, disappointed," LeBreton said. "It's a poor reflection on law enforcement. We take an oath to uphold the law and enforce the constitution of the state and (of) the United States of

## Chapter 42: Jason Kinch, Corey Jackson: Lafayette Parish

America, and when we have an employee who violates that oath as well as the public trust, we act swiftly to remove that employee from a position of authority over our citizens who we are here to serve.[7]

Shock and disappointment aside, in less than two years, a veteran Lafayette Parish Sheriff's deputy who also was a candidate for sheriff in 1999, was arrested in February 2016, accused of paying an employee of the district attorney's office to dismiss DWI charges against defendants.

Ken Franques, Sr., who worked as the public spokesman for former Sheriff Donald Breaux, was a patrol officer for the Maurice Police Department at the time of his arrest. He was one of two persons who were arrested for representing those charged with driving while intoxicated even though neither was an attorney. The two were accused of bribing employees of the district attorney's office with cash and other valuable items in exchange for favorable sentences.[8]

It would, however, take a lawsuit against the Lafayette Parish Sheriff's Office that resulted in a six-figure settlement to uncover a culture of corruption at the Lafayette Parish Correctional Center in May 2013.

In order to reach the $175,000 settlement, former Lieutenant Matthew Thomassee was required to drop his lawsuit, withdraw his complaint filed with the Louisiana Board of Ethics and resign from his job, court documents show. Also included in the agreement was an all-important non-disclosure clause and a stipulation stating the settlement payment was not an admission of guilt on the part of the sheriff's office.[9]

Thomassee's problems started in 2004 or 2005. In his 15th year with the agency, he said he first witnessed a document being falsified by the jail's top ranking official, Warden Rob Reardon. It took about three years before Thomassee, on January 28, 2008, filed an employee misconduct report with Internal Affairs. The issue was only raised then because two deputies at the jail were reprimanded for the same violation, according to Lonnie Murphy, another former correctional center deputy. Thomassee's report, on the other hand, warranted no investigation by Internal Affairs.[10]

Murphy said the falsification of documents was a common practice at the correctional center and that no documents were exempt from the practice but that most times it was done on inmate behavior sheets and housing unit logs, both of which are required for the jail to achieve accreditations from accreditation agencies such as the Commission on

Accreditation for Law Enforcement Agencies and the American Corrections Association (ACA).[11]

While the Louisiana Department of Corrections is quick to issue glowing press releases whenever one of its institutions receives accreditation by ACA, there are strong indications that the prestige of ACA's seal of approval is considerably overblown. ACA, for example is a private organization made up almost entirely of current and former corrections officials and its standards are established with no governmental oversight. Even more significant, according to *Prison Legal News*, an online news service that describes itself as "dedicated to protecting human rights," ACA basically sells its accreditation by charging fees ranging from $8,000 to about $20,000. The amount of the fees depends on the number of days and auditors involved and the number of facilities up for accreditation. In 2011, for example, the $4.5 million it received in accreditation fees represented nearly half its total revenue for the year.

ACA does not offer oversight or ongoing monitoring of correctional facilities, relying instead on policies that comply with the organization's self-promulgated standards at the time of accreditation.[12]

Such lax standards contributed to abuses at the Lafayette Parish Correctional Center which in turn, led to Thomassee's whistleblowing, termination and the ultimate settlement of his litigation against the Lafayette Parish Sheriff's Office.

"One of the criteria for accreditation requires the health authority being on-site on a weekly basis, and that requires signed documentation," Murphy said. In reality, he said, the health authority was at the facility only once a month, but all the documentation showed otherwise. The physician contracted by the Lafayette Parish Sheriff's Office was also the head of the residency program at University Medical Center. So, even though submitted documents showed he was on-site once a week, a more accurate figure would be once a month. Instead, the physician was sending over his medical residents for the weekly visits.[13]

"They weren't the only deputies involved either," Murphy said. Lieutenants would get deputies to sign off on documents. They would do so without even really looking at what they were signing, Murphy said. "To the deputies, they were just following orders, but by signing their names

## Chapter 42: Jason Kinch, Corey Jackson: Lafayette Parish

they too were falsifying documents. For the lieutenants, it was just easier to keep on falsifying instead of actually fixing the problem."[14]

Thomassee was told to just let sleeping dogs lie. But Murphy, in the midst of the investigation, said he was cleaning out a desk and discovered a template for the expeditious falsification of inmate behavior sheets. He said the names of two sergeants who Murphy said were two of the biggest abusers of the document falsification were written on a folder containing the stack of templates.[15]

"Obviously I'd found a packet of quick forgery templates, with blank lines left for the date, time and a spot for writing in a brief sentence," Murphy said. "I found a whole stack of them, and this was while the IA investigation is going on, so I handed it over to (jail commander) Captain (Mike) Roulas, and all he said was, 'What do you want me to do with this?'"[16]

# 43
## Marlin Defillo: NOPD

Marlon Defillo served as Deputy Chief of New Orleans Police and was never a sheriff or deputy sheriff. He is included in this book as the result of a report issued by Louisiana State Police on Defillo's failure to properly investigate the probable fatal shooting of a New Orleans man by New Orleans police following Hurricane Katrina. The charred body of the man and burned-out car in which he was last seen were found days later behind a levee near the spot where he disappeared—a school being used as a staging area by police.[1]

The persistence of the vehicle's owner in locating his car—and the victim—and Defillo's apparent reluctance to pursue the matter resulted in the 33-page report on June 2, 2011, nearly six years following Katrina. Defillo retired soon after the report was issued.[2]

The series of events began in the days immediately following Katrina's landfall on Aug. 29, 2005. A man named William Tanner appeared at NOPD's Public Integrity Bureau (PIB) to file a complaint about the seizure of his personal vehicle. He told police he was driving in the Algiers area when he was flagged down by a man who was assisting a second person who appeared to be injured. The injured person was later identified as Henry Glover. [Defillo would later testify under oath that he was told by a federal agent in June 2008 that witnesses said Glover had been shot by police and that his body, along with the car in which he was riding, had been set fire.]

Tanner said he helped load Glover into his vehicle and that the two men took him to Habans School where he had earlier seen an ambulance and assumed Glover could receive medical care there. Instead, he was met at the school by a group of officers he said appeared to be SWAT members who pointed an assortment of weapons at him and ordered the men away from the vehicle and Glover. Tanner said the officers handcuffed them, placed them on their knees and repeatedly beat them. "At one point the officers were going to beat them again but were stopped by a white female officer who instructed the officers to stop," the report said. She instructed the officers to either take the two to jail or let them go, it said. "At this time, one of the officers retrieved some flares from a building, got inside Tanner's vehicle, and drove away with the injured person still inside the vehicle," the LSP report said.

Tanner, who said the injured person was still alive when he was driven away, said that sometime later he was notified that his burned vehicle had been located between the Mississippi River and a levee. A body, later identified as that of Glover, was inside the car and also burned.

State Police investigators, in interviewing several NOPD officers, were able to ascertain that Defillo made little effort to resolve the reports that Glover had been shot by an officer or that police had burned his body and Tanner's vehicle.

LSP investigators found that Defillo did assign a subordinate to investigate the reports that Glover had been shot and burned by police but did little to follow up with the investigating officer. The State Police report said Rule Four of NOPD policy says:

- Each employee, because of his grade and assignment, is required to perform certain duties and assume certain responsibilities.
- An employee's failure to properly function in either o(r) both of these areas constitutes a neglect of duty.
- An employee with supervisory responsibilities shall be in neglect of duty whenever he fails to properly supervise subordinates.

"Therefore, the allegation of a violation of Rule Four, Performance of Duty, paragraph four, Neglect of Duty on the part of Deputy Chief Defillo is sustained; the allegation is supported by sufficient evidence," the report said.[3]

One of members of the LSP team conducting the investigation said he was called by then-New Orleans Mayor Mitch Landrieu shortly before

## Chapter 43: Marlin Defillo: NOPD

the report was to be released. Landrieu asked how severe the report would be and was told it would be "pretty bad."

"Well, I can't fire him," he said of Defillo.

Landrieu was told the report made no such recommendations, but that it pulled no punches in revealing its findings.

Defillo's father had worked as a driver for Landrieu's father Moon Landrieu when the elder Landrieu was mayor and the current mayor apparently felt politically beholden to the officer. "He's a good officer. He has a family. I can't fire him," he repeated.[4]

Months following his retirement, it was revealed that he had obtained a badge from the New Orleans constable's office and was running a private company that provided coordination of security work and traffic control for the city's movie, film and television production industry. He employed off-duty Orleans Parish sheriff's deputies and officers overseen by the Levee Board and Dock Board because NOPD officers are prohibited from working for private security companies.[5]

# 44

## Lloyd Grafton: An Expert's Perspective

One of the major problems encountered by sheriffs' departments, not only in rural counties and parishes, but large, metropolitan areas as well, is a woeful lack of training for deputies. Often this lack of proper training can produce mixed results that can range from a bumbling Barney Fife-type overreaction to a deadly encounter in situations that could have, should have produced far more favorable results with proper training. And neither are these deficiencies limited to sheriffs' departments.

W. Lloyd Grafton has seen them all. For 23 years, he taught Criminal Justice Administration for four universities and a community policing institute and worked as a contract investigator from 1994 to 2004. In 2013, he was appointed to a six-year term on the Louisiana State Police Commission and he has served as an expert witness in more than 200 cases involving negligent acts, wrongful deaths and excessive force by law enforcement officers.

More than a hired gun for plaintiff attorneys, however, he also spent 21 years as a special agent for the Justice Department's U.S. Bureau of Narcotics and Dangerous Drugs and with the U.S. Treasury as a special agent for the Bureau of Alcohol, Tobacco and Firearms. His specialty was undercover work where not only his success, but his very life depended upon gaining the trust of those he was trying to build a case on.

He once infiltrated the Ku Klux Klan in Baton Rouge. Aware there was a power struggle between the pro-David Duke faction and the anti-Dukes, he ingratiated himself with Duke's rival in nearby Denham Springs, the target of the ATF's investigation and managed to get a firearms conviction against the man. In Tulsa, Oklahoma, he hired himself out as a hit man to an unlicensed abortionist who wanted to kill his partner whom he thought was stealing from him. He even worked with a fellow ATF agent in New Orleans to put down a planned military coup by mercenaries who wanted to turn the Caribbean island nation of Domincia into a criminal's haven.[1]

But the biggest accomplishment of his career was when he posed as a gun dealer and sold a high-powered rifle to a killer hired to assassinate U.S. Senator Howard Baker. The thwarting of the plot was never revealed because, Grafton said, "The entire thing was about a woman." Baker was spared the embarrassment public revelation of the plot would have caused.[2]

Unlike many so-called expert witnesses who manage to consistently gin out opinions that support a plaintiff attorney's position, Grafton picks and chooses his cases carefully. Lest one get the idea that he is a hired gun who routinely spews out reports critical of law enforcement, it should be noted that he often is called simply for consultation on a case. In many cases where liability was in question, he refused to become involved. His entire professional career, after all, was in law enforcement.

A recurring theme in Grafton's reports was a general failure to follow proper procedure in cases involving excessive force, failure to follow routine safety procedures, or failure to provide medical care to prisoners who were sick or injured.

Pressure Point Control Tactics (PPCT) training is mentioned in several of Grafton's reports. Each time, he stressed the lack of and the need for proper training in PPCT, especially in his investigation of events in which prisoners died following the use of force.

Here are some examples taken from the Louisiana Law Enforcement Handbook or from departmental policy and procedure manuals included in several investigative reports compiled by Grafton:

> *A police officer has a duty to perform his function with due regard for the safety of all citizens who will be affected by his actions. His authority must at all times be exercised in a reasonable fashion, and he must act as a reasonable, prudent man under circumstances. But unreasonable or excessive force is a breach of an officer's duty.[3]*
>
> *The decision to use force must be based on reason and necessity, not on emotion. The lawful use of force in any degree must be based on a reasonable judgment that force*

## Chapter 44: Lloyd Grafton: An Expert's Perspective

*is necessary under the circumstances. Therefore, a deputy must always prevent anger from affecting his decision to use force.*[4]

*Force should be used only when it is reasonable to believe that it is immediately necessary. There must be an immediate and reasonable need for the force used. When force in any degree (but particularly deadly force) is used against a suspect, the deputy's actions will be judged on a large part by whether the force was reasonably necessary at the moment of its use. Force, particularly deadly force, should not be used except as a last resort.*[5]
*The subject's injuries must be proportionate to the subject's level of resistance or threat to the officer or another.*
*Restrictions on force are consistent with Supreme Court jurisprudence.*[6]

Other than the Louisiana State Penitentiary at Angola, there is probably no worse place to be incarcerated in Louisiana than in the Orleans Parish Jail. And even that is debatable.

The subject of an extensive investigation by the Civil Rights Division of the U.S. Department of Justice, Grafton found conditions little improved when he was called to investigate the death of prisoner Kerry Washington in 2012. In his report of May 9 of that year, he wrote that "The investigation of Orleans Parish Prison is too lengthy to be addressed in this report. Many of the same conditions found in this report were present when I worked as a federal agent in New Orleans from 1974 to 1990."

It's bad enough that Washington was arrested by the Jefferson Parish Sheriff's Office on April 25 and transferred to the Orleans Parish Prison two days later but not allowed to make a telephone call to his wife to let her know he was in jail until three full days after his arrest, on April 28.

But how bad must conditions at the jail have been that when Washington was killed on the night of April 29, fellow inmates were able to easily pop open their cell doors because of faulty locks? Making matters even worse, the department was fully aware of the condition of the locks.

And how deplorable and negligent must administrative practices of the prison have been that Washington's wife was not informed of her husband's death in the prison for more than two weeks during which time she had repeatedly attempted to contact him while being told he was still an inmate at the prison?[12]

Washington initially was housed on the third floor of the prison but was moved to the second floor after injuring another inmate and being observed with a bloody mouth. He was then moved to the eighth. While on the eighth floor, he was described as becoming combative and was said to have been "rambling incoherently when questioned," Grafton wrote.

He was ordered to be placed in a five-point restraint but efforts to do so were unsuccessful other than placing him in leg shackles because of his "squirming around," according to deputies. At 1:05 a.m., two deputies observed that he was not breathing and less than an hour later, he was pronounced dead at Tulane Medical Center.

"From all of the information I have reviewed concerning this matter," wrote Grafton, "there are many unexplained issues concerning the Orleans Parish Sheriff's Department and the Orleans Parish Prison. I am of the opinion that Kerry Washington was the victim of a beating. The fact that inmates could manipulate the locking and unlocking of their cells helped create the events that cost Kerry Washington his life."[13]

Deputy Dwayne Washington said in his deposition that Kerry Washington was fighting with several inmates when deputies arrived on the third floor and Kerry Washington was handcuffed and taken to the second floor to see a nurse.

After being taken to the eighth floor where Kerry Washington struggled with Deputy Dwayne Washington, Kerry Washington was taken to the tenth floor for evaluation at which time he was ordered placed in a five-point restraint. "If the restraints are not properly applied, it can cause an oxygen deficiency to the restrained individual," wrote Grafton, adding that could explain why Washington was deprived of oxygen "for a period of time leading up to his death."

The autopsy report points out that Kerry Washington's body had lacerations, contusions, a tooth knocked out, abrasions to the neck, back, face, head, chest, lip, side of head, left shoulder, right scapula, right shoulder, his abdomen, both knees, his foot, and deep lacerations across his stomach."[14]

## Chapter 44: Lloyd Grafton: An Expert's Perspective

Moreover, the death certificate listed the cause of death as "respiratory insufficiency."

Grafton said that Washington was "severely and physically abused just shortly before his death. As far as responsibility is concerned, it makes little difference if he was beaten by inmates or deputies—he was in the custody of the Orleans Parish Sheriff's Department."

Deputies maintained that only Washington's legs were shackled. Yet Grafton said the marks and chest abrasions were "where the chest strap would be applied" with the five-point restraint and that the death certificate described the cause of his injuries as "restraint." Grafton said in his report that the physical evidence that caused Washington's death "is simply not explained by the testimony of the Orleans Parish Sheriff's employees nor anyone else involved. I reviewed no reports that would explain the injuries indicated on Kerry Washington's body," he added.[15]

"The U.S. Department of Justice, Civil Rights Division, has been involved in a long investigation known as the 'United States Civil Rights Investigation of the Orleans Parish Prison System," Grafton wrote. "A letter to Sheriff Marlin Gusman dated April 23, 2012, (just four days before Washington's arrest) listed the following findings:

> *Despite our findings and repeated attempts to encourage you to meaningfully address the numerous problems, the already troubling conditions in the Orleans Parish Prison (OPP) are deteriorating. Since we issued our findings letter on September 11, 2009, which identified serious constitutional violations, you have failed to take basic steps to correct the systemic issues that we identified. As this letter demonstrates, urgent and substantial action is required.*

That letter went on to point that:

> *A team of attorneys from the Department of Justice, Civil Rights Division, Special Litigation Section, together with expert consultants in correctional operations and mental health care, just re-inspected OPP on April 3 through (April) 5, 2012 (three weeks prior to Washington's arrest). We found alarming conditions and were distressed that the*

*problems we described in our initial findings letter persist or have worsened.*

The letter, written by Jonathan M. Smith, Chief, Special Litigation Section, consisted of 21 pages and included the following findings:

- Inadequate protection from violence and sexual assault;
- Prisoner-on-prisoner violence and sexual assault;
- Staff members failed to respond to serious violence;
- Inadequate staffing and prisoner supervision;
- Inappropriate use of tier reps;
- Failure to detect weapons;
- Inappropriate co-mingling of violent and non-violent offenders;
- Failure to prevent, detect, and correct excessive use of force and other misconduct;
- Failure to track staff misconduct in an efficient and effective manner;
- Grossly inadequate suicide prevention practices.

"Kerry Washington," Grafton wrote, "did not receive proper care nor was he protected from harm while in the custody of the Orleans Parish Sheriff's Office. The Orleans Parish Sheriff's Office did not perform up to the standards required of responsible law enforcement. In failing to do so, Kerry Washington was deprived of his constitutional rights. The loss of these protections, in my opinion, contributed to the loss of his life."[15]

# Epilogue

Even when sheriffs' departments are dealing with serious issues, humor-laced events do occur, as happened when I was managing editor of the Ruston (Louisiana) *Daily Leader* in the late 1970s not once, but twice, and which involved two separate sheriffs' offices. I was fortunate enough to have covered both events.

The first occurred when a DC-9 loaded with bales of marijuana being smuggled into the country from Colombia crashed onto a rural chicken farm just south of Farmerville in Union Parish, Louisiana. Union Parish is in the northernmost part of the state and abuts the southern border of Arkansas. The pilot of the aircraft was killed in the crash but two other Colombian smugglers wedged themselves between the bales of weed and were cushioned as the aircraft sawed off the tops of pine trees and crashed into the farm. (The owner of the farm is said to have sued over the crash because, he claimed, his chickens were traumatized by the crash and stopped laying—although it is unclear whom he would have sued if, indeed, he actually did.)

As federal, state and local law enforcement officers swarmed the area to investigate the crash and to search for the two survivors, a Union Parish sheriff's deputy, who apparently had not retained much from his high school geography class, spotted one of the smugglers. He stopped his patrol car and called the man over. "Where you from, boy?" he asked the man.

"Señor," answered the still dazed man, "I am from Colombia."

"You know John McKeithen?" the deputy asked, confusing the South American country for the northeast Louisiana Delta town of Columbia, home of the former governor.

"No…"

"Get in th' car, boy, you're under arrest. Everbody in Columbia knows John McKeithen."

And that's how one of the two suspects in the marijuana smuggling plane crash saga was apprehended. At least that's the story as told by a state trooper who was there at the time.

Not that it really mattered. The two were inexplicably made trustees by then-Sheriff Eugene Patterson and one of them walked to a pay phone and called an accomplice to pick them up and the next Patterson heard from them was when he received a thank-you note from Colombia—the country, that is. That's part of the legend that swirled around the plane crash for years and whether or not it is true, there can be little doubt that the Union Parish Sheriff's Office was ill-equipped to deal with international drug smugglers. It was way above their pay grade. One veteran of federal law enforcement officer speculated that Patterson may have received threats to his family, prompting him to allow the Colombians to walk away.

As an interesting postscript to this story, *The Shreveport Times* two days after the crash, ran a small story about two 18-wheelers that pulled into a rural airport in Arkansas. Its occupants tied up the airport manager and his wife, whose residence was at the airport, and stood watching out the window all night as if anticipating an arrival. At dawn, they gave up their vigil and left, leaving the manager and his wife still tied but otherwise unharmed.

Were they awaiting the ill-fated DC-9 that went down in Farmerville and *The Shreveport Times* just failed to connect the dots? That's something we'll never know, but it makes interesting conjecture for amateur sleuths and conspiracy theorists.

The second event, which happened in the same general time frame, evolved from a decency crusade launched by then Lincoln Parish Assistant District Attorney Joe Bleich. Bleich, deeply offended by issues of *Penthouse* and *Playboy* being sold in Ruston convenience stores (or more likely seeing an opportunity to advance his political career), began purchasing one copy of each magazine every month. He would then put on a very public display of holding a court hearing and calling in a local Baptist preacher to gaze upon the latest edition of the magazines from the witness stand and proclaim whether or not he found them to be pornographic, apparently under the premise that the good minister was eminently qualified

## Epilogue

to speak for an entire community on such matters. Once the reverend would affirm that he was offended and that he considered them to be pornographic, the presiding judge would proclaim the magazines to be obscene and order them pulled them from the stores. Of course, the procedure had to be repeated monthly with each new issue of the magazines.

But in his zealousness one month, instead of purchasing single issues, he had deputies seize the entire inventory—before he held his courtroom dog and pony show. Bleich's boss, the local district attorney, was quick to inform him that his actions constituted prior censorship, which is contrary to the First Amendment and that the publications must be returned pronto until Bleich could hold his monthly decency hearing and only then could he confiscate the magazines.

The immediate problem that arose was with one convenience store where deputies had seized ten issues of *Playboy* and *Penthouse* but had inadvertently written "100" on the receipt it gave the proprietor. So, when the magazines were returned, the store was "shorted" 90 copies, according to the receipt. The store owner knew it was just a clerical error but amused, he showed me the receipt. I couldn't resist borrowing the receipt and publishing it on the front page of the paper along with a tongue-in-cheek story about how deputies had "lost" 90 copies of the magazines.

It was all in jest, of course, but Sheriff George Simonton didn't take it that way. The best description of his reaction would be simply to say he popped a blood vessel. Red-faced and breathing fire, he entered the newspaper offices in full-blown fury and holding a crumpled-up copy of the paper in a clinched fist. The ensuing confrontation had him screaming and cursing at me at the top of his lungs. And the madder he got, the more I laughed, which only made him madder. He demanded a page-one apology but never got one.

The district attorney's office, on the other hand, never complained about the story but after that, there were no further decency hearings by the crusading Assistant DA Bleich.

# Notes

## Prologue

1. Maginnis, John, *The Last Hayride*, Gris Gris Press, 1984.
2. North Carolina Sheriffs' Association, *History of the Sheriff*, undated, https://ncsheriffs.org/about/history-of-the-sheriff
3. *Sheriff*, Wikipedia, undated, https://en.wikipedia.org/wiki/Sheriff
4. Ibid.
5. *National Sheriff's Association*, Wikipedia, undated, https://en.wikipedia.org/wiki/National_Sheriffs'_Association
6. *Sheriffs in the United States*, Wikipedia, undated, Sheriff, Wikipedia, undated, https://en.wikipedia.org/wiki/Sheriff
7. Anthony G. "Tony" Falterman, Assumption Parish Sheriff (ret.), interview, March 2019.
8. Ibid.
9. Ibid.

## Chapter 1
## The Kefauver Hearings

1. "Legendary Locals of Metairie, Louisiana" Internet Web page, http://www.websitesneworleans.com/legendarylocalsofmetairie/introductionlegendarylocalsofmetairie.html
2. Ibid.
3. Sifakis, Carl, *The Mafia Encyclopedia*, Da Capo Press, 2005.
4. "Scenes along the Gulf Coast," *Historical Text Archive* Web page, undated, https://historicaltextarchive.com/books.php?action=nextchapter&bid=72&cid=4

5. Ibid.
6. Hunt, Thomas, "Third Interim Report, Part B," American Mafia Website—*Kefauver Committee Interim Report No. 3 to the 82$^{nd}$ Congress*, United States Government Printing Office, 1951, http://www.onewal.com/kef/kef3b.html
7. Ibid.
8. Ibid.
9. Ibid.
10. Ibid.
11. Ibid.
12. Scott, Mike, "Remembering the Beverly, a mob-run playground in Jefferson Parish," New Orleans Times-Picayune, Aug. 13, 2017, http://www.nola.com/300/2017/08/remembering_the_beverly_a_mob-.html
13. Hunt, Thomas, "Third Interim Report, Part B," American Mafia Website—*Kefauver Committee Interim Report No. 3 to the 82$^{nd}$ Congress*, United States Government Printing Office, 1951, http://www.onewal.com/kef/kef3b.html
14. Ibid.
15. Ibid.
16. Ibid.
17. Ibid
18. Ibid.
19. "Brilab jury convicts Carlos Marcello and former Louisiana official," *The New York Times*, Aug. 4, 1981, http://www.nytimes.com/1981/08/04/us/brilab-jury-convicts-carlos-marcello-and-former-louisiana-official.html
20. "Carlos Marcello, 83, Reputed Crime Boss in New Orleans Area, Dies" The New York Times, March 3, 1993

# Notes

## Chapter 2
## Louisiana Sheriffs' Association

1. Louisiana Sheriffs' Association Web page, http://lsa.org/public/home.aspx
2. Louisiana Secretary of State Web page, https://coraweb.sos.la.gov/CommercialSearch/CommercialSearch.aspx
3. Louisiana Sheriffs' Association Web page, http://lsa.org/public/home.aspx
4. Ibid.
5. Business Agenda, Louisiana Sheriffs' Association 2018 Conference, Sandestin, Florida, https://www.lsa.org/LSAconference/2018LSA-Agenda.pdf
6. Social Agenda, Louisiana Sheriffs' Association 2018 Conference, Sandestin, Florida, https://www.lsa.org/LSAconference/2018LSA-SocialAgenda.pdf
7. Campaign Finance Records of the Louisiana Board of Ethics, http://www.ethics.la.gov/CampaignFinanceSearch/SearchResultsByContributions.aspx
8. Financial Statement of the Louisiana Sheriffs' Law Enforcement Program, June 30, 2016, Postlethwaite & Netterville accounting firm, https://app.lla.state.la.us/PublicReports.nsf/4E4DE0027489AE67862580E90072DACA/$FILE/00012F17.pdf
9. Frosch, Craig E., attorney for Usry & Weeks Law Firm, in July 24, 2018, letter to author in response to request for public records.
10. Ibid.

## Chapter 3
## Christopher Columbus Nash, Daniel Wesley Shaw

1. Colfax Massacre, Wikipedia
   https://en.wikipedia.org/wiki/Colfax_massacre
2. Ibid.
3. Ibid.
4. Ibid.

## Chapter 4
## D.J. "Cat" Doucet, Adler LeDoux

1. Gregory, Melissa, "Rapides Sheriff's Office lieutenant fired after arrest," *Alexandria Town Talk*, July 1, 2016.
2. Ibid.
3. Jones, Terry L., Wallace, Ben, "WBR sheriff's deputy arrested in Baton Rouge, accused of soliciting prostitute," *The Baton Rouge Advocate*, Oct. 24, 2014.
4. Ibid.
5. Nelson, Stanley, Barnidge, Matt, and Stanford, Ian, "Cold Case: Connected by violence—the mafia, Klan & Morville Lounge," *The Concordia Sentinel*, July 16, 2009.
6. Ibid.
7. Ibid.
8. Ibid.
9. Ibid.
10. Ibid.
11. Johnson, William, "St. Landry deputy retires after 50 years with sheriff's office," *Gannett Louisiana*, Dec. 28, 2014.
12. Maginnis, John, *The Last Hayride*, Gris Gris Press, 1984.

## Chapter 5

# Notes

## Noah Cross, Frank DeLaughter

1. Noah W. Cross—Cross as Sheriff, http://www.liquisearch.com/noah_w_cross/cross_as_sheriff
2. Nelson, Stanley, "Cold Case: Morville, the KKK, and Frank DeLaughter's criminal pursuits.
3. Aswell, Tom, "On 50th anniversary of Ferriday civil rights killing, read journalist Stanley Nelson's Concordia Sentinel series," *LouisianaVoice*, December 10, 2014, https://louisianavoice.com/2014/12/10/on-50th-anniversary-of-ferriday-civil-rights-killing-read-journalist-stanley-nelsons-concordia-sentinel-series/
4. Mitchell, Jerry, "Small-town editor compelled to solve mystery," *Jackson Clarion-Ledger*, April 27, 2014, http://www.clarionledger.com/story/news/2014/04/26/small-town-editor-compelled-solve-mystery/8235145/
5. Aswell, Tom, "On 50th anniversary of Ferriday civil rights killing, read journalist Stanley Nelson's Concordia Sentinel series," *LouisianaVoice*, December 10, 2014, https://louisianavoice.com/2014/12/10/on-50th-anniversary-of-ferriday-civil-rights-killing-read-journalist-stanley-nelsons-concordia-sentinel-series/
6. Ibid.
7. Aswell, Tom, "On 50th anniversary of Ferriday civil rights killing, read journalist Stanley Nelson's Concordia Sentinel series," *LouisianaVoice*, December 10, 2014, https://louisianavoice.com/2014/12/10/on-50th-anniversary-of-ferriday-civil-rights-killing-read-journalist-stanley-nelsons-concordia-sentinel-series/
8. Ibid.
9. Ibid.
10. Nelson, Stanley, Barnidge, Matt, Stanford, Ian, "Cold case: connected by violence—the mafia, Klan and Morville Lounge," *Concordia Sentinel*, July 16, 2009, http://www.hannapub.com/concordiasentinel/frank_morris_murd

er/cold-case-connected-by-violence-the-mafia-klan-morville-lounge/article_bbbd88a6-4320-11e3-86c7-001a4bcf6878.html
11. Ibid.
12. Ibid.
13. Ibid.
14. Ibid.
15. Ibid.
16. Ibid.
17. Noah W. Cross—Cross as Sheriff, http://www.liquisearch.com/noah_w_cross/cross_as_sheriff
18. Ibid.
19. Nelson, Stanley, Barnidge, Matt, Stanford, Ian, "Cold case: connected by violence—the mafia, Klan and Morville Lounge," *Concordia Sentinel*, July 16, 2009, http://www.hannapub.com/concordiasentinel/frank_morris_murder/cold-case-connected-by-violence-the-mafia-klan-morville-lounge/article_bbbd88a6-4320-11e3-86c7-001a4bcf6878.html
20. Ibid.
21. Ibid.
22. Ibid.
23. Ibid.
24. Ibid.
25. Ibid.
26. "Frank Morris Case," The Civil Rights Cold Case, undated, http://coldcases.org/cases/frank-morris-case
27. Ibid.
28. Nelson, Stanley, Barnidge, Matt, Stanford, Ian, "Cold case: connected by violence—the mafia, Klan and Morville Lounge," *Concordia Sentinel*, July 16, 2009, http://www.hannapub.com/concordiasentinel/frank_morris_murder/cold-case-connected-by-violence-the-mafia-klan-morville-lounge/article_bbbd88a6-4320-11e3-86c7-001a4bcf6878.html
29. "Frank Morris Case," The Civil Rights Cold Case, undated, http://coldcases.org/cases/frank-morris-case
30. Ibid.

## Notes

31. Nelson, Stanley, "Cold Case: Morville, the KKK, and Frank DeLaughter's criminal pursuits," *The Concordia Sentinel*, September 26, 2012, http://www.hannapub.com/concordiasentinel/frank_morris_murder/cold-case-morville-the-kkk-and-frank-delaughter-s-criminal/article_fc40521a-4725-11e3-84d0-0019bb30f31a.htmlIbid.
32. Thibodeaux, Kevin, "Frank DeLaughter," LSU School of Mass Communication, undated, http://www.wafb.com/story/21877926/frank-delaughter
33. Ibid.
34. "Frank Morris Case," The Civil Rights Cold Case, undated, http://coldcases.org/cases/frank-morris-case
35. Ibid.
36. Noah W. Cross, Wikipedia, https://en.wikipedia.org/wiki/Noah_W._Cross#Deputy_Frank_DeLaughter

## Chapter 6
## Willie Waggonner, Vol Dooley

1. Jones, Fredda, "I Remember Jack Favor: From Rodeo Cowboy to Prison Stripes, *Texans United*, February 3, 2012.
2. "Not Guilty, The Christian Ranchman, September/October, 2012, http://www.cowboysforchrist.net/thechristianranchmansep_oct2012.pdf
3. "Victims of the State: Bossier Parish, Louisiana," *Western Louisiana*, April 17, 1964, http://vots.altervista.org/LA/indexW.html
4. "Legal Botch," *Paris (Texas) News*, January 6, 1982.
5. Jack G. Favor v. C. Murray Henderson, May 16, 1972, http://www.leagle.com/decision/1972771348FSupp423_1712/FAVOR%20v.%20HENDERSON

6. "List of Louisiana wrongful convictions overturned since 1966," *Baton Rouge Advocate*, November 23, 2003, http://truthinjustice.org/LA-list.htm
7. "State will not prosecute former Texas rodeo star Jack Favor on the second of two murder charges," *Brownwood (Texas) Bulletin*, May 11, 1974.
8. "Jack Graves Favor," Wrongly Convicted Database Record, *Forejustice*, http://forejustice.org/db/Favor--Jack-Graves-.html

# Chapter 7
# Steve Prator

1. Lau, Maya, "Inmate work program offers jail alternative, takes cut of pay," *The Shreveport Times*, January 7, 2015, https://www.shreveporttimes.com/story/news/local/2015/01/03/inmate-work-program-offers-jail-alternative-takes-cut-pay/21231003/
2. Ibid.
3. Ibid.
4. Bromwich, Jonah Engel, "Louisiana Sheriff's Remarks Evoke Slavery, Critics Say, *The New York Times*, October 12, 2017, https://www.nytimes.com/2017/10/12/us/prison-reform-steve-prator.html
5. Ibid.
6. Ibid.
7.

# Chapter 8
# Bailey Grant, Royce Toney

1. Lane, Emily, "Public corruption in Louisiana 'can't get much worse,' says outgoing FBI New Orleans director," *New Orleans Times-Picayune*, November 6, 2017.

## Notes

      http://www.nola.com/crime/index.ssf/2017/11/public_corruption_fbi_new_orle.html

2. Cold case file of Federal Bureau of Investigation dated April 29, 2010, obtained by LSU School of Mass Communications, http://lsucoldcaseproject.com/wp-content/uploads/2014/10/Mashall-Johns.pdf
3. Ibid.
4. Hamilton, Matthew, "Families sought in cold case," *Monroe News-Star*, Nov. 30, 2009.
5. Cold case file of Federal Bureau of Investigation dated April 29, 2010, obtained by LSU School of Mass Communications, http://lsucoldcaseproject.com/wp-content/uploads/2014/10/Mashall-Johns.pdf
6. Written opinion of Federal Judge Tom Staff, U.S. District Court, Western District, Monroe Division, Jan. 7, 1982.
7. Ibid.
8. Ibid.
9. Ibid.
10. U.S. Department of Justice press release, Feb. 25, 2012, http://cepot-online-criminal-justice-courses.blogspot.com/2012/02/ouachita-parish-sheriff-arrested.html
11. Ibid.
12. Temple, Stacy, Leader, Barbara, "FBI Raids Ouachita Parish, LA Sheriff's Office," *Monroe News-Star*, Feb. 9, 2011.
13. Ibid.
14. "In Court, Sheriff Toney Admits to Having Adulterous Affair," political Internet blog *myarklamiss.com*, March 3, 2011, http://www.myarklamiss.com/news/breaking-news/in-court-sheriff-toney-admits-to-having-adulterous-affair.
15. "Woman Scorned Caused Royce Toney Trainwreck," *Monroe Free Press*, Feb. 26, 2012, https://lincolnparishnewsonline.wordpress.com/2012/02/26/monroe-free-press-woman-scorned-caused-royce-toney-trainwreck/.
16. Gunter, Johnny, "Royce Toney Sentence: Slap on the Wrist," political Internet blog *myarklamiss.com*, Nov. 14, 2012,

http://www.myarklamiss.com/myarklamiss/royce-toney-sentence-slap-on-the-wrist
17. Ibid.
18. Ibid.
19. "Government Consents to New Trial in United States v. Robert "Red" Stevens and Arthur Gilmore, Jr.," news release from U.S. Attorney, Western District of Louisiana, March 5, 2013.
20. Parker, Zach, "Federal prosecutor Griffing faces sanctions over affair," *Ouachita Citizen*, Oct. 12, 2016.
21. Ibid.
22. Ibid.
23. Gunter, Johnny, "Former Ouachita Parish Sheriff's Deputy Hired by ATF," *myarklamiss.com*, September 6, 2012, http://www.myarklamiss.com/myarklamiss/former-ouachita-parish-sheriffs-deputy-hired-by-atf

# Chapter 9
## Bobby Tardo, Duffy Breaux

1. Hackenburg, Liz, "Duffy Breaux, notorious Lafourche ex-sheriff, dies," *Houma Courier*, Dec. 14, 2005. http://www.houmatoday.com/news/20051214/duffy-breaux-notorious-lafourche-ex-sheriff-dies
2. "Former sheriff charged in bomb plot to kill successor," United Press International, Feb. 3, 1989. https://www.upi.com/Archives/1989/02/03/Former-sheriff-charged-in-bomb-plot-to-kill-successor/4693602485200/
3. Gyan, Joe Jr., Semien, John, "Former sheriff held in bombing," *Baton Rouge Advocate*, Feb. 3, 1989.
4. Ibid.
5. Ibid.
6. *Baton Rouge Advocate*, May 1, 1992.
7. Hackenburg, Liz, "Duffy Breaux, notorious Lafourche ex-sheriff, dies," *Houma Courier*, Dec. 14, 2005.

http://www.houmatoday.com/news/20051214/duffy-breaux-notorious-lafourche-ex-sheriff-dies

# Chapter 10
# J. Edward Layrisson, Daniel Edwards

1. First Circuit Court of Appeal, *Harper v. Layrisson*, No. 99 CA 0544, April 10, 2000.
2. Ibid.
3. Ibid.
4. Whipple, Judge Vanessa Guidry, writing for majority in First Circuit Court of Appeal, *Harper v. Layrisson*, No. 99 CA 0544, April 10, 2000.
5. Guidry, Judge John Michael, writing for the minority in First Circuit Court of Appeal, *Harper v. Layrisson*, No. 99 CA 0544, April 10, 2000.
6. Spillers, Charlie, *Confessions of an Undercover Agent*, University Press of Mississippi, 2016.
7. Ibid.
8. United States of America, Plaintiff-appellee, v. Frances Pecora and Nofio Pecoraro, A/k/a Norfio Pecora, Jr., defendants-appellants, U.S. Court of Appeals for the Fifth Circuit - 693 F.2d 421 (5th Cir. 1982), Dec. 1, 1982.
9. Ibid.
10. "Ed Layrisson inherited a bankrupt office, the worst in state history," *The Ponchatoula Times*, Oct. 13, 1983.
11. Anthony G. "Tony" Falterman, Assumption Parish Sheriff (ret.), interview, March 2019.
12. Yee, Aimee, Schon, Sylvia, "Edwards takes office to find IRS puts lien against sheriff's office," Hammond *Daily Star*, July 2, 2004.
13. Ibid.
14. Ibid.

15. Mustian, Jim, Roberts, Faimon A., III, "Why FBI raided Tangipahoa Sheriff's Office, Hammond police HQ; what they took," *The Baton Rouge Advocate*, Dec. 15, 2016.
16. Chatelain, Kim, "FBI raid of Hammond, Tangipahoa police offices tied to drug task force: reports," *The New Orleans Times-Picayune*, Dec. 15, 2016.
17. Mustian, Jim, Roberts, Faimon A., III, "Scandal grows: Embattled DEA agent accused of manipulating witness in double murder case," *The Baton Rouge Advocate*, Oct. 25, 2016.
18. "Tangipahoa sheriff responds to FBI raids on sheriff's office, Hammond PD," WGNO-TV, Dec. 16, 2016.
19. Mustian, Jim, Roberts, Faimon A., III, "Scandal grows: Embattled DEA agent accused of manipulating witness in double murder case," *The Baton Rouge Advocate*, Oct. 25, 2016.

## Chapter 11
## Jeff Landry, Charles Fuselier

1. White, Lamar, "The Napoleon in the Napoleonic Code: Jeff Landry, Louisiana's Attorney General, *CenLamar* Web blog, Oct. 13, 2015. https://cenlamar.com/2017/01/06/the-napoleon-in-the-napoleonic-code-jeff-landry-louisianas-attorney-general-chapter-1/
2. Ibid.
3. Wikipedia. https://en.wikipedia.org/wiki/Jeff_Landry
4. White, Lamar, "The Napoleon in the Napoleonic Code: Jeff Landry, Louisiana's Attorney General, *CenLamar* Web blog, Oct. 13, 2015. https://cenlamar.com/2017/01/06/the-napoleon-in-the-napoleonic-code-jeff-landry-louisianas-attorney-general-chapter-1/
5. Louisiana Secretary of State official election returns. https://voterportal.sos.la.gov/Graphical
6. White, Lamar, "The Napoleon in the Napoleonic Code: Jeff Landry, Louisiana's Attorney General, *CenLamar* Web blog, Oct. 13, 2015. https://cenlamar.com/2017/01/06/the-napoleon-in-the-napoleonic-code-jeff-landry-louisianas-attorney-general-chapter-1/

# Notes

7. White, Lamar, "Jeff Landry: A Plaster Saint of Pay to Play," CenLamar Web blog, March 30, 2017. https://cenlamar.com/2017/03/30/jeff-landry-a-plaster-saint-of-pay-to-play/
8. Jeff Landry, Arena Profile, *Politico*, https://www.politico.com/arena/bio/rep_jeff_landry.html
9. Cobb, Howell, visiting judge, ruling in Craig v. St. Martin Parish Sheriff, United States District Court, Western District Louisiana, Lafayette-Opelousas Division, August 1994, Justia, https://law.justia.com/cases/federal/district-courts/FSupp/861/1290/2261892/
10. Ibid.
11. Ibid.
12. Methvin, Mildred, U.S. Magistrate Judge, ruling in Eugene Thomas, Sr., v. Russell Frederick, United States District Court, Western District Louisiana, Lafayette-Opelousa Division, June 4, 1991, https://law.justia.com/cases/federal/district-courts/FSupp/766/540/1647466/
13. Ibid.
14. Ibid.
15. Ibid.
16. Ibid.
17. Fatherree, Dwayne, "Long-time sheriff called a visionary," The Daily Iberian, March 30, 2016, https://www.iberianet.com/news/long-time-sheriff-called-a-visionary/article_a159cc6c-f68e-11e5-bcf1-f3584b0d703c.html

# Chapter 12
# F. O. "Potch" Didier, Bill Belt

1. Gill, James, "It shouldn't cost so much for inmates to call home," *New Orleans Times-Picayune*, Nov. 2, 2012, https://www.nola.com/opinions/index.ssf/2012/11/it_shouldnt_cost_so_much_for_i.html

2. Ibid.
3. Ibid.
4. Louisiana Secretary of State corporate records.
5. "United States of America versus William O. Belt, Tracy Bryant Belt, and Julie Ann Bernard," copy of Federal Grand Jury Indictment, Aug. 1, 2007.
6. Ibid.
7. "Avoyelles Sheriff Accused of Corruption," KTBS-TV online story, undated, http://www.ktbs.com/story/22354891/avoyelles-sheriff-accused-of-corruption
8. "Mike Small Saves Bill Belt's 'Hide,'" *Cenla News*, Nov. 3, 2010, http://www.cenlanews.com/2010/11/mike-small-saves-bill-belts-hide.html
9. *Hayes WILLIAMS, et al., Plaintiffs-Appellees, v. Edwin W. EDWARDS, Governor, State of Louisiana and Richard L. Stalder, Secretary, Louisiana Department of Public Safety and Corrections, Defendants-Appellants*, No. 91-3559. United States Court of Appeals, Fifth Circuit, June 14, 1992.
10. Ibid.
11. Ibid.
12. Ibid.
13. *"F.O. 'Potch' Didier,"* Wikipedia
14. Ibid.
15. Ibid.
16. Ibid.

# Notes

## Chapter 13
## Jessel Ourso

1. Cruise, Deidre, "Sheriff Jessel Ourso named to Louisiana Justice Hall of Fame, *Plaquemine Post South*, July 8, 2010, http://www.postsouth.com/article/20100708/NEWS/307089958
2. Lockhart, John Michael, "The Ghost of Jessel," The Riverside Reader, June 5, 2014, http://riversidereader.com/2014/06/the-ghost-of-jessel/
3. Ibid.
4. Shepherd, F.E., Wall, Bob, "Ourso Ousted From Office," Baton Rouge State-Times, February 20, 1968
5. Ibid
6. Lockhart, John Michael, "The Ghost of Jessel," The Riverside Reader, June 5, 2014, http://riversidereader.com/2014/06/the-ghost-of-jessel/
7. "Jessel Ourso," *Alchetron Social Encyclopedia*, undated. https://alchetron.com/Jessel-Ourso

## Chapter 14
## Eugene Holland, Chaney Phillips, Ronald "Gun" Ficklin, Jessie Hughes

1. Gill, James, "Sheriffs run afoul of law and order," *New Orleans Times-Picayune*, March 4, 2012, http://www.nola.com/opinions/index.ssf/2012/03/sheriffs_run_afoul_of_law_and.html
2. Eugene Holland obituary, *Baton Rouge Advocate*, December 15, 2010, http://obits.theadvocate.com/obituaries/theadvocate/obituary.aspx?n=eugene-holland&pid=147148077
3. Colona, Dora, "Residents not surprised about sheriff's indictment," *Hammond Daily Star*, August 27, 1997,

http://www.hammondstar.com/residents-not-surprised-about-sheriff-s-indictment/article_3871ae1a-0cde-503d-a749-3b8cd7e8f09b.html
4. Ibid.
5. Ibid.
6. "Mayor takes over as St. Helena sheriff, Associated Press, April 23, 1988, http://www.hammondstar.com/mayor-takes-over-as-st-helena-sheriff/article_6df1a3ef-ed5b-50fb-99a4-a96d41676934.html
7. Ibid.
8. Hunter, Gary, "Louisiana work-release prisoners used by sheriff in chop shop," Prison Legal News, February 15, 2008, https://www.prisonlegalnews.org/news/2008/feb/15/louisiana-work-release-prisoners-used-by-sheriff-in-chop-shop/
9. Hunter, Gary, "Louisiana work-release prisoners used by sheriff in chop shop," Prison Legal News, February 15, 2008, https://www.prisonlegalnews.org/news/2008/feb/15/louisiana-work-release-prisoners-used-by-sheriff-in-chop-shop/
10. Ibid.
11. Interview with Ken Pastorick, August 21, 2017.
12. Hunter, Gary, "Louisiana work-release prisoners used by sheriff in chop shop," Prison Legal News, February 15, 2008, https://www.prisonlegalnews.org/news/2008/feb/15/louisiana-work-release-prisoners-used-by-sheriff-in-chop-shop/
13. Ibid.
14. Gates, Paul, "Former sheriff 'Gun' Ficklin sentenced to 63 months," WAFB-TV, Baton Rouge, February, 2005, http://www.wafb.com/story/7264845/former-sheriff-gun-ficklin-sentenced-to-63-months
15. Gates, Paul (2008-06-27). "First African-American sheriff in St. Helena Parish history sworn in, WAFB-TV, Baton Rouge, June 27, 2008.
16. "Deputy arrested on child rape charges," WWL-TV, New Orleans, July 18, 2007.

# Notes

## Chapter 15
## Dale Rinicker

1. Mason, Cody, "Too Good to be True: Private Prisons in America," *The Sentencing Project*, January 2012, http://sentencingproject.org/wp-content/uploads/2016/01/Too-Good-to-be-True-Private-Prisons-in-America.pdf
2. Louisiana Sheriff Busted in Private Prison Scheme, *Prison Legal News*, July 15, 2000, https://www.prisonlegalnews.org/news/2000/jul/15/louisiana-sheriff-busted-in-private-prison-scheme/
3. Records of U.S. Fifth Circuit Court of Appeals, Oct. 13, 1999.
4. Louisiana Secretary of State corporate records.
5. Records of U.S. Fifth Circuit Court of Appeals, Oct. 13, 1999.
6. Ibid.
7. Ibid.
8. Ibid.
9. Ibid.
10. Ibid.
11. Ibid.
12. Ibid.
13. U.S. Attorney's Office, Western District of Louisiana, news release, April 1, 2014. https://archives.fbi.gov/archives/neworleans/press-releases/2014/former-east-carroll-parish-sheriff-pleads-guilty-to-aiding-a-felon-in-possissing-a-firearm
14. Louisiana Secretary of State election statistics.

## Chapter 16
## Norm Fletcher

1. "Former sheriff pleads guilty to charges stemming from inmate's escape," Associated Press story of August 3, 1989.
2. Maginnis, John, *The Last Hayride*, Gris Gris Press, Baton Rouge, Louisiana, 1984.
3. Ibid.

## Chapter 17
## Irvin "Jif" Hingle

1. Maldonado, Charles, "Hingle faces federal corruption charges," *Gambit Magazine*, October 5, 2011, http://www.bestofneworleans.com/blogofneworleans/archives/2011/10/05/hingle-faces-federal-corruption-charges
2. Joint press release by FBI and U.S. Attorney's Office, October 5, 2011, https://archives.fbi.gov/archives/neworleans/press-releases/2011/plaquemines-sheriff-charged-with-conspiracy-to-commit-mail-fraud-and-bribery
3. Ibid.
4. Zurik, Lee, "Emails paint a picture of parties and potential corruption," WVUE Fox 8, New Orleans, undated, http://www.foxwilmington.com/Global/story.asp?S=17221178
5. Ibid.
6. Ibid.
7. Ibid.
8. Ibid.
9. Ibid.
10. Zurik, Lee, "Will feds raise the pressure on Hingle?" WVUE Fox 8, New Orleans, March 30, 2012, http://www.fox5vegas.com/Global/story.asp?S=17221994
11. Ibid.
12. Ibid.
13. Ibid.
14. News release by U.S. Attorney for the Eastern District of Louisiana Jim Letten, Nov. 30, 2011.
15. Alexander-Bloch, Benjamin, "Former Plaquemines Parish Sheriff Jiff Hingle sentenced to nearly 4 years on corruption charges," *New Orleans Times-Picayune*, Feb. 25, 2016, http://www.nola.com/crime/index.ssf/2013/07/former_plaquemines_parish_sher_2.html

## Notes

16. Zurik, Lee, "Hingle to jail, taxpayers pay him $400k," WVUE Fox 8, New Orleans, undated, http://www.fox8live.com/story/23448052/lee-zurik-investigation-hingle-to-jail-taxpayers-pay-him-400k
17. Reutter, David, "Plaquemines Parish Jail Grand-Opening Faces Shuttered Wasteful Cells," *Prison Legal News*, Aug. 4, 2016, https://www.prisonlegalnews.org/news/2016/aug/4/plaquemines-parish-jail-grand-opening-faces-shuttered-wasteful-cells/

## Chapter 18
## Mike Tregre, Wayne Schaeffer

1. Kopplin, Zack, "Louisiana Sheriffs Hid a Gun That Could Free a Man and Then Blamed Hurricane Katrina," *The Daily Beast*, August 9, 2016. https://www.thedailybeast.com/louisiana-sheriffs-hid-a-gun-that-could-free-a-man-and-then-blamed-hurricane-katrina
2. Ibid.
3. Louisiana Secretary of State official election results, October 22, 2011. https://voterportal.sos.la.gov/Graphical
4. Bacon-Blood, Littice, "St. John sheriff deputized wife, 2 children, broke law, watchdog says," New Orleans Times-Picayune, August 9, 2016. http://www.nola.com/crime/index.ssf/2016/08/metro_crime_commission_says_st.html
5. Mustian, Jim, "'I did what I saw was done previously': St. John sheriff to revoke law enforcement credentials he awarded wife, children amid accusations of nepotism," *New Orleans Advocate*, August 9, 2016. http://www.theadvocate.com/new_orleans/news/crime_police/article_49f8ce0e-5daa-11e6-aa2c-8f7fb4329c76.html

## Chapter 19
## Albert D. "Bodie" Little

1. "Winn Parish Sheriff under investigation," KSLA-TV, Shreveport, Feb. 16, 2011, http://www.cbs46.com/story/14042951/winn-parish-sheriff-under-investigation
2. "Former Winn Parish sheriff convicted in drug case," Associated Press, Feb. 25, 2012, http://www.nola.com/crime/index.ssf/2012/02/former_winn_parish_sheriff_con.html
3. Finley, Stephanie A, "Former Winn Parish sheriff sentenced 13+ years in prison," Press release, U.S. Attorney's Office, Western District of Louisiana, Aug. 17, 2012, https://www.justice.gov/sites/default/files/usao-wdla/legacy/2013/04/03/wdla20120817.pdf
4. "Former Winn Parish sheriff convicted in drug case," Associated Press, Feb. 25, 2012, http://www.nola.com/crime/index.ssf/2012/02/former_winn_parish_sheriff_con.html
5. "I ain't a crook," *Topix Winnfield* blog, May 15, 2011, http://www.topix.com/forum/city/winnfield-la/TLE32TR4DHAIDO1NV
6. "Former Winn Parish sheriff convicted in drug case," Associated Press, Feb. 25, 2012, http://www.nola.com/crime/index.ssf/2012/02/former_winn_parish_sheriff_con.html
7. "Winn Parish Sheriff under investigation," KSLA-TV, Shreveport, Feb. 16, 2011, http://www.cbs46.com/story/14042951/winn-parish-sheriff-under-investigation

# Notes

## Chapter 20
## Sid J. Gautreaux

1. Morris, Randa, "Sheriff Busted for Illegal Quotas Claims 'Ignorance Of The Law,'" Addicting Information: The Knowledge You Crave, May 9, 2015, http://addictinginfo.org/2015/05/09/sheriff-busted-for-illegal-quotas-claims-ignorance-of-the-law-as-defense-video/
2. Grindley, Lucas, "Sheriff Claims He Didn't Know Anti-Sodomy Laws Weren't Valid Anymore," *Baton Rouge Advocate*, July 29, 2013.
3. Samuels, Diana, "East Baton Rouge Sheriff's Office 'made mistakes' in arrests of gay men at Baton Rouge," *New Orleans Times-Picayune*, July 30, 2013.
4. Grindley, Lucas, "Sheriff Claims He Didn't Know Anti-Sodomy Laws Weren't Valid Anymore," *Baton Rouge Advocate*, July 29, 2013.
5. Samuels, Diana, "East Baton Rouge Sheriff's Office 'made mistakes' in arrests of gay men at Baton Rouge," *New Orleans Times-Picayune*, July 30, 2013.
6. McDonough, Katie, "Are states still enforcing unconstitutional anti-sodomy laws?" *Salon.com*, April 9, 2013.
7. Grindley, Lucas, "Sheriff Claims He Didn't Know Anti-Sodomy Laws Weren't Valid Anymore," *Baton Rouge Advocate*, July 29, 2013.
8. Ibid.
9. Ibid.
10. Samuels, Diana, "East Baton Rouge Sheriff's Office 'made mistakes' in arrests of gay men at Baton Rouge," *New Orleans Times-Picayune*, July 30, 2013.

## Chapter 21
## Newell Normand, Harry Lee, Frank Clancy

1. Pompilio, Natalie, "Lee ignores rule against associating with criminals," *New Orleans Times-Picayune*, Nov. 16, 1999.
2. Author's interview with Genny May, U.S. Marshal of the Eastern District of Louisiana and a former intelligence officer for Louisiana State Police, Feb. 5, 2018.
3. Opinion No. 92-132, Louisiana Board of Ethics for Elected Officials, Oct. 27, 1994.
4. Gill, James, "Harry Lee: the company he keeps," *New Orleans Times-Picayune*, April 6, 1994.
5. Warren, Bob, "Lee goes to bat for Caracci—defends connections at hearing on a.-Ace," *New Orleans Times-Picayune*, April 1, 1994.
6. Samples of Harry Lee quotes, *New Orleans Times-Picayune*, April 2, 2000.
7. "Sex scandal could cost Steven Seagal his fake badge," *New York Post*, April 26, 2010, http://nypost.com/2010/04/26/sex-scandal-could-cost-steven-seagal-his-fake-badge/
8. Ibid.
9. Lemons, Stephen, "Steven Seagal resigned rather than face an IA investigation, according to Sheriff Newell Normand," *Phoenix New Times*, March 18, 2011, http://www.phoenixnewtimes.com/blogs/steven-seagal-resigned-rather-than-face-ia-investigation-according-to-sheriff-newell-normand-6499604
10. Ibid.
11. Hunter, Michelle, "Jefferson Parish Sheriff Newell Normand denies he is target of federal probe," *New Orleans Times-Picayune*, Aug. 1, 2016, http://www.nola.com/politics/index.ssf/2016/08/jefferson_parish_sheriff_newel_7.html
12. Russell Gordon, "Wife of sheriff who helped Gov. John Bel Edwards win election, lands Superdome contract months later," *New Orleans Advocate*, Sept. 1, 2016,

## Notes

http://www.theadvocate.com/new_orleans/news/politics/article_f1aee8de-7094-11e6-ac14-1778e75efd0b.html
13. Ibid.
14. Vargas, Ramon Antonio, Sledge, Matt, "Joe McKnight killing probe defended by police; questions mount over confessed shooter's release," *New Orleans Times-Picayune*, Dec. 2, 2016, http://www.theadvocate.com/new_orleans/news/crime_police/article_10f45128-b8b8-11e6-a8d6-fbec74f0a74c.html?sr_source=lift_amplify
15. Ibid.
16. DeBerry, Jarvis, "At Joe McKnight press conferences Sheriff Newell Normand is angry and oblivious," *New Orleans Times-Picayune*, Dec. 10, 2016, http://www.nola.com/crime/index.ssf/2016/12/mcknight_sheriff_press_confere.html
17. Ibid.
18. Ibid.
19. Lane, Emily, "Jefferson Parish Sheriff Newell Normand announcement retirement," *New Orleans Times-Picayune*, July 25, 2017, http://www.nola.com/crime/index.ssf/2017/07/newell_normand_jefferson_paris.html
20. White, Lamar, Weaver, Katie, Turk, Leslie, "Overboard! One Louisiana Businessman. Four Politicians. And A Scandal That Is Slowly Unfolding," The Bayou Brief, July 26, 2017. http://bayoubrief.com/2017/07/26/overboard-one-louisiana-businessman-four-politicians-and-a-scandal-that-is-slowly-unfolding/

## Chapter 22
## Charles Foti, Marlin Gusman

1. "Orleans Parish Sheriff's Office," Legislative Audit Report, Louisiana Legislative Auditor, March 30, 2016.
2. "Orleans Parish Prison: A Big Jail with Big Problems," undated ACLU publication, https://www.aclu.org/other/orleans-parish-prison-big-jail-big-problems
3. Ibid.
4. "Troubled jail at center of Orleans Parish sheriff's race," Martin, Naomi, New Orleans Times-Picayune, Jan. 16, 2014, http://www.nola.com/politics/index.ssf/2014/01/troubled_jail_at_center_of_orl.html
5. "Orleans Parish Prison: A Big Jail with Big Problems," undated ACLU publication, https://www.aclu.org/other/orleans-parish-prison-big-jail-big-problems
6. Ridgeway, James, Casella, Jean, " 'Complete lawlessness' at Orleans Parish Prison," *Mother Jones*, April 6, 2012, https://www.motherjones.com/politics/2012/04/new-orleans-parish-prison-conditions-lawsuit-splc/
7. Ridgeway, James, Casella, Jean, "America's 10 Worst Prisons: NOLA, *Mother Jones*, https://www.motherjones.com/politics/2013/05/10-worst-prisons-america-orleans-parish-opp/
8. "Southern Poverty Law Center files federal lawsuit against Louisiana sheriff to end prisoner abuse at jail," Southern Poverty Law Center news release, April 1, 2012, https://www.splcenter.org/news/2012/04/02/southern-poverty-law-center-files-federal-lawsuit-against-louisiana-sheriff-end-prisoner
9. Letter to Orleans Parish Sheriff Marlin Gusman from Jonathan Smith, U.S. Justice Department, April 23, 2012.
10. Ibid.
11. Letter to U.S. District Judge Lance Africk from New Orleans attorney Mary E. Howell, March 11, 2013.

## Notes

12. "Justice Department Files for Contempt and Requests Receiver to Operate Orleans Parish Jail," U.S. Department of Justice news release, April 25, 2016, https://www.justice.gov/opa/pr/justice-department-files-contempt-and-requests-receiver-operate-orleans-parish-jail
13. "Federal Judge Expresses Frustration in New Orleans Jail Reform Litigation," *Prison Legal News*, December 2017, https://www.prisonlegalnews.org/news/2017/dec/5/federal-judge-expresses-frustration-new-orleans-jail-reform-litigation/

# Chapter 23
# Dallas Cormier

1. Jefferson Davis Parish Sheriff's Office Web page. http://jdpso.org/history.php
2. "Ex-Sheriff seeks pardon to hunt," *New Orleans Times-Picayune*, Aug. 13, 1994. https://collateral.medium.com/jeffdavis8/dallas-cormier-federal-indictment.pdf
3. Ibid.
4. St. Ores, John, "JD sheriff indicted on 36 charges," *Lake Charles American Press*, July 27, 1990.
5. Jones, Mike, "Former JD sheriff placed on probation," *Lake Charles American Press*, March 30, 1993.
6. St. Ores, John, "JD sheriff indicted on 36 charges," *Lake Charles American Press*, July 27, 1990.
7. Jones, Mike, "Former JD sheriff placed on probation," *Lake Charles American Press*, March 30, 1993.

## Chapter 24
## Jeff Britt, Ricky Jones

1. Audit report of Tensas Parish Sheriff's Office by Louisiana Legislative Auditor's Office, Dec. 9, 1998.
2. Ibid.
3. Ibid.
4. Ibid.
5. Ibid.
6. "Tensas Sheriff Indicted in Jail Beating," *The Baton Rouge Advocate*, February 27, 1998.
7. "Sheriff's Beating Case Ends in Hung Jury," *Dallas Morning News*, July 11, 1998.
8. "Tensas Sheriff Indicted in Jail Beating," *The Baton Rouge Advocate*, February 27, 1998.
9. *The Baton Rouge Advocate*, June 9, 1999.
10. Crowder, Carla, "Private firm has seen riot, escapes, drugs at prisons it operates," *Prison Talk* Web page, April 15, 2003, http://www.prisontalk.com/forums/showthread.php?t=13274
11. Ibid.
12. Ibid.
13. Russell, Gordon, Crisp, Elizabeth, "Gov. Edwards pardons ex-sheriff with felony record, appoints him to board governing car dealers," Baton Rouge Advocate, Aug. 19, 2018, https://www.theadvocate.com/baton_rouge/news/politics/article_3bbbf70c-a0de-11e8-a69c-ab023a8e364f.html
14. List of Louisiana locations by per capita income," Wikipedia. https://en.wikipedia.org/wiki/List_of_Louisiana_locations_by_per_capita_income
15. Flaherty, Jordan, Morial, Jacques, "Did a White Sheriff and District Attorney Orchestrate a Race-Based Coup in a Northern Louisiana Town?" HuffPost, May 26, 2010. https://www.huffingtonpost.com/jordan-flaherty/did-a-white-sheriff-and-d_b_514707.html
16. Ibid.

# Notes

17. Ibid.
18. Louisiana Legislative Audit Report, Town of Waterproof, Aug. 27, 2008. https://www.lla.la.gov/PublicReports.nsf/DF10A23CB968CFA9862574B10062FB07/$FILE/00004C58.pdf
19. "Crazed Waterproof (sic) Louisiana Police Chief Miles Jenkins and Mayor Bobby Higginbotham Arrested, Charged After Running Federally Funded Speed Trap Town," anonymous undated blog *Our Tax Dollars At Work*. https://ourtaxdollarsatwork.wordpress.com/2009/02/22/crazed-waterproof-louisiana-police-chief-miles-jenkins-and-mayor-bobby-higginbotham-arrested-charged-after-running-federally-funded-speed-trap-town/
20. "Excessive Fine Enforcement," Louisiana Legislative Auditor report in response to House Concurrent Resolution 204, June 6, 2007. https://www.thenewspaper.com/rlc/docs/2007/la-speedtraps.pdf
21. Flaherty, Jordan, "The Black mayor of Waterproof, Louisiana, has spent nearly a year behind bars without bail," Bayview, National Black newspaper, March 25, 2011. http://sfbayview.com/2011/03/the-black-mayor-of-waterproof-louisiana-has-spent-nearly-a-year-behind-bars-without-bail/
22. Ibid.
23. Flaherty, Jordan, Morial, Jacques, "Did a White Sheriff and District Attorney Orchestrate a Race-Based Coup in a Northern Louisiana Town?" HuffPost, May 26, 2010. https://www.huffingtonpost.com/jordan-flaherty/did-a-white-sheriff-and-d_b_514707.html
24. Author's interview of Higginbotham, Dec. 8, 2011.
25. Flaherty, Jordan, "Conviction of Black Mayor Overturned by U.S. Court of Appeals in Case Closely Watched by Civil Rights Activists, Huffpost, June 25, 2012, https://www.huffpost.com/entry/conviction-of-black-mayor_b_1454458

## Chapter 25
## Scott Franklin

1. "Summary of the 'Jena Six' Case, Discover the Networks, 2007. http://www.discoverthenetworks.org/Articles/summaryofthejenasixcase.html
2. "Drug Bust or Racist Revenge in Louisiana?" *African American Newsletter*, undated. http://newamericamedia.org/2010/05/drug-bust-or-racist-revenge-in-louisiana.php
3. Ibid.
4. "Jena:-Re-do Jena?" *Commonwealth for a Free Moral Society*, undated. https://commonwealthfreemoralsociety.wordpress.com/jenas-unfinished-business/jena-re-do-jena/
5. "Operation Option Three Hits Jena," *Revolution*, April 4, 2010. http://www.revcom.us/a/197/Jena-en.html
6. Ibid.
7. "Drug Bust or Racist Revenge in Louisiana?" *African American Newsletter*, undated. http://newamericamedia.org/2010/05/drug-bust-or-racist-revenge-in-louisiana.php

## Chapter 26
## Jack Strain

1. Pagones, Sara, "In stunning fall for former lawman, ex-St. Tammany Sheriff Jack Strain charged with rape, incest," *New Orleans Advocate*, June 11, 2019.
2. Pagones, Sara, "Former St. Tammany sheriff spent nearly $500K on work-release facility before handing it over to friends," *New Orleans Advocate*, Nov. 7, 2016.
3. Ibid.
4. Ibid.

## Notes

5. Pagones, Sara, "Operator of Tammany shuttered work-release outfit trying to force sheriff to settle," *New Orleans Advocate*, May 20, 2015.
6. Sheriff Jack Strain interview with WDSU-TV, New Orleans, June 2006, https://www.youtube.com/watch?v=5aqsFUK12I0
7. Tim Wise, "Little Man with a Gun in His Hand: an Open Letter to Sheriff Jack Strain, of St. Tammany Parish, Louisiana, *Black Commentator*, July 13, 2006, http://www.timwise.org/2006/07/little-man-with-a-gun-in-his-hand-an-open-letter-to-sheriff-jack-strain-of-st-tammany-parish-louisiana/.
8. Jim (Jimi) Izrael, NPR interview by Madeleine Brand on Day to Day, July 10, 2006.
9. Lohr, David, "The 13 Racist Police E-mails You Didn't Read," *Huffington Post*, April 9, 2015, http://www.huffingtonpost.com/2015/04/09/st-tammany-parish-sheriffs-office-racist-emails_n_7027274.html
10. Chiri, Kevin, "Sheriff Jack Strain says intimidation charges are all political," *St. Tammany West News*, May 11, 2015.
11. Election statistics provided by the Louisiana Secretary of State, http://www.sos.la.gov/ElectionsAndVoting/GetElectionInformation/FindResultsAndStatistics/Pages/default.aspx
12. Moore, Katie, "New questions about tax dollars spent to fix up Slidell jail facility," WWL-TV news story, Nov. 8, 2016, http://www.wwltv.com/news/local/new-questions-about-tax-dollars-spent-to-fix-up-slidell-jail-facility/349418551

## Chapter 27
## Clay Higgins

1. Pierce, Walter, "Clay Higgins resigned from OPD in 2007 on cusp of major disciplinary measures," *The Independent*, Sept. 29, 2016,

http://theind.com/article-24002-Clay-Higgins-resigned-from-OPD-in-2007-on-cusp-of-major-disciplinary-measures.html
2. Turk, Leslie, "Capt. Clay fails the fact-check," The Independent, Nov. 4, 2016, http://theind.com/article-24189-Capt-Clay-fails-the-fact-check.html
3. Kopplin, Zack, "Uniform misconduct: Inside the rise and possible fall of 'The Cajun John Wayne,'" *The Independent*, Oct. 4, 2016.
4. Ibid.
5. Pierce, Walter, "Guidroz to Higgins: 'Put your big boy pants on,'" The Independent, Oct. 4, 2016.
6. "Michael Cohen Testifies Before House Oversight Committee," *Fox News Insider*, Feb. 27, 2019.
7. Bobby Guidroz, St. Landry Parish Sheriff, interview with author, April 22, 2019.
8. Kopplin, Zack, "Uniform misconduct: Inside the rise and possible fall of 'The Cajun John Wayne,'" *The Independent*, Oct. 4, 2016.
9. Turk, Leslie, "Higgins skipped taxes—and child support," *The Independent*, Nov. 17, 2016.
10. Raymond, Laurel, "House Republican calls for mass killing of 'radicalized Islamic' suspects," *ThinkProgress*, April 14, 2017.
11. Nelson, Louis, "Louisiana congressman criticized for selfie video in Auschwitz gas chamber," *Politico*, July 5, 2017.

# Chapter 28
# Rodney Arbuckle

1. Purpera, Daryl G., Louisiana Legislative Auditor, letter to DeSoto Parish Sheriff Rodney Arbuckle, April 9, 2014. https://www.lla.la.gov/PublicReports.nsf/943A27922B989F2686257CB600487865/$FILE/00038F29.pdf
2. Corporate filings, Louisiana Secretary of State https://coraweb.sos.la.gov/CommercialSearch/CommercialSearchDetails.aspx?CharterID=677675_C2F4B136CE

## Notes

3. Ibid.
4. Sterritt, James R., attorney for DeSoto Parish Sheriff Rodney Arbuckle, letter of October 28, 2013, in response to Louisiana Legislative Auditor's Office's October 10, 2013, draft investigative audit report.
5. Purpera, Daryl G., Louisiana Legislative Auditor, letter to DeSoto Parish Sheriff Rodney Arbuckle, April 9, 2014. https://www.lla.la.gov/PublicReports.nsf/943A27922B989F2686257CB600487865/$FILE/00038F29.pdf
6. Ibid.
7. Sterritt, James R., attorney for DeSoto Parish Sheriff Rodney Arbuckle, letter of October 28, 2013, in response to Louisiana Legislative Auditor's Office's October 10, 2013, draft investigative audit report.
8. *Louisiana Code of Governmental Ethics* http://ethics.la.gov/Pub/Laws/ethsum.pdf
9. Purpera, Daryl G., Louisiana Legislative Auditor, letter to DeSoto Parish Sheriff Rodney Arbuckle, April 9, 2014. https://www.lla.la.gov/PublicReports.nsf/943A27922B989F2686257CB600487865/$FILE/00038F29.pdf
10. *Louisiana Code of Governmental Ethics* http://ethics.la.gov/Pub/Laws/ethsum.pdf
11. Purpera, Daryl G., Louisiana Legislative Auditor, letter to DeSoto Parish Sheriff Rodney Arbuckle, April 9, 2014. https://www.lla.la.gov/PublicReports.nsf/943A27922B989F2686257CB600487865/$FILE/00038F29.pdf
12. Sterritt, James R., attorney for DeSoto Parish Sheriff Rodney Arbuckle, letter of October 28, 2013, in response to Louisiana Legislative Auditor's Office's October 10, 2013, draft investigative audit report.

## Chapter 29
## Joseph Reed Bueche

1. Stegall, Amber, "Pointe Coupee deputy arrested for malfeasance in office," WAFB-TV, Baton Rouge, Louisiana, August 8, 2013. http://www.wafb.com/story/23085987/pointe-coupee-deputy-arrested-for-malfeasance-in-office

## Chapter 30
## Willy Martin

1. Curth, Kimberly, "Fox 8 Investigates: Officers with troubling backgrounds rehired by different agency," WVUE-TV, New Orleans, Louisiana. http://www.fox8live.com/story/35502168/fox-8-investigates-officers-with-troubling-backgrounds-re-hired-by-different-agency
2. Ibid.
3. Ibid.
4. Ibid.

## Chapter 31
## Greg Champagne, Julius "Ducky" Sellers, Jr.

1. Interview with W. Lloyd Grafton, January 15, 2017.
2. Bacon-Blood, "St. Charles deputy 'grossly exceeded' speed limit in fatal wreck, State Police say, *New Orleans Times-Picayune*, Jan. 21, 2014.
3. Ibid.
4. Interview with W. Lloyd Grafton, January 15, 2017.
5. Champagne, Greg, "President's Podium: Dakota Access Pipeline," National Sheriffs' Association Web page, Nov. 1, 2016,

# Notes

http://www.sheriffs.org/blog/Presidents-Podium-Dakota-Access-Pipeline

6. Verdin, Monique, Foytlin, Cherri, "Letter to Greg Champagne in Response to Comments About Standing Rock," Bold Louisiana Web page, Dec. 1, 2016, http://boldlouisiana.org/letter-to-sheriff-greg-champagne-in-response-to-comments-about-standing-rock/

## Chapter 32
## Louis Ackal

1. Grafton, Lloyd, report on shooting of Michael Jones, October 26, 2009.
2. Ibid.
3. Ibid.
4. Richmond, U.S. Rep. Cedric L., letter to U.S. Attorney General Loretta Lynch, May 19, 2015.
5. *Daily Iberian*, March 19, 2017.
6. Broussard, Donald D., e-mail to author dated March 25, 2017.
7. *Daily Iberian*, March 19, 2017.
8. Broussard, Donald D., e-mail to author dated March 25, 2017.
9. Grafton, Lloyd, report on shooting of Michael Jones, October 26, 2009.
10. Ibid.
11. Ibid.
12. Ibid.
13. Ibid.
14. Ibid.
15. Ibid.
16. Ibid.
17. Ibid.
18. Watts, Amanda, "Iberia, Louisiana sheriff accused of having inmates beaten," CNN, March 11, 2016.
19. Ibid.

20. Ibid.
21. Richmond, U.S. Rep. Cedric L., letter to U.S. Attorney General Loretta Lynch, May 19, 2015.
22. Rappleye, Hannah, "Shocking Trial, but Louisiana Sheriff Cleared of Civil Rights Abuses," NBC News, Nov. 5, 2016, http://www.nbcnews.com/news/us-news/shocking-trial-louisiana-sheriff-cleared-civil-rights-abuses-n678031
23. Ibid.
24. Associated Press, "Acquittal for Louisiana sheriff whose deputies beat inmates," *New Orleans Times-Picayune*, Nov. 5, 2016 http://www.nola.com/crime/index.ssf/2016/11/acquittal_for_louisiana_sherif.html
25. Fatherree, Dwayne, "Seven former IPSO officers sentenced in DOJ probe," *The Daily Iberian*, March 28, 2017.
26. Ibid.
27. Author's interview with Victor White, Jr., June 2018.
28. Litigation information provided by New Orleans law firm of Usry & Weeks in documents provided by attorney Craig E. Frosch in letter of July 24, 2018 pursuant to public records request submitted to Louisiana Sheriffs' Association.
29. Ibid.
30. Hargrove, Thomas, Murder Accountability Project.
31. Ibid.
32. Ibid.
33. Simerman, John, "$3 million in new payouts as Iberia Parish Sheriff's Office settles more abuse suits," Acadiana Advocate, March 2, 2019.
34. Ibid.
35. Ibid.
36. Ibid.

# Notes

## Chapter 33
## Mike Couvillon

1. *Origin of the Sheriff*, Pendleton County (Kentucky) Sheriff's Office Web page, http://sheriff.pendletoncounty.ky.gov/aboutus/Pages/OriginoftheS.aspx
2. "Corruption Accusation over Sheriff's new home; sheriff defends purchase," KATC-TV news story, May 23, 2014 (updated March 23, 2015), http://www.katc.com/story/28591121/corruption-accusation-over-sheriffs-new-home-sheriff-defends-purchase
3. Ibid.
4. Louisiana Revised Statute 42:1113(A), http://ethics.la.gov/Pub/Laws/ethiclaw.pdf#page=7&zoom=auto,-40,792
5. "Corruption Accusation over Sheriff's new home; sheriff defends purchase," KATC-TV news story, May 23, 2014 (updated March 23, 2015), http://www.katc.com/story/28591121/corruption-accusation-over-sheriffs-new-home-sheriff-defends-purchase
6. Ibid.
7. Advisory Opinion No. 83-254 of the Commission on Ethics for Public Employees, Nov. 15, 1983, http://ethics.la.gov/EthicsOpinion/DocView.aspx?id=8566&searchid=a48b0fee-49bc-4d5d-a178-df2d61329f90&dbid=0
8. Opinion No. 97-092, Louisiana Board of Ethics, March 16, 1998, http://ethics.la.gov/EthicsOpinion/DocView.aspx?id=829&searchid=c8b4b3fd-6f7f-438b-b5ab-271a0cce14c0&dbid=0
9. Louisiana Legislative Financial Report, Vermilion Parish Sheriff's Office, Nov. 22, 2016, https://www.lla.la.gov/PublicReports.nsf/DC37B8819FB5CCB9862580CE005C99F8/$FILE/00012659.pdf
10. Consent Order 2014-762, Louisiana Board of Ethics, Dec. 16, 2016, http://ethics.la.gov/EthicsOpinion/DocView.aspx?id=362290&searchid=5155abf3-5f66-440b-b0f7-2999a1af40af&dbid=0
11. "Mike Couvillon re-elected Vermilion Parish Sheriff," KATC-TV news story, Oct. 24, 2015,

http://www.katc.com/story/30342799/mike-couvillon-re-elected-vermilion-parish-sheriff

# Chapter 34
# Jack Stephens

1. Barker, Kim, "Spillionaires: Profiteering and mismanagement in the wake of the BP oil spill," *ProPublica,* April 13, 2011, https://www.propublica.org/article/spillionaires-profiteering-mismanagement-in-the-wake-of-the-bp-oil-spill
2. Ibid.
3. Ibid.
4. Ibid.
5. "Head of the Metropolitan Crime Commission says his group is interested in a possible study of the St. Bernard Parish criminal justice system," news release from St. Bernard Parish Sheriff's Office, January 23, 2015. http://sbso.org/head-of-the-metropolitan-crime-commission-says-his-group-is-interested-in-a-possible-study-of-the-st-bernard-parish-criminal-justice-system/
6. Purpura, Paul, "Former St. Bernard Parish sheriff's deputy indicted in corruption probe," *New Orleans Times-Picayune*, Aug. 4, 2015, http://www.nola.com/crime/index.ssf/2015/08/st_bernard_parish_appointee_an.html
7. Ibid
8. Myers, Ben, "Indictment against former St. Bernard sheriff's deputy quashed," *New Orleans Times-Picayune*, May 31, 2016, http://www.nola.com/crime/index.ssf/2016/05/indictment_against_former_st_b.html
9. Author's interview of Rafael Goyeneche, III, head of the New Orleans Metropolitan Crime Commission, November 27, 2017.
10. "4 St. Bernard Parish Prison correctional officers indicted for inmate's death," WGNO-TV report, Dec. 3, 2015,

# Notes

   http://wgno.com/2015/12/03/4-st-bernard-parish-prison-correctional-officers-indicted-for-inmates-death/
11. "St. Bernard Sheriff Jack Stephens retires, says he's 'seen it all,'" New Orleans Times-Picayune, July 1, 2012. http://www.nola.com/crime/index.ssf/2012/07/st_bernard_sherif f_jack_stephe_1.html

# Chapter 35
# Austin Daniel

1. *Priscilla Lefebure v. Barrett Boeker, Assistant Warden Louisiana State Penitentiary, individually and in his official capacity, West Feliciana Parish, Samuel D. D'Aquilla, 20$^{th}$ Judicial District Attorney, J. Austin Daniel, Sheriff, West Feliciana Parish, Insurance Company DOES 1-5, DOES 6-20*, United States District Court, Middle District of Louisiana, Dec. 21, 2017.
2. Ibid.
3. Ibid.
4. Toohey, Grace, "Expert: DA's omission of rape kit in case against Angola assistant warden 'shocking…unbelievable,'" *Baton Rouge Advocate*, Mar. 14, 2017, http://www.theadvocate.com/baton_rouge/news/courts/article_09b 2b6d2-08e2-11e7-ab3b-efd5ca6a70ef.html
5. Ibid.
6. Ibid.
7. Toohey, Grace, "West Feliciana Parish sends rape kit in case against Angola warden to be tested after months in possession," Baton Rouge Advocate, June 26, 2017, http://www.theadvocate.com/baton_rouge/news/crime_police/articl e_1e84fa10-5ac8-11e7-bbde-b7432a3f5cd4.html
8. Ibid.
9. *Priscilla Lefebure v. Barrett Boeker, Assistant Warden Louisiana State Penitentiary, individually and in his official capacity, West*

Feliciana Parish, Samuel D. D'Aquilla, 20*th* Judicial District Attorney, J. Austin Daniel, Sheriff, West Feliciana Parish, Insurance Company DOES 1-5, DOES 6-20*, United States District Court, Middle District of Louisiana, Dec. 21, 2017.
10. Nakamoto, Chris, "Sheriff's office admits to mistake after not sending rape kit off for testing," WBRZ-TV, Baton Rouge, LA., June 26, 2017, http://www.wbrz.com/videos/investigative-unit-sheriff-s-office-admits-to-mistake-after-not-sending-rape-kit-off-for-testing/
11. *Priscilla Lefebure v. Barrett Boeker, Assistant Warden Louisiana State Penitentiary, individually and in his official capacity, West Feliciana Parish, Samuel D. D'Aquilla, 20*th* Judicial District Attorney, J. Austin Daniel, Sheriff, West Feliciana Parish, Insurance Company DOES 1-5, DOES 6-20*, United States District Court, Middle District of Louisiana, Dec. 21, 2017.

# Chapter 36
# Wayne Morein, Eddie Soileau

1. *Investigation of the Ville Platte Police Department and the Evangeline Parish Sheriff's Office*, Report of U.S. Department of Justice, Civil Rights Division, Dec. 19, 2016.
2. Ibid.
3. Mustian, Jim, "In Evangeline Parish arrest scandal, civil liberties took back seat to decades of tradition," *Baton Rouge Advocate*, Dec. 31, 2016, http://www.theadvocate.com/acadiana/news/crime_police/article_6981deec-ceb5-11e6-bacf-63ebea1d8c26.html?sr_source=lift_amplify
4. *Investigation of the Ville Platte Police Department and the Evangeline Parish Sheriff's Office*, Report of U.S. Department of Justice, Civil Rights Division, Dec. 19, 2016.
5. Heier, Michael, Opinion 16-0159, Louisiana Attorney General's Office, Dec. 6, 2016.

# Notes

## Chapter 37
## Jerry Larpenter: Terrebonne Parish

1. Quinn, Rob, "Sheriff Raids House to Find Online Critic," *Newser* Web page, August 5, 2016, http://www.newser.com/story/229188/sheriff-raids-house-to-find-online-critic.html
2. Author, "Gordon Dove: fox in the House Natural Resources Committee henhouse, or perhaps it's just Louisiana Jindaltics as usual," *LouisianaVoice*, June 1, 2014, https://louisianavoice.com/2014/06/01/gordon-dove-fox-in-the-house-natural-resources-committee-henhouse-or-perhaps-its-just-louisiana-jindaltics-as-usual/
3. "Terrebonne Sheriff trying to use criminal statute to unmask online critic," WWL-TV, August 3, 2016, https://www.wwltv.com/article/news/local/lafourche-terrebonne/terrebonne-sheriff-trying-to-use-criminal-statute-to-unmask-online-critic/287169610
4. Ibid.
5. Author interview with former Louisiana Governor Edwin Edwards, October 2016
6. Editorial, *Houma Daily Courier*, August 7, 2016
7. Moore, Katie, "Terrebonne Sheriff reaches 'compromise' with blogger in 1st Amendment lawsuit over illegal search," WWL-TV, September 7, 2017, https://www.wwltv.com/article/news/local/investigations/katie-moore/terrebonne-sheriff-reaches-compromise-with-blogger-in-1st-amendment-lawsuit-over-illegal-search/472063049
8. Opinion 12-0187, Louisiana Attorney General, February 7, 2013
9. Opinion of Louisiana Ethics Commission, 1995
10. Corporate records of Louisiana Secretary of State
11. Opinion of Louisiana Ethics Commission, 2011

12. "Authement v. Larpenter,' Court of Appeal of Louisiana, First Circuit, 97 CA 0579 and 97 CA 0580, May 15, 1998 decision, https://caselaw.findlaw.com/la-court-of-appeal/1271098.html
13. Official Oath of Office, December 18, 1981, https://tomaswell.files.wordpress.com/2018/06/oath-of-office.pdf
14. Author interview with Denham Springs, Louisiana, City Judge Jerry Denton, June 2018
15. Ibid

# Chapter 38
# The Costs of Bad Sheriffing

1. Frosch, Craig E., attorney for Usry & Weeks Law Firm, in July 24, 2018, letter to author in response to request for public records.
2. Author interview with Victor White, Sr., June 2018.
3. Christopher Butler v. Iberia Parish Sheriff's Office, United States District Court, Western District of Louisiana, Case No. 6:2014cv00228, February 10, 2014.
4. Ray Trosclair v. Louis Ackal, et al, United States District Court, Western District of Louisiana, Case No. 6:2017cv00470, March 29, 2017.
5. Franseen, Jeane, Lee, Ashley, "Louisiana State Police Taking Over Death Investigation," *myarklamiss.com*, June 23, 2015, https://www.myarklamiss.com/crime/update-louisiana-state-police-taking-over-death-investigation/153553066
6. Samuels, Diana, "Kenner door-to-door sales business wins $600,000 in lawsuit," *New Orleans Times-Picayune*, January 20, 2016, https://www.nola.com/business/index.ssf/2016/01/kirby_vacuum_lawsuit_kenner_do.html
7. Frosch, Craig E., attorney for Usry & Weeks Law Firm, in July 24, 2018, letter to author in response to request for public records.

## Notes

8. Laurie Segura v. Louis Ackal and Iberia Parish Sheriff's Department, United States District Court, Western District of Louisiana, Case No. 6:15-cv-02480

## Chapter 39
## George D'Artois

1. Kozak, Brad, "When cops go bad I: the tale of George D'Artois," The Truth About Guns, October 19, 2011, http://www.thetruthaboutguns.com/2011/10/brad-kozak/when-cops-go-bad-i-the-tale-of-george-dartois/
2. *The Shreveport Times*, May 19, 1974.
3. Kozak, Brad, "When cops go bad I: the tale of George D'Artois," The Truth About Guns, October 19, 2011, http://www.thetruthaboutguns.com/2011/10/brad-kozak/when-cops-go-bad-i-the-tale-of-george-dartois/
4. Patton, Devon, "Anne Brewster & George D'Artois in a story of murder or suicide," KTBS-TV, March 3, 2015, http://www.ktbs.com/story/28254676/ann-brewster-george-dartois-in-a-story-of-murder-or-suicide
5. Kozak, Brad, "When cops go bad I: the tale of George D'Artois," The Truth About Guns, October 19, 2011, http://www.thetruthaboutguns.com/2011/10/brad-kozak/when-cops-go-bad-i-the-tale-of-george-dartois/
6. Ibid.
7. Ibid.
8. Author's notes from position as then-labor reporter for the *Baton Rouge State-Times*.
9. "D'Artois ordered by Fant to appear in court Oct. 13," *Minden Press-Herald*, October 4, 1976.
10. "D'Artois letter revealed," *Minden Press-Herald*, December 20, 1978.

11. "George Wendell D'Artois," *Find a Grave*, http://www.findagrave.com/cgi-bin/fg.cgi?page=gr&GRid=15628059
12. "D'Artois Trial Ordered," *The Monroe News-Star*, April 5, 1977.
13. "George Wendell D'Artois, Find a Grave, http://www.findagrave.com/cgi-bin/fg.cgi?page=gr&GRid=15628059
14. Stonecipher, Elliott, "Jim Leslie: the delay—denial?—of justice," *RealShreveport.com*, http://realshreveport.com/jim-leslie-the-delay-denial-of-justice/
15. Ibid.
16. Ibid.
17. Ibid.

# Chapter 40
# John Guandolo, Keith Phillips and Ekko Barnhill

1. Piggott, Stephen, "Disgraced Ex-FBI Agent Guandolo to Train Louisiana Law Enforcement Next Week," *Southern Poverty Law Center Hatewatch*, March 1, 2017, https://www.splcenter.org/hatewatch/2017/03/01/disgraced-ex-fbi-agent-john-guandolo-train-louisiana-law-enforcement-next-week
2. Gill, James, "John Guandolo's new line of work," *Baton Rouge Advocate*, Jan. 19, 2015, http://www.theadvocate.com/new_orleans/opinion/james_gill/article_6b271022-163a-5fa2-9c42-6815d9968534.html
3. Ibid.
4. Piggott, Stephen, "Disgraced Ex-FBI Agent Guandolo to Train Louisiana Law Enforcement Next Week," *Southern Poverty Law Center Hatewatch*, March 1, 2017, https://www.splcenter.org/hatewatch/2017/03/01/disgraced-ex-fbi-agent-john-guandolo-train-louisiana-law-enforcement-next-week

# Notes

5. Ibid.
6. Ibid
7. Minora, Leslie, "Dallas EPA Investigator Would Do Anything for Love. Yes, Even *That*, *Dallas Observer*, Oct. 14, 201, http://www.dallasobserver.com/news/dallas-epa-investigator-would-do-anything-for-love-yes-even-that-7125461
8. Ibid.
9. Roberts, Michael, "Dedicated and determined at Barnhill Orchards," *Arkansas Times*, Sept. 23, 2015, http://www.arktimes.com/arkansas/dedicated-and-determined-at-barnhill-orchards/Content?oid=4087607
10. Minora, Leslie, "Dallas EPA Investigator Would Do Anything for Love. Yes, Even *That*, *Dallas Observer*, Oct. 14, 201, http://www.dallasobserver.com/news/dallas-epa-investigator-would-do-anything-for-love-yes-even-that-7125461
11. Ibid.
12. Miller, Heather, "Ex-EPA agent gets prison time for lying under oath," *The Ind.*, March 29, 2012, http://theind.com/article-9914-ex-epa-agent-gets-prison-time-for-lying-under-oath.html

# Chapter 42
# Jason Kinch and Corey Jackson

1. "Corrupt Cops in Louisiana Arrested but Released," Waste and Corruption News, April 14, 2015, http://www.wasteandcorruption.us/
2. "Louisiana State Trooper and Lafayette Sheriff's Deputy Arrested on Racketeering Charges: Warrant Out for former CEO of Knight Oil Tools," KATC-TV, April 12, 2015, http://www.katc.com/story/28783245/louisiana-state-trooper-and-lafayette-sheriffs-deputy-arrested-on-racketeering-charges
3. Ibid.
4. Joint press release by Louisiana State Police and Lafayette Parish Sheriff's Office, May 26, 2016.

5. "Louisiana State Trooper and Lafayette Sheriff's Deputy Arrested on Racketeering Charges: Warrant Out for former CEO of Knight Oil Tools," KATC-TV, April 12, 2015, http://www.katc.com/story/28783245/louisiana-state-trooper-and-lafayette-sheriffs-deputy-arrested-on-racketeering-charges
6. WAFB-TV story, April 4, 2015.
7. Schneider, Alyssa, "The CEO of Knight Oil Tools has turned himself in to authorities after a warrant was issued for his arrest," WAFB-TV, April 14, 2015.
8. "New details in DA's Office DWI scandal arrests," KATC-TV, Lafayette, May 18, 2017.
9. Flanagan, Patrick, "Caught up in the Cover-up," *IND Monthly*, Oct. 1, 2013, http://theind.com/article-15044-caught-up-in-the-cover-up.html
10. Ibid.
11. Ibid.
12. Friedmann, Alex, "How the Courts View ACA Accreditation," *Prison Legal News*, October 10, 2014. https://www.prisonlegalnews.org/news/2014/oct/10/how-courts-view-aca-accreditation/
13. Flanagan, Patrick, "Caught up in the Cover-up," *IND Monthly*, Oct. 1, 2013, http://theind.com/article-15044-caught-up-in-the-cover-up.html
14. Ibid.
15. Ibid.
16. Ibid.

# Chapter 43
# Marlon Defillo—NOPD

1. Investigation into alleged misconduct of Deputy Chief Marlon Defillo, Louisiana State Police, June 2, 2011.
2. McCarthy, Brendan, "NOPD's no. 2 cop Marlon Defillo retires from force," New Orleans Times-Picayune, July 21, 2011,

## Notes

   http://www.nola.com/crime/index.ssf/2011/07/marlon_defillo_resigns_from_ne.html
3. Investigation into alleged misconduct of Deputy Chief Marlon Defillo, Louisiana State Police, June 2, 2011.
4. Interview with member of LSP investigative team who asked that his identity be kept confidential.
5. McCarthy, Brendan, "Marlon Defillo is still coordinating police details for movie sets," New Orleans Times-Picayune, Feb. 6, 2012, http://www.nola.com/crime/index.ssf/2012/02/marlon_defillo_is_still_coordi.html

## Chapter 44
## Lloyd Grafton

1. Bell, Stewart, *Bayou of Pigs*, John Wiley & Sons Canada, Ltd., 2008, pp. 144-146.
2. Interview with W. Lloyd Grafton, January 15, 2017.
3. Law Enforcement Handbook.
4. Ibid.
5. Ibid.
6. Ibid.
7. Grafton, W. Lloyd, written report on investigation of *Cheryl Washington and Kerrionne Nicole Washington vs. Martin Gusman, Criminal Sheriff, Orleans Parish, Docket No. 2007-3308, Div. B-15*, May 9, 2012.
8. Ibid.
9. Ibid.
10. Ibid.
11. Ibid.

# Index

Abbott, Jeremiah, 169
Abramoff, Jack, 149
Ackal, Louis, ix, 250
AFL-CIO, Louisiana, 218
Africk, Federal District Judge Lance, 136
Ahrens, Garrett Andrew, 176
Alexander, Leonardo, 99
Alford, Tony, 239
Allen, Calhoun, 255, 259
Allyson, June, 7
American Civil Liberties Union of Louisiana, 114
American Corrections Association (ACA), 280
Amigo Enterprises Inc., 222
Anderson, Jennifer, 241
Anderson, Wayne, 240
*Andy Griffith Show*, 173
Angelle, Scott, 177
Angelo, Darren, 95
Anthony, Ted, 177
Arbuckle, Rodney, 179
Arceneaux, David, 243
Ardoin, David, 240
Arlene & Joseph Meraux Charitable Foundation Inc., 222
Army Corps of Engineers, 195
Arnold, Chuck, ix
Arpaio, Joe, ix, 120
Attorney General, Louisiana, 244
Augustine, Althea, 215
Auschwitz Memorial and Museum, 178
Auschwitz,, 178
Austin Sales and Service, Inc., 126
Austin, Lucien Roy, 125

Authement, Aubrey, 245
B & D Auto Sales, 85
Baca, Lee, ix
Bailey, Robert, 153
Baker, U.S. Sen. Howard, 288
Ballard, Brent, 21
Baloney, Geri, 66
Baloney, Quendi, 66
Barker, Justin, 152
Barnhill, Ekko, 264
Barnidge, Matt, 29
Barousse, Homer Ed, 251
Barron, Birdie Ellen, 56
Bates, Fred, Jr., 91
Batiste, Arizona, 99
*Baton Rouge Advocate*, 62, 81, 105, 112
*Baton Rouge State-Times*, 23
Battaglia, Edwin, 251
Bayou Bridge Pipeline, 198
*Bayou Brief*, 267
Beard, Hazel, 39
Becnel, Debra, 224
Bell, Mychal, 152
Belt, Bill, 73
Belt, Tracy, 73
Bender, Stacy, 21
Benetech Software, 93
Bennett, Aaron, 93
Bensley, Tom, 111
Bergeron, Ralph, 51
Bernie, Sue, 228
Berry, Bert, 251
Bethancourt, Judge Randal, 239
Beverly Club, 6, 9
Blakes, Rakeem, 206
Blanchard, Eric, 215

Blanco, Kathleen, 121
Bleich, Joe, 294
Bluhm Legal Clinic, Northwestern University School of Law's, 137
Blumberg, Mark, 211
Board of Ethics, Louisiana, 102
Boatner, John, 77
Boeker, Barrett, 227
Bold Louisiana, 194
Bonnett, George, 168
Bordelon, Gary, 126
Borne, Wilkes & Rabalais law firm, 251
Bosch, John, 4
Boudreaux, Bernard, 68
Bourg, Frank, 2
Boustany, Charles, 65, 177, 202
Boyte, Frederick "Bo", 47
BP (British Petroleum), 221
Bradley, Shandell, 250
Breaux, Donald, 279
Breaux, Duffy, 51
Brewster, Ann, 256
Bridgewater-Norman, Shawn, 121
Brilab investigation, 12
Briley, Dudley, 3
Britt, Jeff, 143
Broussard, Bret, 212
Broussard, Donald, 205
Broussard, Sye, 239
Brown, Andy, 251
Brown, Gwyn, 100
Bueche, Joseph Reed, 185
*Bunkie Record*, 77
Bureau of Alcohol, Tobacco and Firearms, 287
Bureau of Alcohol, Tobacco and Firearms (ATC), 208
Bureau of Alcohol, Tobacco and Firearms (ATF), 52, 152
Bureau of Narcotics and Dangerous Drugs, U.S., 208, 287
Bureau of Safety and Environmental Enforcement, 177
Burghoff, Gary, 7
Burns approached *The Shreveport Times*, 259
Burns, Robert, 212
Burns, Sam, 259
Burrescia, Jimmie, 58
Bussie, Victor, 218
Butler, Carl, 99
Butler, Christopher, 212, 250
Bynum, James "Big Jim", 35
Byrd, Mike, ix
Caddo Correctional Center, 40
Cajun Callers of Bayhills, Inc., 74
Caldwell, Buddy, 66
Capital City Alliance, 114
Capone, Al, 3
Capps, Grayson, 160
Captain Higgins Gear Company, LLC., 176
Caracci, Frank, 117
Caracci, Mark, 118
Carrier, Robbie Bethel, 214
Carter, Jimmy, 77
Cash, Dr. Artis, 256
Castillo, Allan Neal, 179
Caviness, Gene, 45, 49
Cawthon, Joe, 36
Cazabat, Alphonse, 17
Celestine, Stephanie, 209

# Index

Center for Investigative Reporting, 28
Central Louisiana Communications, Inc., 74
Chaffe McCall law firm, 121
Champagne, Greg, 189
Charisse, Cyd, 7
Chauvin, Douglas, Jr., 244
Chennault, Gen. Claire, 25
Chesser, Bill, 47
Civil Rights Division, U.S. Justice Department, 211
Clancy, Frank, 1, 7, 11
*Clarion-Ledger*, 27
Clark, Beau, 229
Clark, Cori Leigh, 85
Clark, Tyrone, Sr., ix
Clinton, Bill, 120
Club Forest, 5, 7
CNL Cigarettes, 247
Cobb, Judge Howell, 67
Cohen, Michael, 176
Cohen, Mickey, 12
Colombia, 293
Columbia, Louisiana, 293
Comeaux, James, 210
Commission on Accreditation for Law Enforcement Agencies, 72, 280
*Commonwealth for a Free Moral Society*, 154
Concerned Citizens of St. Tammany (CCST), 169
*Concordia Sentinel*, 23
*Concordia Sentinel, The*, 26
Conner, Rachel, 149
Cook, Chuck, 44, 49
Cook, Yancey, King & Galloway law firm, 181, 251
*Cop Watch*, 49
Copeland, Larry, 5
Copes, Gary, 145
Cormier, Dallas, 139
Costello, Frank, 6
Cournoyer Cadillac, 248
Couvillon, Mike, 217
Craig, Howard, 67
Crane, Bob, 7
Crigler, Judge John, 150
Cross, Noah, 25, 28, 31
Cross, Pearson, 217
Cruise, Dee, 81
CTNN (Craig Taffaro, Newell Normand), 123
Cuccinelli, Ken, 112
Culp, Larry Glen, 46
Culp, Laurie Schween, 46
Cumbey, Floyd Edward, 35
Curth, Kimberly, 187
D'Aquilla, Sam, 227
D'Artois, George, 25, 255
*Daily Iberian*, 206
*Daily Sports Wire*, 5
Dakota Access Pipeline, 189
*Dallas Observer*, 265
Daniel, Austin, 227
Daughters of the American Revolution (DAR), 30
David, Tarik, 209
Davidson, Robert, 179
Davis, Gov. Jimmie, 26
Davis, Michael K., 45
Davis, William C., 31
Dawsey, Barry Edward, 84

Dawson, Dana Rev., 7
Daye, Anthony, 212
DeBerry, Jarvis, 122
Deepwater Horizon, 66, 95, 221
Defillo, Marlon, 283
Delahoussaye, Terry, Sr., 214
DeLaughter, Frank, 26, 28, 31, 33
Delay, Tom, 149
Delgado, John, 112
Delta Security, 95
Department of Justice, Civil Rights Division, U.S., 291
Department of Public Safety and Corrections, 242
Desona Dairy-Corbin Planting Company, 87
Deutsch, Florian, 21
Didier, F.O. "Potch", 76
Ditch, Dr. Carl, 201
Dixie Finance Corporation, 7
Dixie Mafia, 259
Dixon Correctional Institute, 243
Dodd Law Firm, 251
Dodd, William F., 246
Doherty, Judge Rebecca, 265
Domincia, 288
Dominick, Andre, 224
Dooley, Vol, 35
Doucet, Cat, 3, 21, 22, 23, 24, 29, 81
Dove, Gordon, 239
Dove, Jackie, 239
Downer, Hunt, 65
Downs, J. Earl, 255
Drane, Judsen Lee "Blackie", 31
DRC Group, 94
Drug Enforcement Agency Task Force, 107

Drug Enforcement Agency, U.S. (DEA), 107
Duet, Eddie, 52
Duhé, Bo, 206
Duke, David, 160, 287
Dupuis, Butch, 68
East Carroll Correctional Systems, Inc. (ECCS), 87
East Carroll Detention Center (ECDC), 87
Edmonson, Mike, 224
Edwards, Daniel, 55, 59, 61, 262
Edwards, Edwin W., 81, 117, 241
Edwards, Frank, xiv, 55, 59
Edwards, Gov. John Bel, 40, 55, 66, 121, 145, 170, 262
Edwards, Jules, 273
Ellis, Frank, 203
Entrekin, Todd, ix
Epps Detention Center, 88
Equality Louisiana, 114
Ernst, Cy, 9
Ethics Commission, Louisiana State, 244
Etienne, Dalton, 70
*Eunice New Era*, 22
Falkenheiner, W.C., 30
Falterman, Anthony G. "Tony", xiv, 60
Fannin, Jim, 108
Fant, Judge John F., 257
Favor, Jack, 35
Fernandez, Anthony, Jr., 222
Fewell, Richard, 44, 49
Ficklin, Ronald "Gun", 84
Finley, U.S. Attorney Stephanie, 108

# Index

Fire Apparatus Specialties, 244
First Circuit, LLC, 244
Flagg, Fannie, 7
Fleet Intermodal, 95
Fleniken, Judge William, 258
Fletcher, Norm, 91
Flournoy, Howell, 255
Foil, Franklin, 57
Fontaine, Joan, 7
Fort Laramie Treaty, 196
Fortunato, John, 120
Foti, Charles, 133
Foytlin, Cherri, 194
Franklin, Scott, 151
Franques, Ken, Sr., 279
Freeman, Reef, 29
Frosch, Craig, 16
Fryer, Milford, 81
Fuentes, Kristy, 95
Fuller, Ed, 31
Fuller, William Herbert, 42, 43
Fuller, Zennie William, 42
Funderburk, Ike, 217
Fuselier, Charles, 67, 81
Gallow, Perry, 173
Garber, Mark, 269
Gary, Ted, 139
Gasser, Ronald, 122
Gautreaux, Sid J., 112
Gemelli, Angelo, 4
Gene Autry Rodeo, 35
Gibson, Willie Charlie, 42
Gill, James, 73
Gillen, Tom, 60
Gilley, Mickey, 25
Gilmore, Arthur Jr., 48
Glover, Henry, 283

Godwin, Laymon, 44
Gonzales, Judge Doug, 257
Gourgues, Jarrod, 223
Goyeneche, Rafael, 94, 101, 137, 188, 221
Grafton, Lloyd, 201, 287
Grant, Bailey, 41
Graugnard, GeorgeAnn, 100
Grayson, Brett, 275
Great Sioux Nation, 196
Griffing, C. Mignonne, 45
Griffing, Mignonne, 47
Griffith, Rusty, 258
Guandolo, John, 261, 264
Guidroz, Bobby, 175, 267
Guidry, John Michael, 57
Guidry, Robert, 117
Guidry, Shane, 123
Gulf State, LLC, 130
Gunter, Johnny, 47
Gupta, Vanita, 136
Gusman, Marlin, 291
Gusman, Marlin N., 125
Guste, Attorney General William, 24, 259
Guste, William, 107
Gutierrez & Hand law firm, 251
Habans School, 283
Haik, U.S. District Judge Richard, 264
Hall, Lestage & Landreneau law firm, 251
Hammond Daily Star, 26, 60
Hammond Police Department, 61
Haney, John, 68
Hanna, Sam, 26
Hanson, Brandy, 158

Hanson, David, 157
Hargrove, Thomas, 214
Harrell, Bruce, 60
Harris, Angel, 40
Harvey Gulf, 123
Hassert, Brad, 169
Hataway, Leonard R. "Pop", 81
Hathaway, Don, 39
Haydel, Scott, 68
Hebert, Racheal, 228
Hebert, Toby, 213
Hebert, Troy, 49
*Heinert, Paul*, 193
Henderson, C. Murray, 36
Hewitt, Curt, 23, 29
Hidalgo, Brent, 244
Higginbotham, Mark, 146
Higgins, Clay, 173, 267, 269
Higgins, Rebecca Lee, 176
Hilton, Jim, x
Hines, David, 250
Hingle, Irvin "Jif", 93
Hobbs Act, 48
Hodge, Lawrence, ix
Holland, Eugene, 83
Hornsby, Federal Magistrate Judge Mark, 109
Horseshoe Lake, 29
*Houma Daily Courier*, 241
Howard, Samuel, 153
Howell, Mary, 134
*Huffington Post*, 168
Hughes, Jessie, 86
Hunt, Thomas, 2
Iberia Parish Correctional Center, 208
Illing, Scott, 170

Immigration and Naturalization Service, 146
Infinity Communications, Inc., 74
Internal Revenue Service Criminal Investigation Division, 94
International Association of Police Chiefs, 5
Internet Background Check System database, 180
Isakson, Robert, 94
Izrael, Jim, 168
Jackson, Corey, 278
Jackson, Jackie, 80
Jackson, James, 85
Jackson, Jesse, 152
Jails on Demand, 95
James, Biff, 65
Jasmine, Madeline, 101
Jefferson, William, 149, 261, 264, 268
Jena Six, 151
Jenkins, Miles, 146
Jindal, Bobby, 121
John Curtis High School, 121
Johnson, Arte, 7
Johnson, Joseph, 3
Johnson, Joseph D., 74
Johnson, Rae Ellen, 74
Jones, Albert, III, 209
Jones, Karl, 144
Jones, Marcus, 155
Jones, Michael, 203, 207
Jones, Ricky, 147
Jones, Tina, 154
Jordan, Glen, 88
Juneau, Judge Jeanne, 224
Justice Department, U.S., 28

# Index

Justice for Victor White III Foundation, 205
Kastel, Phil "Dandy", 6
Keathley, Raymond, 31
Keen, Clifford "Skip", 158
Keen, Jarret, 158
Keen, Skip, 157
Kefauver Committee, 7, 9
Kefauver, Sen. Estes, 1
Kelley, T.P., 259
Kellogg, Gov. William Pitt, 17
Kelly, Pat, ix
Kemp, Duncan, 58
Kennedy, John N., 49
Kimball, William, 256
Kinch, Jason, 278
King, Loretta, 135
*Kirchmeier, Kyle*, 193
Knight Oil Tools, 277
Knight, Bryan, 277
Knight, Mark, 277
Knight, William, 139
Ku Klux Klan, 26, 29, 42, 43, 287
Kyle, Dan, 143
LaBauve, Howard, 10
*Lafayette Advertiser*, 278
Lafayette Metro Narcotics Task Force, 277
Lafayette Parish Correctional Center, 278
Lafittel, Jean, 3
Lafourche Novelty Company, 247
Lafrance, Michael, 96
Lagniappe and Castillo Research and Investigations, 179
Lamour, Dorothy, 7
Lancaster, J.B., 80

Landrieu, Mitch, 284
Landrieu, Moon, 285
Landry, Jeff, 65, 124, 273
Landry, Nelson, Jr., 214
*Laney, Paul*, 193
Lansky, Meyer, 6
Laperouse, Cody, 212
Larpenter, Jerry, 239
Larpenter, Priscilla, 239
Lartigue, Neal, 236
LaSalle, Byron Benjamin, 210, 212
LaSalle, C.O., 210
Layrisson, Ed, 60
Layrisson, Edward, 55
Leblanc, Craig, 174
LeBreton, Art, 278
Leche, Daniel, 51
LeDoux, Adler, 24
Lee, Harry, 81, 117, 119
Lee, Martiny and Caracci Law Firm, 118
Lee, Rev. Robert Jr., 33
Leger, Chad, 270
Leger, Jonathan, 159
Leija, Kim, 46
Leslie, Jim, 256
Letten, Jim, 93
Levy, Jim, 77
Lewis, Jerry, 99
Lewis, Jerry Lee, 25
Lexington (Kentucky) *Herald Leader*, 168
*LIFE Magazine*, 29
Little, Albert D. "Bodie", 107
Local Agency Compensation Enforcement (LACE), 182
Long, Earl K., 23

Louisiana Association of Business and Industry (LABI), 257
Louisiana Correction Services, 145
Louisiana Department of Corrections, 39
Louisiana Department of Public Safety and Corrections, 84, 88
Louisiana Department of Safety and Corrections, 14
Louisiana Justice Hall of Fame, 81
Louisiana Political Hall of Fame, 72
Louisiana Political Museum and Hall of Fame, 81
Louisiana Sheriffs' and Deputies' Political Action Committee, 15
Louisiana Sheriffs' Association, 13, 242
Louisiana Sheriffs' Association (LSA), xiv
Louisiana Sheriffs' Association Risk Management Program, 118
Louisiana Sheriffs' Law Enforcement Program (LSLEP), 15, 213, 249
Louisiana Sheriffs' Mounted Posse Association, Inc., 13
Louisiana Sheriffs' Risk Management Program, 15
Louisiana Stadium and Exposition District (Superdome Commission), 121
Louisiana State Penitentiary at Angola, 36
Louisiana State Penitentiary Museum Foundation, 81
Louisiana State Police, 152
Louisiana State Prison at Angola, 227
Louisiana Tactical Police Officers' Association's (LTPOA), 262
Louisiana Tech University, 26, 218
Louisiana United International, 169
Love, Hartwell, 26
LSA (Louisiana Sheriffs' Association), 13
LSU Law Enforcement Institute, 255
Lynch, Loretta, 201
MacArthur Justice Center, 137
Mader, Christian, 269
Madison Square Garden, 35
Mafia, 259
Maggio, Ross, 75
Maginnis, John, *24*
Malkiewiez, Cody, 187
Manship School of Mass Communications, LSU, 28
Manual, Russell, 277
Marcello, Anthony, 11
Marcello, Carlos, 6, 9, 11, 23, 29, 117, 247, 256
Marquar, Kendal, 131
Martin, Willy, 187
Martiny, Danny, 118
Mauffray, Judge J.P., 152
McCarthy, Sen. Joe, 262
McClendon, Marshall, 51
McDaniel, Raymond, 259
McDonald, Janis, 28
McDowall, Roddy, 7
McGoffin, Gary, 273
McGuire, Thomas, 11
McKeithen, John, 240, 293

# Index

McKeithen, John J., 79
McKnight, Joe, 121
McLindon, John, 212
McMahon, Royce, 218
McMillan, Jack, 147
McNabb, Alton Hoyt, II, 85
McNabb, Michelle, 217
Meraux, L.A., 3
Methvin, Federal Magistrate Judge Mildred "Mimi", 70
Metropolitan Crime Commission, New Orleans, 94, 101, 137, 188, 221
Middleton, Charles K., 270
Miller, Ann, 7
Miller, Beauregard, 7, 8
Minacore, Calogero (Carlos Marcello), 12
Minora, Leslie, 265
Miranda, Carmen, 7
Mitchell, Jerry, 27
Mody, Lori, 261
Moity, Warren, 10
*Monroe News Star*, 42
Montgomery, Warren, 157
Moran, Justin, 63
Morgel, Dorothy, 87
Morris, Frank, 27, 32, 33
Morris, John, *23*
Morrison, DeLesseps S., 6
Morville Lounge, 29
Mosca's Restaurant, 248
Mouriz, Brandon, 95
Murphy, Lonnie, 279
NAACP Legal Defense and Educational Fund, 40
Nagin, Ray, 268

Nash, Christopher Columbus, 17
*Natchitoches Parish*, xiii, 91
National Crime Information Center, 91
National Police Officers Association of America, 255
National Response Center, 198
National Sheriffs' Association, 72
Needham, Patrick, 3
Nelson, Levi, 18
Nelson, Stanley, 23, 26
Nelson, Willie, 120
Ness, Eliot, 3
Nevils, Chris, 107
*New Orleans Advocate*, 158
New Orleans Jazz and Heritage Festival (Jazz Fest), 127
New Orleans Police Department, 5
*New Orleans Times-Picayune*, *23*, 41, 73, 112
Newman, Emerson, 83
Newman, Jean, 83
Nguyen, Kayden, 120
Nielsen, Brandon, 101
Noel, Clarence, 92
Normand, Newell, 119
Northeast Delta Correction Services, 88
Northeast Louisiana Correction Services, Inc., 88
Northshore Workforce Solutions, 159
Nowell, Edward, 99
Nungesser, Billy, 123
O'Mary, Paul, 68
O'Neal, Shaquille, 269
Obama, Barack, 65

Opelousas Police Department, 173
Operation Third Option, 153
Organized Crime Control Act, 51
Ortego, Bill, 174
Ortego, Dana, 239
Ortego, Debbie, 239
Ouachita Correctional Center, 47
Ouachita Parish Police Jury, 44
Ourso, Jessel, 79
Ourso, Mitch, 81
Ozenne, Curtis, 203
Ozenne, Gilbert, 7, 10
Pace, Julius, 5
Padgett, Louis H. Jr., 35
Palmer, Gerald, 251
ParaTech, 223
Pardons, Louisiana State Board of, 145
Parish Oilfield Services LLC., 222
Parker, Bruce, 114
Parker-Brown, Belinda, 168
Pastorick, Ken, 85
Patterson, Eugene, 294
Paxton, James, 147
Peace Officers Standards and Training (POST), 102
Peace Officer's Standards in Training (POST), 72
Peachey, Marlin, Jr., 159
Pecoraro, Frances, 58
Pecoraro, Nofio, Jr., 58
Pecoraro, Nofio, Sr., 58
Pelican Marine, 123
Perez, Pete, 7
Perrilloux, Scott, 63, 84
Perrodin, Janet, 206
Pfeifer, John, 29, 33

Phillips, Chaney, 83
Phillips, Keith, 264
Pineville Police Department, 152
Pinion, Randy, 56
Poissot, O.C. "Coonie", 33
Polite, U.S. Attorney Kenneth, 136
Pontchartrain Cadillac, 248
Pope, Brian, 177, 267
Poretto, Joseph, 9
Pouchie, Yule, 187
Powell, Jane, 7
Prator, Steve, 39
Pressure Point Control Tactics (PPCT), 288
Price, Judge O.E., 36
Price, O.E., 35
Prince Murat Hotel, 257
*Prison Legal News*, 137, 280
Prison Litigation Reform Act, 228
Private Security Examiners, Louisiana State Board of, 127
Promotek, LLC, 244
Provosty, Sadler & Delaunay law firm, 251
Public Service Commission, Louisiana, 177
Pulitzer Prize, 28
Purpera, Daryl, 125, 182
Racketeer Influenced and Corrupt Organizations Act (RICO), 48
Ramos, Steven T., 176
Raye, Martha, 7
Reagan, Ronald, 77
Reardon, Rob, 279
Register, Robert, 17
Reyer, George, 5
Richard, Andre, 174

# Index

Richardson, John, 259
Richey, W.H., Mr. and Mrs., 35
Richmond, U.S. Rep. Cedric, 201
Ricker, Christopher, 159
Ricks, Percy Lee, 68
Riddle, Charles, 76
Rinicker, Dale, 87
Robicheaux, Marcus, 204, 215
Roedel Parsons Koch Boache Balhoff & McCollister law firm, 121
Roedel, Larry, 121
Roemer, Charles, 12
Romero, Cesar, 7
Romero, Eddie, 70
Rothkamm-Hambrice, Rosemary, 177
Roulas, Mike, 281
Rowan, Mike, 49
Rowley, Celestine "Dutch", 5, 7
Rozands, Charlton P., 245
Rozands, Mae, 246
*Ruston Daily Leader*, 293
Ryland, Jane, 128
Saadi Haberdashery, 248
Saadi, George, 248
Sallet, Jeffrey, 41, 62
Savoy, Gerald, 209, 212
Schaeffer, Allan Wayne, 99
Schiff, Leslie, 48
Schnyder, Paul, 99
Schon, Sylvia, 60
Schuler, Marsha, 259
Scott, Chad, 62
Scott, Roger, xv
Scott, U.S. District Judge Nauman, 30

Seagal., 120
Seagal, Steven, 176
Seale, James Ford, 28
Searcy, J.R., 46
Secretary of State, Louisiana, 158
Segura, Laurie, 251
Sellers, Derrick, 215
Sens, John, 132
Sexual Trauma Awareness & Response (STAR), 228
Sharpton, Al, 152
Shaw, Daniel Wesley, 17
Shelley, Jay, 28
Sheriffs' and Police Training School Association of the State of Louisiana, 13
Shield Land, 52
*Shreveport Times*, 257, 294
Shumate, Mark, 90
Silver Dollar Group, 28
Simmons, Kevin, 85
Simonton, George, x, 295
Sioux Reservation, 190
Small, Mike, 75
Smith, Howard K., 25
Smith, Randy, 157
Smith, Randy, Jr., 168
Snowdy, J. Sterling, 101
Snyder, Robert C., 218
Soileau, Eddie, 236
Songe, Elmore, 245
Sonnier, Robert, 204
Southern Louisiana Communications, Inc., 74
Southern Poverty Law Center, 28

Southwestern Legal Foundation, Southern Methodist University, 255
Spencer, Arthur Leonard, 33
St. Bernard Parish Prison, 224
St. Tammany Workforce Solutions, 158
Stagg, Judge Tom, 44
Standing Rock, North Dakota, 190
*Stanek, Rich*, 194
Stanford, Ian, 29
Stanley, Aaron, 56, 57
State Bond Commission, 108
State Ethics Board, 218
State Penitentiary at Angola, Louisiana, 289
State Police Commission, Louisiana, 287
State Police Criminal Investigation Unit, Louisiana State Police, 185
Stephens, Jack, 221
Sterritt, James R., 181
*Steven Seagal, Lawman*, 120
Stevens, Robert "Red", 48
Stewart, Dennis, 85
Stewart, Rynika, 126
Stonecipher, Elliott, 258
Strain, Jack, 157
*Sullivan v. New York Times*, 240
Swaggart, Jimmy, 25
Syracuse University College of Law, 28
Taffaro, Craig, 123
Taffaro, Craig, Jr., 222
Taffaro, Craig, Sr., 222
Tanner, William, 283
Tardo, Cyrus "Bobby", 51

Tensas Detention Center, 145
Terrebonne Levee District, 241
*The Black Commentator*, 160
*The Democratic Voice*, 60
The Independent, 268
*The Last Hayride,*, 24
The Spot, *23*
Theriot, Roy, 80
Thibodeaux, Charles, 3
*ThinkProgress*, 178
Thomas, Craig, 174
Thomas, Danny, 7
Thomassee, Matthew, 279
Thompson, Daquentin, 213, 250
Three Rivers Wildlife Management Area, 258
Tidwell, Mitchell, 85
*Times of Acadiana*, 24
Tingle, Allen, 158
Toney, Royce, 41, 45
Torres, Bud, 185
Townsend, Taylor, 66, 109
Treasury, U.S., 287
Treen, Dave, 240
Tregre, Arthur, 189
Tregre, Jared, 101
Tregre, Mike, 100
Triche, Edie, 102
Triche, Jeremy, 101
Trosclair, Howard, 213, 250
Trump, Donald, 176, 177
Tullier, John Jr., 51
Turner, Lana, 7
U.S. Drug Enforcement Administration, 61
U.S. Justice Department, Civil Rights Division, 231

# Index

U.S. Marshal Fugitive Task Force, 152
*Understand the Threat* (UTT), 262
United Houma Nation of Louisiana, 194
United States Civil Rights Investigation of the Orleans Parish Prison System, 291
University Medical Center, 280
University of Louisiana Lafayette, 217
Ursin, Gerald, Jr., 126
Used Motor Vehicle Commission, 146
Usry & Weeks law firm, 249
Usry & Weeks Law Firm, 15
UST Environmental Service, 67
Vaccarella, Lisa, 224
Vallee, Rudy, 7
Vance, U.S. District Judge Sarah R., 96
Veillon, Dallas, 189
Verdin, Monique, 194
Vidrine, Hubert, 264
Vitter, David, 55, 121, 170, 177, 202
Volz, John, 52
Waggonner, U.S. Rep. Joe, 35
Waggonner, Willie, 35
Waitz, Joe, III, 239
Waitz, Joe, Jr., 239
Wallace, Catrina, 153
Walter, Federal Judge Donald E., 212

Walters, Reed, 154
Washington, Donald, 74
Washington, Dwayne, 290
Washington, Kerry, 289
Watson, Jeff, 189
Webster, William, 10
Welker, David, 94
Wells, James B., 36
Werther, Jennifer, 170
West Carroll Parish Detention Center, 88
Whipple, Vanessa Guidry, 57
White Citizens Council, 256
White League, 19
White, Lamar, 65, 267
White, Victor, III, 201, 250
White, Victor, Jr., 211, 212, 250
Wilkerson, Steven Britt, 274
Williams, Billy, 32
Williams, Lucinda, 160
Williams, Nat, 86
Williams, Timothy, 224
Wilson, Ron, 148
Wooton, Ernest, 93
Worley, Jo Ann, 7
WVUE-TV, 187
WWL-TV, 195, 224
Wyly, "Captain Jack", 87
Yates, Donald Lee, 35
Yee, Aimee, 60
YouTube, 175
Zurik, Lee, 94

www.ingramcontent.com/pod-product-compliance
Lightning Source LLC
Chambersburg PA
CBHW021134230426
43667CB00005B/107